Jumbo Puzzle Book 2

Play these other great puzzle books by USA TODAY:

USA TODAY Sudoku

USA TODAY Everyday Sudoku

USA TODAY Crossword

USA TODAY Logic

USA TODAY Sudoku X and Mini Sudoku

USA TODAY Word Roundup & Word Search

USA TODAY Word Play

USA TODAY Jumbo Puzzle Book

USA TODAY Picture Puzzles

USA TODAY Everyday Logic

USA TODAY

JUMBO
Puzzle Book 2

400 Brain Games for Every Day

Andrews McMeel
PUBLISHING®

Andrews McMeel Publishing
a division of Andrews McMeel Universal
1130 Walnut Street, Kansas City, Missouri 64106

www.andrewsmcmeel.com

20 21 22 23 24 PAH 18 17 16 15 14

ISBN: 978-0-7407-8539-9

puzzles.usatoday.com

Attention: Schools and Businesses

Andrews McMeel books are available at quantity discounts with bulk purchase for educational, business, or sales promotional use. For information, please e-mail the Andrews McMeel Publishing Special Sales Department: specialsales@amuniversal.com.

CONTENTS

USA TODAY

Can't get enough of USA TODAY puzzles?

You can play:

- In the USA TODAY newspaper

- At puzzles.usatoday.com

- By downloading the FREE USA TODAY app (Get it on Google Play or iTunes)

- By downloading the FREE USA TODAY Crossword app (Get it on Google Play or iTunes)

INTRODUCTION

For hours of mind-pumping brain games, we offer this eclectic mix of word and number puzzles: traditional crosswords, logic, Sudoku, Word Roundup™, and Hidato™. This hefty tome includes enough puzzles to work one per day for a year's worth of brain fitness. We can't promise better brain function, but you will enjoy hours of fun and entertainment.

Happy puzzling!

BAKER'S HUMOR
By Frances Burton

ACROSS
1 It can reveal your worry
6 Plain of Jars locale
10 It comes before a storm
14 Arctic wear
15 Frightful giant
16 Bicolor treat
17 Start of a baker's quip
19 It allows you to keep your place
20 Behavioral quirk
21 Pertaining to birth
22 Grind, as teeth
23 Tangles
25 Brit's raincoat
26 Cease partner
27 Colorful flower
31 Baker's quip (Part 2)
34 Private address
37 First lady
38 It gets the ball off the ground
39 Baker's quip (Part 3)
46 Choice cut
47 Smile derisively
51 Dinosaur's start
52 Fetch
54 Impostor's cover
57 Sheet of printed matter
58 16 1/2 feet
59 Needing mending
60 End of the baker's quip
62 Slender instrument
63 Alan or Cheryl
64 Have young
65 Convalesce
66 Vaulted cathedral area
67 TV twins' name

DOWN
1 Dealt with maliciously
2 Native of the Aloha State
3 Puts up
4 Other name indicator
5 Taint
6 Tony winner Lenya
7 Eastern potentates
8 Type of vaccine
9 Place to make a scene
10 Rustic pipe
11 Geographical datum
12 See-through item
13 Former woolly bear
18 Florentine poet
22 Comedian's cache
24 Twain's talent
25 Cartoon voice Blanc
27 Overloaded, as a fuse
28 Brazil, e.g.
29 Anger
30 It's OK on board
32 Unskilled worker
33 It's on some hallowed walls
34 Praises for products
35 Paste some find tasty
36 Possession indication
40 Harvested
41 Monopolizes
42 Imposing
43 Up and about
44 Windstorm
45 Start of Cain's query
48 Dangers
49 Come about
50 Show embarrassment
52 Crucifixes
53 Dodge
54 Bit of nuclear physics
55 In the human brain it may be temporal or frontal
56 Club in a bag
57 Uproar
60 Pt. of FSU
61 Linden or Holbrook

STARTUP FUNDS
By James Sajdak

ACROSS
1 No bull, yet?
5 Times Square eatery
11 Kettle and others
14 Word in a bibliography
15 Special Forces units
16 Layoff tool?
17 Where silents could be seen
19 Bug or badger
20 Feinted on the ice
21 Freshly cut, as bluegrass
22 Lean (on)
23 Kind of kick
25 Abalone fancier
27 He or she may be a hack
32 Trans-Atlantic carrier
35 Cannes cash
36 Type of knife
37 URL beginning
39 Noncom nickname
42 Jaguar models
43 Kin of 71-A
45 Matador's opponent
47 Elm and Oak, briefly
48 Muscular ride
52 Behavioral sci.
53 Bacon selections
57 It may be a seat at a barn dance
59 Turns sharply from a straight course
62 Jim Henson creation
63 Secret of the vain, perhaps
64 Slotted shoe
66 Clean up at the table
67 Bottom line, usually
68 Words with problem or chance
69 Encouraging word
70 Gathered together
71 ___II razor

DOWN
1 Positive type of attitude
2 Completely unfamiliar
3 Lollipop portions
4 Spy ware?
5 Canal mule
6 Molecular component
7 Overhaul
8 Korean auto maker
9 Stadium-crowd-shot shout
10 IRS ID
11 Nonconformists
12 Olympian jump
13 Extremely alluring
18 Crane canine
22 Kick back
24 Earthbound avians
26 Cowboy Ritter
28 Slice of history
29 Glinda the Good's domain, in film
30 Editorial notation
31 Pre-kickoff ritual
32 Huge court presence
33 Alaskan island
34 Like some gowns
38 Dissect grammatically
40 Infantile syllable
41 Demonstrates fallibility
44 Piggery
46 Prefix meaning "bone"
49 Inflammatory condition of the skin
50 Thick-skinned herbivores
51 Off-course
54 Certain to get
55 Michelangelo sculpture
56 Block of ice on a glacier
57 Treat gently
58 Fit of fever
60 Big cat's prey
61 Nostalgic song ending
64 Coat in a pan
65 Crown Victoria

ODD COUPLE
By Lynn Lempel

ACROSS

1 It can put you in your place
6 Having the right stuff
10 Start to take flight
14 Address with a st. but no st.
15 End to be attained
16 Lung division
17 Foul-up
18 Teeny bit
19 They may ring a bell
20 Start of a quip about a marital mismatch
23 Barley brew
26 On tenterhooks
27 Mortarboard doodad
28 Missionary winner of the Nobel Peace Prize
30 Jazzy job
31 It can be rubber or brass
32 Marital mismatch quip (Part 2)
39 Speaker's digression
41 Clumsy guy
42 Rudely assertive
43 Marital mismatch quip (Part 3)
46 Stinging response to an insult?
47 Oddjob's creator, Fleming
48 Be in a sticky situation?
50 Airbag activator
54 Comparative phrase
56 Reggae relative
57 End of the marital mismatch quip
60 No great shakes
61 One way to keep one's hair dry
62 Tally mark
66 Utah Lake city
67 Not well-grounded?
68 Blow a gasket
69 Nike alternative
70 One place kids play
71 It's for suckers

DOWN

1 Records that are not that hard to break
2 One billion years, in geology
3 Atty. group
4 A resting place
5 Oozes forth
6 Part of the winemaking process
7 Plundered treasure
8 Parts of the music scale
9 Like some waistbands
10 Gem imperfections
11 Heartthrobs
12 It may be humble
13 Kind of code
21 Dutch cheese town
22 Prepare to advance on a fly
23 You cannot swat a fly without it
24 Collar attachment
25 Sesame Street prankster
29 Maelstrom
30 Best Picture and Best Song of 1958
33 Funny King
34 Diehard fan
35 Frat recruiting event
36 Archipelago parts
37 Pool hustler
38 Hard-driving personality
40 Actor/director Von Stroheim
44 Erode
45 Parting words
49 Events, happenings, etc.
50 Comforting words
51 Clayton of "The Lone Ranger"
52 Watched the birdie
53 They split when smashed
54 Dangerous reptile
55 Three-time Masters winner
58 Space race acronym
59 Plunder
63 It's in some pits
64 Calculating one, briefly
65 Shape with cutting blows

NOT FOR SQUARES
By Carol Lachance

ACROSS

1 An unwanted lasting impression
5 Old West challenge
9 A hundred smackers
14 Shout of triumph
15 Avis lead-in
16 Butler's woman
17 "Shane" star Ladd
18 In ___ (worked up)
19 Humidifier emission
20 Subject of a sighting
23 Able-bodied
24 Tough wood
25 Mariner's worry
29 Brown ermine
31 Black-hearted
33 Leave widemouthed
34 They may be blown in boxes
36 Words of denial
39 Boundary between the North Temperate and North Frigid zones
43 A judge, at times
44 Mrs. Muir's beau
45 Kind of agent
46 It means everything
48 Computer operating system of old
52 Far-famed
55 Formerly Portuguese Indian territory
57 "Roll Over Beethoven" rock grp.
58 Awards since 1944
61 Exonerate
64 Fan fave
65 Ending for "peek" or "bug"
66 Tony of "Taxi"
67 Last of the Stuarts
68 Metric weight
69 Quire of manuscript pages
70 Broker's grp.
71 Espied

DOWN

1 Fills positions for
2 "Heads or tails"
3 Words with "remember" or "celebrate"
4 Hindu noble
5 Progresses at a slow, boring pace
6 It may accompany a mug shot
7 Plane measure
8 Energetic dance of the '60s
9 Thirteen witches
10 Glass fragment
11 Mushy fare
12 El Dorado treasure
13 Feather adhesive
21 One may commune with it at times
22 Tortoise-shell cat
26 Judge's seat
27 Military no-show
28 Network of veins, e.g.
30 Many miles away
32 Churchill's trademark
35 Dead Sea document
37 Dark and gloomy
38 Food scraps
39 Waiflike
40 Supersized sandwich
41 Toward China
42 Hair knots
47 Strip down the highway
49 "Little" redhead with a straw hat
50 Soccer stadium cheer
51 "Already?"
53 Staring intently
54 Mineral used to soften water
56 Checked out the chicks
59 "So Big" author Ferber
60 Acorn droppers
61 Org. that handles outbreaks
62 Mekong dweller
63 Kind of user

5

NO DEAL
By Diane C. Baldwin

ACROSS

1 Jersey baby
5 Part of a sultan's household
10 Absurd talk
14 Island festivity
15 Bakery come-on
16 Hodgepodge
17 Out of sync
20 Name for an unknown
21 Do a farrier's work
22 Loyal subject
23 Secluded valley
24 On the schedule
26 Sentence ending
29 Lingo
30 "Sad to say . . ."
31 Conversation piece?
32 Banned pesticide
35 Aren't on the same page
39 Explosive letters
40 Soap units
41 Character builder?
42 Faux pas
43 Crossed, as a stream
45 Fashion edge
48 Be an omen of
49 Witch prop
50 Two-person sled
51 Sprain treatment
54 With nothing in common
58 Tract of wet ground
59 Muscular
60 Fail to trade
61 Honey bunch
62 Identical socks, e.g.
63 Like typical Monday crossword puzzles

DOWN

1 Decent, so to speak
2 Its body is painted
3 Dainty trim
4 A fight may make it fly
5 Discussed thoroughly (with "out")
6 It may result from a burning desire
7 Double Dutch item
8 Aussie ratite
9 Do damage to
10 Prompting the hook
11 "Full House" twins
12 Prolonged attack
13 Tricked, slangily
18 Where to get a Nobel Prize
19 It has solar heating
23 General idea
24 Gambits
25 Ocean route
26 Warsaw ___, 1955 alliance
27 Verve
28 Spout angry words
29 See-through
31 Tea from Sri Lanka
32 Closing document
33 Unit of force
34 ___ off (furious)
36 Be frugal
37 Become worthy of
38 Grimm beast
42 Splits to unite?
43 Old-fashioned ones
44 Lyric poems
45 Thermonuclear blast maker
46 Bert's Muppet pal
47 Bond portrayer
48 Mesa relative
50 Use weights
51 Creative notion
52 Copyright symbols
53 Lay eyes on
55 Electric resistance measure
56 It makes waves
57 Truman's successor, popularly

HEADLINERS
By Lynn Lempel

ACROSS

1 Oscar winner for "Cactus Flower"
5 Not burning the mouth
9 Defeat
14 Moises in the majors
15 Resurgently
16 Office in the city
17 Computer component
19 West Point greenhorn
20 Welcome warmly
21 Work on one's knight moves?
23 Cote members
24 Goa garb
26 Some legumes
28 Pretty penny
31 Org. you can get a charge out of
33 Dole's Senate successor
34 Happy associate
35 Tubular pasta
36 Calendar listings
39 Still to be paid
40 Bob Marley classic
42 "Common" chapter of history
43 Like cloudless nights
45 Mephisophelean
46 Kind of fish or flower
47 Bookworm, in stereotypes
48 Permissive reply
49 Like batting-practice balls
50 Remove, as cargo
53 Vacation purpose, often
55 Cherished position in auto racing
56 Cat alarms?
58 Some of Granny's kids, perhaps
62 Last word of "The Farmer in the Dell"
64 High-altitude phenomenon
66 Reasons to bring out the National Guard
67 Little dipper?
68 Its members include Canada and Luxembourg
69 It's headless

70 Sips of sambuca, e.g.
71 Cervine male

DOWN

1 "Funny ___ or funny peculiar?"
2 "Curse the luck!"
3 Have an effect
4 One with no pockets
5 Blemish the finish of
6 Set in motion
7 "The Periodic Table" novelist Primo
8 Think anxiously about something
9 One is at home
10 Board with a thumb hole
11 Like some accounts
12 Swedish inventor of dynamite
13 Slip cover?
18 Forensic tool
22 Put on the air

25 Reason for savings
27 Film source, sometimes
28 Inserts
29 Lummox
30 Where to find some old ships
32 Dancer Alvin
35 Masked swashbuckler
37 Definitely the case
38 Beach pileup
41 Pass beyond
44 Gives in, as to pressure
49 Complete reversals
50 Dizzying gallery fare
51 Page number
52 Mustard type
54 Emulated Jack Horner
57 Prefix for meter
59 Shipshape
60 Some parting words
61 Clean air hurdle
63 "___ Beso" (1962 hit)
65 Plea from the sea

FILL TO THE MAX
By Fred Jackson III

ACROSS

1 Horse feature
5 Native Alaskan
10 Koosh competitor
14 Tan and Lowell
15 It's model material
16 Snoopy peer
17 Impromptu jazz performance
19 Weight room units
20 The same partner
21 Word with "bank" or "love"
22 Some butcher shop orders
24 Not for everyone
26 Long, narrow inlet
27 They can be found in a den
34 Seize by force
37 Follows a recipe direction
38 Final resting place, for some
39 "Star Trek" navigator
40 Dill and marjoram
41 "Dies ___" (Day of Wrath)
42 What a jilted woman may exclaim
43 Animal with a ringed tail
44 Amazed by (with "of")
45 Make final preparations?
48 Casual greetings
49 Honor for Peyton Manning
53 Danish seaport, birthplace of Hans Christian Andersen
56 Schoolyard challenge
58 Big galoot
59 Silent film star Negri
60 Bucks, cabbage, dough, etc.
63 Egyptian symbol of life
64 Where a Chicago touchdown may be cheered
65 "Rowan & Martin's Laugh-In" comedian Johnson
66 Result of downsizing
67 "___ it!" ("Hooray for us!")
68 Locale in a Beatles song

DOWN

1 Student's choice
2 Appliance maker
3 Shea player, for short
4 Serpentine letter
5 Sponges do it
6 Word with "laugh" or "straw"
7 Nobelist and author Wiesel
8 They troupe for the troops
9 Hissy fits
10 "Nothing doing!"
11 First place
12 Marriage, for one
13 Parker who played Daniel Boone
18 Come out in the long run
23 Boring items
25 Very light brown
28 Use choice words
29 Magna ___
30 Earth's is elliptical
31 Supernatural glow
32 Sticking point, metaphorically
33 Where dummies sit
34 Quantico initials
35 One involved in litigation
36 Part of a skeleton
40 Pokey
41 Abbr. appropriate for JFK and LAX
43 Corp. money managers
44 Archipelago units
46 Avian chatterboxes
47 Kind of income
50 Decants
51 Rapids transits
52 Bid
53 Australia's national gemstone
54 Ready to serve
55 Some lodge members
56 Type of giveaway
57 Prefix meaning "gas" (Var.)
61 Baseball scoreboard letters
62 19th letter of the Greek alphabet

DIMENSIONS
By Gloria &
Larry Hanigofsky

ACROSS
1 Apply plaster
5 Italian sauce
10 Wile E. Coyote's brand
14 Mountain in Thessaly
15 Fosters
16 Fashionable
17 Three long ones
20 Kind of space
21 Useful Latin abbr.
22 Chuang-tzu principle
23 Word with "too happy"
26 Inner city concern
28 Eliot's Jennyanydots, e.g.
31 Blamed one
33 Crown
37 Specialty
39 Kind of student
41 Heart-stopping incident
42 Three big ones
45 Anoint
46 Moth's legacy
47 Capone tracker
48 Most current
50 With neither profit nor loss
52 Hog heaven
53 Twenty quires
55 Anagram for seek
57 The heart of Jerusalem?
60 One who sincerely flatters
62 Sponsorship
66 Three short ones
70 Item for a woman's travel
   bag, perhaps
71 Another suitor
72 Liveliness
73 Permeate
74 Flavorful
75 It can be quite an impression

DOWN
1 It has an uphill battle
2 Ancestor of the Edomites
3 Has no presence
4 Filled with a great quantity
5 Historic beginning
6 Sinuous swimmer
7 Successful pitch
8 Meadowlands contests
9 Warren Report name
10 Miracle for a duffer
11 Net activity
12 Flaky rock
13 Reverberate
18 Some edible legs
19 Like robins' eggs
24 NASA scrub
25 Habitat for humanity
27 City south of Atlanta
28 Secret group
29 Where Kings go to beat the
   Heat
30 Precept
32 Chevy truck model
34 Throws caution to the wind
35 Surrealist Max
36 Like some divorces
38 Less inept
40 Dig (into)
43 What ushers do, sometimes
44 Raise a stink?
49 Comes to a point
51 Type of tide
54 News providers
56 Stitched
57 Applications
58 Planned setting
59 Fit of chills and fever
61 Letters on a letter
63 It's over 32 miles per hour
64 ___ the Terrible
65 Enraptured
67 Kind of roof
68 Half a bar order
69 Form of English

TWISTED FOOT
By Sefton Boyars

ACROSS
1 Largest county in Ireland
5 Street protest sound
10 Commencement time?
14 Doomsayer's sign
15 Eagle's retreat
16 Fulminate
17 Indication of a hit show
18 Beldam
19 Emanating glow
20 Prepared for a big move, in a way
23 Something to cast
24 It may whoop it up at night
25 A hasty escape
28 Dover and Gibraltar
32 Klutz
35 Mixologist on "The Love Boat"
37 One of a skeletal pair
38 Charity festivity
39 Ray Charles or Otis Redding, based on who you ask
42 Upper hand
43 Dieter's portion
44 Consociate
45 Marshal under Napoleon
46 Short-legged hounds
48 Dipsomaniac
49 Frodo's friend
50 Common Mkt.
52 Recuperate
61 Vineyard unit
62 Ancient Scandinavians
63 Wheel contact
64 Bowler's feature
65 Cockatoo's pride
66 Hound's handle
67 Eats late
68 Ones from the kitchen can be good
69 Collar type

DOWN
1 Bubbly, brown potable
2 Not include
3 Loan quarters to?
4 Squeeze some dough
5 Seal of approval
6 Where you are on a map
7 Highest salaried baseball player
8 One of a noted sailing threesome
9 Pass the bar?
10 Southern speech pattern
11 Apply crudely
12 Indian tourist city
13 The four seasons?
21 Kid of 1950s TV
22 Sounds of pain
25 Equate
26 Dramatic device
27 Run-down and filthy
29 Stratagems
30 At ___ for words
31 Occupied
32 Saharan sanctuary
33 Member of the supremes?
34 Gem side
36 ID datum
38 Smoking evidence?
40 Fiery dance
41 Mulled over
46 "A Christmas Carol" cry
47 Dogmas
49 Curbs
51 Rub the wrong way
52 Hands-on workplaces
53 Non-clashing color
54 Make a false step
55 It's given to the wise
56 Vowel-rich cookie
57 Once-mighty initials
58 Important theater sign
59 Gucci of fashion
60 "Mila 18" author Uris

FRACTIONS
By Carol Lachance

ACROSS

1 Weapon of two balls and a cord
5 Unruffled
9 Carefree walk
14 Tennessee's state flower
15 Sunburn soother
16 Actress Garson
17 Chromosome part
18 Entre ___ (confidentially)
19 Dislike intensely
20 Fractional amount
23 "Anchors Aweigh" gp.
24 Ready alternative
25 Reporter who uses shoe leather
28 Think highly of
30 Muddy enclosure
32 Man-mouse link
33 Quartz or flint
35 In a lather
37 Part of Captain Kidd's treasure
40 Isaac's mother
41 Eggnog spice
42 Mil. address
43 W.C. Fields persona
44 Casual eatery
48 Hit song from "Flashdance"
51 Proscribe
52 Enter the one-legged race
53 Organizational offshoot
57 Sandbank
59 War of the Roses house
60 Ballpark figure expression
61 Remote button
62 Peer of Dashiell
63 Cornelius and Zira, e.g.
64 On pins and needles
65 Positioned a golf ball
66 Nothing more than specified

DOWN

1 California vacation spot
2 Blackmailer's words
3 Winter coat feature
4 "Hold on ___!"
5 Cuddle up
6 Among the clouds
7 Lummox
8 Come together, as gears
9 Visibly shocked
10 Top man, in spoofs
11 Mammoth
12 Sign of early August
13 Blow it
21 Add vitamins to
22 Bridge expert Culbertson
26 In ___, going nowhere
27 Get a little shut-eye
29 Far from terra firma
30 Search, as for talent
31 Heaviest U.S. president
34 "Money ___ object!"
35 Doing double-time
36 Items in an Easter basket
37 Smurf patriarch
38 Settles, as an issue
39 Got on board
40 "Casablanca" pianist
43 ___-fi (film type)
45 Famous Olympian Jim
46 Word with "Rebel" in a Duane Eddy song title
47 Go against
49 "Too rich for my blood!"
50 Kegler locale
51 "Mr. Television"
54 Duma refusal
55 Ran like the wind
56 Be a gadabout
57 Bath bath
58 Chewbacca's friend

GADGETRY
By Mike Wittman

ACROSS

1 Courted a ticket
5 Fake sword, sometimes
9 Furniture wood
14 Violist's clef
15 Emulated Miss Daisy
16 "Androcles and the Lion" setting
17 Chef's gadget
19 "American Graffiti" quaffs
20 Parts of drum kits
21 It may be tidy
23 One foot forward
24 They may be left on doorsteps
26 Kind of calm
28 Chef's gadget
33 Dungeon objects
34 Dances in the grass?
35 Conciliatory offering
38 It makes hair stand on end
39 Aired an encore presentation of
40 Wednesday's Child is full of it
41 Bald spot's cover?
42 1992 presidential debate participant
43 Achieve a magician's goal
45 Chef's gadget
47 One of three states
50 Bedevils
51 Come up against
52 Naval pronoun
55 Gave a smooch to
59 Gave a hand
61 Chef's gadget
63 Magic, notably
64 Safety installation
65 Testimonial dinner, perhaps
66 It's abrasive
67 Risky place to live?
68 It was once, once

DOWN

1 Anatomical holders
2 Try not to be taken by surprise
3 Sicilian hothead?
4 Hotel employee
5 Quite fast, in music
6 Stones' Wood
7 Lyrical poems
8 Home of Machu Picchu
9 Part of a rotating shaft
10 Mistake eliminator
11 It's at the river's end
12 Begins the betting
13 Like the speech of a person with a cold
18 Decaying bog mosses
22 Disney film set in China
25 Field of knowledge
27 Early Nintendo gaming platform, briefly
28 "When ___ fly!" ("It'll never happen")
29 Cookie that debuted in 1912
30 Let the cat out of the bag
31 They're in a cash register in Berlin
32 Pleased as punch
35 Acronym on some jackets
36 Behave like lava
37 House of Lords member
39 Clarinet vibrators
42 Common fraternity letter
43 Debate with
44 Rub the right way
45 Knife expert
46 Turkey call
47 Dish out gazpacho, e.g.
48 Strong structural support
49 Tremble in fear
53 Where you are on a map
54 "Gadzooks!"
56 Telephone button
57 Slippery sea critters
58 Mild oath of frustrationw
60 Give it a go
62 Where a musician earns his money

THE DOCTOR IS . . . ON?

By Debbie &
Steven Ginzburg

ACROSS

1 What a borrower carries
5 Cornerstone abbr.
10 Legislative decisions
14 Letters on the cross
15 Something close to your heart?
16 Winemaker's aboveground storage
17 Black Hills st.
18 Bed boards
19 Ding
20 TV doctor known for a "keen" wit?
23 Destructive current
24 IRS and IRA expert
25 TV maker with a canine mascot
28 Cunning
29 Flying nuisance
32 Request
34 TV doctor "at home" with unusual cases?
36 Part of a magician's phrase
39 Victorian, for one
40 Some deli orders
41 TV doctor who "lifts" self-esteem?
46 Dangles a carrot in front of
47 Where the buck stops
48 Airport screening org.
51 Easy mark
52 Extra NFL periods
54 Hallowed
56 TV doctor working with a "flock" of interns?
60 Wearing cross-trainers, perhaps
62 Reveal
63 Roundish
64 New Zealand fruit or bird
65 Jungle vine
66 Weapon in the game Clue
67 "___ It Romantic?"
68 Beatific being
69 Scott of an 1856 Supreme Court case

DOWN

1 Postprandial chore
2 Ultimate conclusion
3 Very muscular
4 Rikki-___-Tavi
5 No-brainer
6 Foot part
7 Word with "sand" or "speed"
8 Room at the top
9 It doesn't include overtime
10 Current letters
11 Jovial
12 You might get one in a booth
13 Command to a guest
21 MIT grad, perhaps
22 Hasty, as a decision
26 Haggling topic
27 Greek war god
30 "Happy Days Are Here Again" composer
31 Set fire to
33 Port city in Japan on Osaka Bay
34 Horrified sound
35 Not at all well-done
36 Sights when losing a yacht race
37 La ___ Tar Pits
38 Reduce activity
42 ". . . like ___ not!"
43 "Great Expectations" heroine
44 Weapons cache
45 Biweekly tide
48 Howard of "Gandhi"
49 It's a wrap?
50 Thoroughly confused
53 Yarn unit
55 Three notes, often
57 Revise
58 One way to go to a dance
59 Sharpen, as a skill
60 Be seen among moguls?
61 Common possessive

FINDING NEMO
By Frank Virzi

ACROSS

1 It may be on the staff
5 Austen and Flaubert heroines
10 Source of low pitches
14 Munich mister
15 Frosty eyes?
16 ___ mater
17 She married Charles Lindbergh in 1929
19 Card or Met, briefly
20 "We're off ___ the wizard"
21 10th-anniversary material
22 "___ Mio"
23 Skid row woe
25 Fledgling
27 Worked like a dog
31 "Norma ___"
32 "Hang on . . ."
38 Ball, buff or bass ending
39 Basketball Hall-of-Famer Thomas
40 Drops of golden sun, on music scales
41 I before E except after C, and others
46 Creator of Rosemary and her baby
47 "No argument here"
48 Preliminary performance
53 Some NCAA basketball players
54 Nouveau ___
55 Blow the whistle
57 Billy and the kids?
61 Inter ___
62 Time it takes for you to get here?
64 Skelton's Kadiddlehopper
65 Section of a long poem
66 Grievous sound
67 Period in office
68 Emphatic agreement
69 CPR pros

DOWN

1 Friendly talk
2 Carson's successor
3 Airborne fish eaters
4 Liberty
5 Prefix with system or sphere
6 "Beetle Bailey" creator Walker
7 Cheech of Cheech and Chong
8 Unescorted
9 San Antonio-to-Laredo dir.
10 Wailer of Gaelic folklore
11 Brass, e.g.
12 Fuse ore
13 Indian wrap
18 Part of MGM
22 Outback gem
24 Meeting for exchanging information
26 Lover of Eurydice
27 Weaving machine
28 Soon, ere now
29 Nota ___
30 Half of a '50s sitcom couple
33 Actor Cage, familiarly
34 Wee ones
35 Bottle rocket paths
36 Come across as
37 Verb for Virgil
42 Soccer superstar
43 Heraldic border
44 Sign of late summer
45 Treater's phrase
48 Expanse of land
49 Moon valley (Var.)
50 Worse for winter driving
51 Fictional Heep
52 It could be added to the 57-Across clue
56 Head of Paris
58 Small matter
59 Just one of those things?
60 Worker IDs
62 Sgt., e.g.
63 Parts of yrs.

LIVE AND LEARN
By Robert H. Wolfe

ACROSS
1 Miracle-___ (garden brand)
4 Sophisticated U.S. detection aircraft
9 Some come from a fountain
14 Underwater shocker
15 "My Dinner with Andre" director
16 ___ Ann (Lily Tomlin character)
17 Start of a reputed quote from 34-Down
20 Weatherperson's adjective
21 William with the bow
22 Part of Hispaniola
23 Quote (Part 2)
28 Stepfather of John F. Kennedy, Jr.
29 Say "tut-tut"
31 Staff note after fa
32 Grayish brown
33 Actress Plummer
36 Polishes
39 Played the part of
40 Some buildings with corporate names
41 Frankincense and myrrh, but not gold
42 Go head-to-head
43 Verge
44 Emulate a landscaper
47 Quote (Part 3)
51 Father, Son and Holy Ghost, e.g.
53 AK or HI, once
54 Become conscious
55 End of the quote
60 Bye, somewhere
61 Nuclear physicist Enrico
62 About 22 degrees
63 Industrious sorts
64 Many a preadolescent
65 HS equivalency test

DOWN
1 Japanese consort
2 Try, try again?
3 A King of Norway
4 Distinctive element of many of 34-Down's novels
5 Gradually decrease
6 Steak partner
7 155, to some
8 Boil
9 It's placed between the knees
10 "Island of the Blue Dolphins" author Scott
11 Three sheets to the wind
12 Balance provider, for short
13 Indebted to the pot, in poker lingo
18 Spot checker?
19 Vintage vehicle
23 Drinks tea, perhaps
24 Alphabetic trio
25 It is not, really
26 Bump on a branch
27 In a happy mood
30 Color qualities
32 Like a heartless man of film
33 Soon, poetically
34 Writer who inspired Faulkner
35 Hotel room fixtures, for short
36 Sitarist Shankar
37 Land of the leprechauns
38 They're found in a yard
39 Falco of "The Sopranos"
41 NHL Hall-of-Famer Bobby
43 Deprived, as of happiness
44 Feeling of pleasure and enjoyment
45 Like a low-scoring hockey tie
46 Wrote
48 Novocain predecessor
49 "Song of the South" uncle
50 Word before or after "pan"
52 Ship deserter
54 Peak of perfection
55 Amount of chewing gum
56 Words with a ring to them?
57 Railroad unit
58 Early moisture
59 Moist finish?

MAKING THE CUT
By Lynn Lempel

ACROSS
1 High school class
5 Scribes' supplies
9 No longer a couple
14 Salad option
15 Tape measure part
16 Burger alternatives
17 26 fortnights
18 Dojo blow
20 Med school grad
22 Brazil resort, familiarly
23 Kipling novel
24 Routine monotony
28 Russian-born Israeli politician
30 Cartoon baby found on a doorstep
31 Wet thoroughly
33 Asian celebration
34 Spoke gushingly
37 The "U" in UHF
38 Holder for blazing logs
40 Logical start?
43 Chemist Pasteur
44 Three-faced film heroine
47 Rock layers
49 "The Last King of Scotland" portrayal
51 Design description
52 Shady shooter's advantage
55 Qty.
56 Key in the corner
57 Untold centuries
58 Mental block?
62 Warm, in a game
65 ___ the above
66 Fighting like mad
67 Peruvian of yore
68 "No Strings Attached" band
69 McEntire album title
70 Jambalaya, e.g.

DOWN
1 Home on the farm
2 Rainbow component
3 Planning to lose?
4 Free conditionally
5 Peeve
6 PBS supporter
7 Olympian gymnast Strug
8 Done in
9 Downed
10 Mount into the Grand Canyon
11 Hurting the most
12 Not as cramped
13 Salt meas.
19 Liz Taylor's third
21 Nicosia native
24 Clock change inits.
25 Impress deeply
26 Apparatus
27 Come unstitched
29 Abbr. on a nutritional label
32 Alfresco
35 One of a personal trio
36 Priestly figure of Gaul
38 Share
39 General helper
40 Balaam's rebuker
41 London cathedral designed by Wren
42 All aquiver
44 Distinguished
45 London theater Old ___
46 Detroit-to-Toronto dir.
48 Pub quaffs
50 Gorgeous Greek of lore
53 Coveted statue
54 Keen
58 Wasn't brave
59 Co. known for breasts and legs
60 Overalls part
61 Zeta-theta link
63 You may draw one
64 Bitterly cold

BORN ON THE 4TH OF JULY

By Verna Suit

ACROSS

1 Camp cook's meal
6 Gives a hoot
11 Do the math
14 Rose-colored dye
15 Town near Bangor
16 Top clock number
17 Movie producer born July 4, 1885
19 Office PC linkup
20 NASCAR advertiser
21 Feet found in English verse
22 Designer Geoffrey
24 Farming prefix
25 Folksinger Pete
26 Songwriter born July 4, 1826
31 Break a commandment
32 Coffeehouse containers
33 Mom's command
36 Haley or Trebek
37 Altar locales
39 Buddhist monk
40 Mal de ___ (seasickness)
41 What models need
42 "The Tortoise and the Hare" writer
43 Talk show host born July 4, 1943
47 Polish capital
49 Western star Calhoun
50 Mr. T's TV outfit
51 Vatican-related
53 Eisenhower, familiarly
56 Big or little digit
57 Orchestra leader born July 4, 1911
60 Untold centuries
61 Lorne Greene in "Battlestar Galactica"
62 Impostor
63 Some NFL linemen
64 Ascended, as from the grave
65 Some recipe amts.

DOWN

1 "Fantasia" frames
2 Owl's comment
3 "The jig ___!"
4 Weeks in a Roman year?
5 Deep perception
6 Garden-variety
7 Casbah resident
8 Orbison and Rogers
9 Newport News-to-Hampton dir.
10 Palate refreshers
11 Wheel goo
12 "Cheers" character
13 Place for a short-order cook
18 Naked
23 AAA's opposite?
24 Summit
25 ID nos.
26 Fraudulent operation
27 Painted metalware
28 Some yuletide decor
29 Made into an alloy
30 Rock hound's find
34 Love personified
35 Bite-size Spanish appetizer
37 What there oughta be
38 Monetary unit of Afghanistan
39 Impose a tax
41 Grade school subject
42 Transport by helicopter
44 That girl, in Spain
45 Annie, for one
46 Gallivant
47 Well-managed resource?
48 On ___ (doing some heavy drinking)
51 School gps.
52 Highest point
53 Sorts
54 Refuse to release
55 Flubs
58 Uganda's Amin
59 Experimental area

PAY UP
By Allan E. Parrish

ACROSS
1 Film dwarfs' refrain
5 Wilson in "Mrs. Doubtfire"
9 Emulate a bouncer
14 College of Thomas Gray and William Pitt
15 "Go Tell ___ the Mountain"
16 Large marine eel
17 Funambulist's tool
18 ___ bath (therapeutic treatment)
19 Criminals, in the station house
20 "Tennessee Flat Top Box" singer
23 Gold, in Guatemala
24 Advertising award
25 Comedian with a bowler hat
27 Start of a Latin 101 trio
29 Woodstock lineup
32 Airport listing, for short
33 They may all be off
35 Patron saint of sailors
37 Some vacation destinations
41 Personnel investigation
44 Landlady of classic TV
45 Three of a kind?
46 Dull discomfort
47 Canal locale
49 Took it on the lam
51 What you may need after a breakdown
52 Undesirable payment status
56 Soybean product
58 Small, Dogpatch-style
59 Underwater weapon
64 In ___ (befuddled)
66 "Arrivederci"
67 Purposely burn
68 "Werewolves of London" vocalist
69 Russian city near the Kazakhstan border
70 Quartet with a defection
71 Ancestors of domestic donkeys
72 Haitian's head
73 Workers need them (Abbr.)

DOWN
1 Adult German male
2 Title start of a Langston Hughes poem
3 It's child's play
4 Center of Miami
5 Incorrect name
6 End in ___ (require overtime)
7 On-campus mil. group
8 GI from Down Under
9 Forceful
10 Coffee, in slang
11 Flamboyant Flynn of film fame
12 Blue Grotto island
13 "Iron Mike" of boxing
21 Fifth day of Kwanzaa
22 "___ had so many children"
26 Old-time Turkish title
27 Clerical title
28 It's verboten to a vegan
30 Trudge tediously
31 Blue cartoon character
34 Clay pigeon sport
36 Characteristic of Nash's "lama"
38 Angry dads, at times
39 Reverberate
40 Distort
42 Makes happy
43 Certain low-calorie cola
48 Wish otherwise
50 Homer Simpson's catchword
52 Public square
53 Adjutants
54 Russians and Ruthenians, e.g.
55 Florida attraction
57 Doesn't just diet
60 "Stop the clock!"
61 ". . . why ___ thou forsaken me?"
62 Positive market move
63 Cupid, to Athena
65 Pulitzer dramatist Akins

SWEET DREAMS
By Lynn Lempel

ACROSS

1 Words from a well-known caller
6 London or Pisa attraction
11 End of the MLB season
14 AKC certificate notation
15 Do a parental job
16 "Straight away!"
17 Future flavor of 59-Across
19 Tony winner Wallach
20 Fizzy fountain fare
21 Seine feeder
22 Tea extra
24 Mountain route
26 Great pretenders get them
27 Daily production quantity of 59-Across
32 Data holder
33 Rat Pack name
34 Jazz style
37 Designated successor
38 Island terrorized in "Jaws"
40 Browser's site
41 Sugary suffix
42 Ad writer's honor
43 He drummed up "Help!"
44 Big sales time for 59-Across
48 Disorderly disturbance
50 Clump of hair
51 Pool divisions
52 Nautical platform
54 Feuding
58 Bars in the supermarket?
59 Nickname of the treat with its 100th anniversary on July 7, 2007
62 Fan letdown, temporarily
63 Blank tapes?
64 Secretary of Perry
65 Bradley and McMahon
66 Historical info
67 Display disdain, in a way

DOWN

1 Cloned computers
2 "The Three Tenors," for example
3 Convey
4 Symbolic figure of speech
5 Summer setting at Penn Sta.
6 Statement of obvious fact
7 Clodhoppers
8 Youngman offered his
9 Subj. for some foreigners
10 Captures, as a fish
11 Versatile musician
12 Paint choice
13 Jenna and Barbara, e.g.
18 Full of promise
23 Earth-friendly prefix
25 It spits out cabbage
26 Big name in cosmetics
27 Many check for it by saying "Hello!"
28 Old mid-month date
29 Parts of returns, often
30 Dostoyevsky masterpiece (with "The")
31 Enable
35 Gymnast Korbut
36 Wily maneuver
38 "Light" and "dark" orders
39 1/60th of an hr.
40 In error
42 Didn't go together
43 TD verifier
45 Crackerjack
46 They're produced by hives
47 Zap
48 Marcher's instrument, perhaps
49 Transit type
52 "Aw shucks!"
53 "To be," to Tiberius
55 Turkish bath decoration
56 Archipelago part
57 Ruler of yore
60 It's a ballpark figure
61 PGA driving distances

BE PREPARED
By Allan E. Parrish

ACROSS

1 Industry magnate
5 Little troublemaker
9 Popular British comedy, informally
14 Sheltered spot
15 Wide-spouted mantel piece
16 Beef designation
17 Emergency item
19 Horse-racing prize
20 Horse halter
21 Backer
23 Pursued an academic specialty (with "in")
26 Actress Ekland
27 Los Angeles suburb
28 Tet celebrant, generally
30 Gentle-lamb connection
33 Desert transports
35 Camper's protection
36 Wind of a sort
37 Mann's "The Magic Mountain" locale
38 Mammoth feature
40 Alphabetic run
41 Minute
42 Not kosher
43 Certain train car
45 Patriotic org.
46 Fictional sleuth Nero
48 Well partner
49 "Chain Gang" singer
51 Artificially formal
53 It separates Kazakhstan and Uzbekistan
55 Bumble Bee offering
56 It's not to one's credit
57 Emergency item
62 Dig for data
63 This, in Tijuana
64 God of love
65 What new parents lose
66 Dwell on anger
67 Mental fog

DOWN

1 "Proud Mary" grp.
2 San Diego draw
3 Gardner of Hollywood
4 Popular St. Valentine's Day gift
5 Contradict
6 Kigali is its capital
7 ___ Lingus
8 "Very well, mademoiselle"
9 Designate
10 Main impact of an attack
11 Emergency item
12 Playground outburst
13 Stadium call
18 Wild
22 Mischievous activities
23 Some parrots
24 Springtime bloomer
25 Emergency item
29 Personal possessions, informally
31 Record holder?
32 Hitchcock of Hollywood
34 Swimmer's choice
39 Lets go
40 Gathered and arranged
42 Ballroom dance
44 It sank in Havana Harbor
47 Monticello, for one
50 Branch of the United Nations?
52 "Presumed Innocent" creator
53 Makes a contribution
54 It holds the line
58 Calif. clock setting
59 Nest egg component, often
60 "Frasier" character
61 Nationality ending

HUH?
By Carol Lachance

ACROSS

1 Slalom obstacles
6 It might turn over a new leaf
10 Sacked out
14 Make ashamed
15 Windows alternative
16 Queen of the opera
17 Voyager Polo
18 Inadvisable action
19 "By the Time ___ to Phoenix"
20 Imaginary creature
23 Training area
26 Yoga class requirement
27 "___ the word!"
28 Post-hurricane worker, say
30 Bart and Maggie's sister
31 The Trojans of the NCAA
34 Move like sludge
35 Bait fish
37 Redhead's secret?
39 Something whose name is not known
42 Synagogue scripture
43 Wallet filler
44 "Little Women" woman
45 Trendy
46 Queries
48 A source of the Mississippi
50 Pizarro's Peruvian
51 Laila of boxing
52 Hardly gregarious
53 Its name is forgotten
57 Thespian's quest
58 Italia's capital
59 On TV he had heroes
64 ___ dixit
65 Guitarist Clapton
66 How often the postman rings?
67 Drink made with honey
68 Carrel, e.g.
69 Brief but vigorous fight

DOWN

1 Herd of humpbacks
2 Legal org.
3 La Brea goo
4 PC key
5 "I'll believe it when I see it"
6 Charge
7 Soon, to a bard
8 Royal with a golden touch
9 A book of Moses
10 "Vaya con Dios"
11 Texas city, familiarly
12 First name in stunts
13 Your first one may be blind
21 Hard-nosed
22 City near Boys Town
23 It comes in spurts
24 "Anybody home?"
25 "The Magic Flute" composer
29 Greek cheese
30 Asian monks
31 Except on the condition
32 Tattletale
33 China, in Polo's time
36 Bitless bridle
38 Isle of exile
40 China's largest river
41 Culinary hot stuff
47 Spooked
49 Acrobat's hose
50 "___ a drink"
51 "From ___ to a King"
53 Quick haircut
54 It remained in Pandora's box
55 Rick's love in Casablanca
56 "Jake's Thing" author Kingsley
60 "I ___ you one"
61 "Skedaddle!"
62 Do not delay
63 The One in "The Matrix"

SURE STARTS
By Gail Grabowski

ACROSS
1 Less-than-lovely ladies
5 Lock not on a door
10 Memo abbreviation
14 Code that's not a secret
15 One making overnight deliveries
16 Ipanema person?
17 Certain royal servant
19 Waffle brand
20 Quarters
21 Square, updated
22 Fall on Pikes Peak?
23 Fare you toss
25 CSI test site
27 Sufficient, in Dogpatch
29 Gilligan's Island feature
32 Dick's love
35 One way to enjoy a game
38 "Me, too!"
39 German expletive
40 Distribute, as cards
42 Stick up
43 Witchy woman
45 Mass seating
46 Big fusses
47 Win the pie contest
49 "The Wizard of Oz" co-star
51 Bottled spirits
54 Throws a party for
57 Broke the news
59 Amounting to nothing
61 Ranchero's rope
63 Chunks of history
64 United maintenance group
66 Branch structure
67 It has regular drawings
68 Immodest look
69 Fair-to-middling
70 City on the Ruhr
71 Spiraling current

DOWN
1 "Funny ___ or funny strange?"
2 Ishmael's people
3 Salami choice
4 Tack room items
5 Inspection org. since November 2001
6 Eaves dropper?
7 Put a stop to
8 Back in the navy?
9 Item of biblical attire
10 Way back when
11 One place for advertising
12 Golden Fleece ship
13 Farm implement
18 Like the Grinch
24 Put one over on
26 Stay to the finish
28 Ruckus
30 Melville effort
31 Calligrapher's fine points?
32 Tamale alternative
33 Non-clashing color
34 Belt holder
36 Pub pour
37 Cry of pain
40 Member of Frank's "Rat Pack"
41 Wild blue yonder grp.
44 Must
46 Magazine feature
48 Prickly sensation
50 It's sometimes rounded up
52 Currency west of the Urals
53 Vegas attractions
55 Like mugs and trophies
56 Warhorse
57 Addition column
58 Sandwich cookie name
60 Minstrel's instrument
62 Off the beaten track
65 Start to stop?

FISH TAILS?
By Carol Lachance

ACROSS

1 Junkyard hue?
5 Noted bow-carrier
10 Get an ___ effort
14 Crawl at a snail's pace
15 Piece for practice
16 Lee of desserts
17 Polar chunk
18 Fixed farm fowl
19 From the beginning
20 "Why did you go fishing?" response
23 Oahu patio
24 Paulo or Tome
25 "Thrilla in Manila" winner
28 Mag. staff
29 Place to put all hands on
33 Enters cyberspace
35 City that hosted the first Grand Prix in 1906
37 Sidesplitter
38 Music teacher's question for Charlie?
43 Manual consultant
44 Stashed away
45 Smack with a book, e.g.
48 McGregor of "Moulin Rouge"
49 Swinger's choice
52 Join in a quilting bee
53 Sound after slaking one's thirst, perhaps
55 Salad green
57 Fisherman's "OK, I guess I'll do it"
62 Taj Mahal stopover
64 "The Sopranos" matriarch
65 Attending to the matter
66 Practice origami
67 "___ else fails . . ."
68 Foxy dwellings
69 "Et voila!"
70 Big dipper
71 Slight advantage

DOWN

1 Thumb through the Yellow Pages, e.g.
2 Sell off quickly
3 Views with contempt
4 Fraternity letter
5 Singer Winans
6 The 45th of 50
7 Insect in its cocoon
8 Fan mail recipients
9 Bad response from a credit card company
10 Old Testament twin
11 A Disney film with dancing elephants
12 Miner's strike
13 Unpleasantly wintry
21 Baseball's Nomo
22 Heckler's word
26 Large diving bird
27 Passionate about
30 Exotic farm-bird
31 Play with "Memory"
32 Notre Dame legend Rockne
34 Crossword component
35 Vega's constellation
36 Tube interference
38 Spoils shares
39 1975 victor over Connors at Wimbledon
40 The Americas, in 1500
41 Another Notre Dame legend, Parseghian
42 Shilling's five
46 Crow cry
47 "The Prophet" author
49 Conked on the noggin
50 Kind of price
51 Hazardous fly
54 Mt. Carmel overlooks it
56 ___ Island Red
58 "Mary ___ little lamb . . ."
59 Spot on the tube
60 Cash cache
61 In fine fettle
62 Toward the stern
63 "Can you ___ little faster?"

TWISTED ENDS

By Frank Virzi &
Sue Clark

ACROSS

1 Realtor's favorite word
5 Beetle Bailey's boss
10 First Best Actor winner Jannings
14 Table spread
15 Marginally ahead
16 Gamma preceder
17 Muscle-building Maidenform products?
20 Lennon's "ocean child"
21 LAX posting
22 Poli-___ (college major)
23 Scoreboard abbr. at Jacobs Field
24 Pun responses, perhaps
26 His and her
28 Historic periods in which big heads flourished?
32 Swashbuckler Flynn
33 Gets a cat to leave
34 The Gramophone Company Ltd., today
35 Suppress
37 Patient replies?
40 Minneapolis suburb
42 Myopic cartoon character
44 Some really rotten garage services?
49 Conger hunter
50 Make college attendance official
51 "Platoon" setting, briefly
52 "Israfel" poet's monogram
54 Bach's "Toccata and Fugue ___ Minor"
55 First name among famous lyricists
58 Remain loyal to wildebeests?
62 Architect Saarinen
63 Author of "The Principles and Practice of Medicine"
64 Sea eagle
65 June 6, 1944
66 Food and shelter, for two
67 Elvis' daughter

DOWN

1 Arty area of Manhattan
2 Lena of "Chocolat"
3 Big name in blocks
4 If Homer stubs his toe, he goes "___!"
5 Kinda
6 Like one battery terminal
7 Soak flax
8 Hands-over-the-eyes words
9 Grand in scope
10 Flow partner
11 "Moon River" lyricist Johnny
12 Napoli locale
13 Tools for some surgeons
18 Problem for Pauline
19 Explosive liquid, for short
24 Day-___ (fluorescent paint brand)
25 Like some modern carpets
27 "___ a real nowhere man . . ."
28 Capital of Chile?
29 Kind of wrestling
30 One of the Four Forest Cantons
31 Geological span
35 Round Table title
36 At peace
37 In the past
38 In what way?
39 Letters of distress
40 Summer in the south of France
41 Jeter of the Yankees
42 Card combos
43 It comes between the U.S. and U.K.
44 Became rigid
45 Like some pools
46 New York city
47 Soaked in salt water
48 Solitary sorts
53 Like ___ of bricks
55 Cross letters
56 They're made only at home
57 On the briny
59 Coquettish
60 Cheer for a matador
61 Become cohesive

BE HONEST
By Norm Guggenbiller

ACROSS
1 Amorist
6 "My Cup Runneth Over" singer
10 Fresh-daisy link
13 Some cop show scenes
15 Charm
17 Business mailings to every address, e.g.
19 Tofu base
20 It may be on the house?
21 Tears apart
22 Uncle Sam poster word
23 According to
25 Word with "out" and "for"
26 Without delay
31 Overcome utterly
32 Brazilian destination
33 "S.O.S." group
37 Uzbekistan's ___ Sea
38 Like this puzzle's theme?
40 Sort of hammer
41 List type
42 Sweet-smelling necklace
43 Ambergris source
44 Type of detective
48 Retirement agcy.
51 Hold title to
52 Thames pullers
53 Funnel-shaped
55 Puff adder relatives
56 Crude shelter
59 Sure thing, in court
63 Some big chickens
64 Pheasant female
65 Botch things
66 Right on the map
67 Twosomes

DOWN
1 Some TV screens
2 Mississippi tributary
3 What results may do
4 Language suffix
5 Take back
6 Words with "early age" or "impasse"
7 Damage superficially
8 Certain lodge brother
9 Lead-in for Madre or Leone
10 Acid type
11 Wall Street index, for short
12 Gloomy, depressed feeling
14 Police leader?
16 Canonized mlle.
18 Addictive amphetamine, familiarly
22 Belt
23 Suffering partner
24 Battle of Endor fighter
26 Sharp blow
27 "Comin' ___ the Rye"
28 Peruse
29 It comes after the bride
30 Posh crafts
34 Hardly thrilling
35 It's full of hay
36 Bowls over
38 Tear or stain
39 Cayuse controller
43 Woolen fabric
45 Track down
46 Bobby's blackjack
47 Receive with enthusiasm
48 What players keep
49 Deep sleep
50 Something to lend
54 November winners
55 Lil' helper
56 Syllables of derision
57 Played for a sucker
58 Till pile
60 Orchestra-funding org.
61 Laura and Phil, for two
62 Small, low island

PEOPLE FOOD
By Timothy Parker

ACROSS
1 1796 Napoleonic battle site
5 Hip-hop repertory
9 Birds, collectively
13 Desktop trash can, e.g.
14 A throw into the dugout, e.g.
16 Barbershop call
17 Apt entree for Sawyer?
19 Big wine valley
20 Most bothersome
21 Expert on spars and stars
23 "The Incredible Hulk" creator
24 Obsolete repro machine
25 "Pah-pah" preceder
26 Discourteous
27 Kind of dog
30 Ones going through a stage?
33 Originated
34 Whisper one's affection
35 Wildcatter's find
36 No mere cold snaps
38 Stop wondering
39 Court or church phrase
40 Linger
41 Scots Gaelic
42 Agent, colloquially
43 Bit of nuclear physics
44 It may be flipped
46 "Don't give me that!"
48 Falls for a recently married woman?
52 In whatever way
54 Navigation units
55 School for martial arts
56 Apt dessert for White?
58 "What died?" provocation
59 Usher's post
60 Dry as dust
61 Caught in the act
62 Grade school door sign
63 Palomino's pace, sometimes

DOWN
1 Uncoventional sibilations
2 The Brady Bunch, e.g.
3 ___ one-eighty (turns around)
4 Tangled up, as laces
5 Cash in, as coupons
6 Crop up
7 Fall lead-in?
8 Junior, for one
9 Vanity Fair photographer Leibovitz
10 Apt entree for Wilde?
11 Former Canadian athlete
12 Dipper part
15 Leftover matter
18 About 2.2 pounds
22 Shouts of endorsement
24 Warm and humid
26 Territory
28 Forfeiture
29 Symbol of servitude
30 Rope fiber
31 Supportive assistant
32 Apt meal for Louis?
33 Word in some temperature readings
36 State since 1890
37 Variety of grape
41 Most high-strung
44 Tropical vines (Var.)
45 Songwriter's poetic meter
47 Like Samson, thanks to Delilah
48 Word with "opened" or "married"
49 Take up a leg, e.g.
50 Campy, perhaps
51 Heretofore
52 Chaotic happenings
53 Point in a network
54 Nothing special
57 Item in one's chest

DAYDREAMING
By Carol Lachance

ACROSS

1 Puts the kibosh on
6 Overwhelm
11 ___ du Diable
14 Bagel flavor
15 Edmonton player
16 Without further delay
17 Place for a happy meteorologist?
19 British water closet
20 Hire
21 Narcissist's love
22 "Shoot!"
23 Operation Overlord launch
25 Some bow ties
27 Moreover
30 Sorrows
32 "Pret-a-Porter" actor Stephen
33 First word of a Beatles song title
34 Type of chair
35 Provide with work
38 Bygone telephone device
40 Condensed wrap-up
42 Sticky strip
43 Tent-shaped home
45 Sullivan and Asner
46 Kwanzaa day
47 Infantile remark
48 Ready to hit the hay
49 River in central Europe
50 The Kettles of filmdom
53 Exec's note
55 Mountains between Germany and the Czech Republic
56 Gaelic language
58 Sean Penn film
62 Husband of Fatima
63 '60s sci-fi series
65 Type of mother
66 Big social gathering
67 Krugerrand measure
68 Chang's conjoined twin
69 Coup ___
70 Where the sun don't shine?

DOWN

1 Owlish greeting
2 The King of Siam's employee
3 Show affection, dog-style
4 Holy city?
5 Fancy hairnet
6 Fastest way to a new lawn
7 Team data
8 They can be resident or non-resident
9 The Wizard of ___ Park (Thomas Edison)
10 Shape in advance
11 Watching the Teletubbies?
12 Fast partner
13 Moon of Endor citizens
18 Left in the dark
24 Arthurian times
26 Pt. of USDA
27 Sitcom legend Alan
28 Son of Eric the Red
29 Staring at celebs on the red carpet?
31 Roast host
35 Former manager of The Beatles
36 Ron Howard role
37 Anniversary unit
39 City northwest of Soissons
41 He raised Cain
44 Walked the runway
48 Long-eared hound
49 Tuba's toot
50 He defeated Lee at the Battle of Gettysburg
51 "Stormy Weather" composer
52 Show evidence
54 Halloween stock
57 Lab burner
59 Poet Teasdale
60 Pt. of USNA
61 Parcel (out)
64 Hairy Addams cousin

CLASSIC!
By Fran & Lou Sabin

ACROSS
1 Dizzy's jazz style
4 Heavy lifter
9 Biblical queen's land
14 Fraternity letter
15 Sleeper's concern
16 Oscar-winning Marisa
17 Film classic of 1939
20 Spurs
21 Group protest participant
22 ___ mater
23 Men-goats of myth
25 Sawbones' gp.
28 Pipe cleaners
30 Code word?
33 Cookie jar theft
35 Change for the better
36 Film classic of 1965
42 Drunk as a skunk
43 "Waiting for the Robert ___"
44 Most hackneyed
47 Gobi and Kalahari
52 And more, briefly
53 Sieve feature
55 Mel's Diner waitress
56 Chemical salt
59 Kind of colony
60 Classic film of 1954
64 Nancy Drew author Carolyn
65 New Hampshire state flower
66 Tea addition
67 Sin city?
68 Crops, as a snapshot
69 Buttons with an Oscar

DOWN
1 One wanting something for nothing
2 Peter who played Lawrence
3 Jipijapa hat
4 Punny answer to "Why are birds so noisy?"
5 Troy, N.Y. college
6 Tunnel builder
7 India's Jawaharlal
8 Gourmand's delight
9 "Don't touch!" editorially
10 Gordie of NHL fame
11 U.A.E. members
12 Oscar winner Kingsley
13 Financial support
18 Mild, yellow cheese
19 Place for a run
23 Mannheim missus
24 Speller's phrase
26 Warm weather wear
27 Current status
29 Wear down
31 Marriages may change some
32 Ostrichlike bird
34 White House monogram, 1953–61
36 Carry
37 Trumpet man Al
38 Drew out
39 Two of a kind
40 Ye-Shoppe go-between
41 Honoraria
45 Robert of "Jaws"
46 Reduces to junk
48 Penultimate fairy tale word
49 "The Bathers" painter
50 Hypnotic condition
51 Like many nuts
54 Admit
57 "___ you don't!"
58 Exercise judgment
59 Cpls., once
60 Approves, briefly
61 Opposite of "paleo"
62 Ivy Leaguer
63 Music genre

TURNING IT ON
By Randall J. Hartman

ACROSS

1 Its capital is Dispur
6 Best Picture of 1958
10 Tickled pink
14 Medicinal herb
15 Saudi Arabia neighbor
16 Choir attire
17 Part of Hispaniola
18 Ginger portrayer on "Gilligan's Island"
19 World-famous garden
20 1969 hit by Blood, Sweat and Tears
23 Boozehound
24 Bowler, for one
25 Say again
29 Strait-laced
31 Ovine entreaty
34 Video game pioneer
35 Film critic Pauline
36 Guitarist Clapton
37 Mystical dancer
40 Country cabin components
41 Requirement
42 Donovan McNabb, notably
43 Orlando-to-Miami dir.
44 Declare with conviction
45 Salon jobs
46 Freudian topic
47 007 creator Fleming
48 Situation with high personnel turnover
55 Draw a line in the sand, perhaps
56 MasterCard rival
57 White heron
59 Land of leprechauns
60 Harrow rival
61 Actress Verdugo
62 Race assemblage
63 Compos mentis
64 Bowling alley button

DOWN

1 Vesuvius output
2 They may be high or open
3 Barbershop cut
4 Proposal opponent
5 Windjammer sheet
6 "10-4"
7 Poker player's declaration
8 Predatory group
9 Before long
10 Welcome
11 Rock band?
12 Brother of Seth
13 Place to curl up and hibernate
21 Part of a famous soliloquy
22 Scene-stealer
25 Singer Lou
26 Cultural values
27 Legendary Satchel
28 Lets in an unearned run
29 Cell alternative
30 Funny Foxx
31 Places for drunken sailors
32 Seating request
33 You may get these in the long run?
35 Capped part
36 "Blackboard Jungle" author Hunter
38 Calls for
39 Moore octet
44 In the past
45 Hardly the most prestigious paper
46 Big social gathering
47 Cockamamie
48 Like a condor in the wild
49 War of 1812 lake
50 "La Dolce ___" (Fellini film)
51 "The Heat ___"
52 Go beyond a once-over
53 Hematite and galena
54 Russo of "The Thomas Crown Affair"
55 Rep. opponent
58 Make lace

NOVEL MISSIONS
By Diane C. Baldwin

ACROSS
1 Indian royalty (Var.)
6 Lay eyes on
10 Restless yearning
14 Blazing
15 ___ contendere
16 Herd mama
17 Superhero's exploit
19 Something to cop
20 Magician's declaration
21 Warbled in the Alps
23 Camel's cousin
26 Pastoral poems
27 Sleuth's task
32 Tennis star Nastase
33 Shenanigan
34 Carte words
37 Pussyfoot
40 Wallet bill
42 Call for help
43 Words to live by
47 Let loose
48 Tragedian's intent
51 Old photo hue
54 Relative, but not by blood
55 Munitions cache
57 Meeting of spiritualists
62 Steep, rugged cliff
63 Romance hero's aim
66 Casting assignment
67 Charlotte Bronte's Jane
68 Sticker
69 Hand-holders
70 Dizzy, James or Jimmy
71 Gives the impression of
   being

DOWN
1 Throaty utterance
2 Place to worship from
3 Hipster's jargon
4 Greek war god
5 Agree out of court
6 Needle point?
7 Lay down the lawn
8 Perform on stage
9 It may "rock the cradle"
10 Stand in the way of

11 Running figure
12 Angler's basket
13 Coin toss call
18 "Felix ___" (George Eliot
   title)
22 Dancing spot
24 "What did I tell you?!"
25 Board game tokens
27 Forms a lap
28 Hodgepodge
29 They're sometimes read
30 Old pro
31 Succor in a storm
34 Diva Gluck
35 Wolf's shelter
36 Word with "liberal" or
   "martial"
38 Bermuda border
39 Remarkable time
41 Grant's foe
44 Harmful look
45 Cub Scout unit
46 Cruet contents, often

48 Fief holders
49 Humorous poet Ogden
50 Thick woolen fabrics
51 Pelvic bones
52 Faux pas
53 Praise from David
56 Past one's prime
58 "The Morning Watch"
   author
59 Congenial
60 Study hard for exams
61 Building wings
64 Refrain syllable
65 Commandments number

FEEL THE BURN
By Raymond Hamel

ACROSS
1 "Who's Afraid of Virginia ___?"
6 "In the Bedroom" director Field
10 Latin lesson word
14 Mumbai's country
15 "Cannery Row" author
17 Catchphrase of diet expert Susan Powter
19 ___ favor (please)
20 Financial belt-tightening
21 Not favoring
22 Insolent act
23 Skier's lift
24 Mishandle an opportunity
28 Humanities degs.
31 Boxers' attire
32 "We Three Kings of Orient ___"
33 Hit the road
34 Impressively great
35 Dermatologist's concerns
37 Fleece-bearing craft
38 Run for, as public office
39 ___ polloi
40 Sous chef, at times
41 Sound after a pinprick
42 Screening room command
45 Shatner role
46 Gluten-containing grains
47 Tack on
50 Mental fog
51 ___ chi
54 Place the first words of 17, 24 and 42-Across are heard
57 Previously
58 Antibody producer
59 Namath's last team
60 Indy 500 winner Luyendyk
61 "… the ___ completion of their appointed rounds"

DOWN
1 Smoke curl
2 Not snowed by
3 Stinky smell
4 Pouty protruder
5 Big money contributors
6 Dangerous fly
7 Classic TV tosspot
8 Feral shelter
9 Puts out of commission
10 Neighbor on "Bewitched"
11 Israel's Golda
12 Congressional business
13 Terrier type
16 Kind of base
18 Period of quiet
22 Tiny bit
23 Patisserie product
24 Gown
25 What trainees need to learn
26 Village Voice awards
27 TV hotel owner Fawlty
28 Word of gratitude, somewhere
29 Feature of some Christmas trees
30 Thunderous event
33 Very thin models
35 Phylum of humans
36 Part of an egg
40 Emulates Holmes
42 Shampooing step
43 Perfectly
44 Like a smoke-filled room
45 Laments loudly
47 Somewhere over the rainbow
48 Bread eaten with hummus
49 Teen's big event
50 "Bobby" co-star Moore
51 Hired ride
52 "In your dreams, pal!"
53 "___ This a Lovely Day" (Irving Berlin song)
55 Pine relative
56 Dispirited

TV LAND
By Frances Burton

ACROSS
1 Relaxation
5 Carpentry joint
10 Party offerings
14 What's more
15 "So long"
16 Mine entrance
17 That special leader?
18 Staggers
19 Golfer's quest
20 Four flush
21 "Gilmore Girls" place
23 Bumpkin
25 Construction lifts
26 Consecrate
28 Ruckus
30 Avoid ignorance
31 Executive's incentive
32 Gear tooth
35 Some square dancers
36 Drill for penetrating rock
37 Spelunker's haunt
38 Word in a Maugham title
39 Prince Charming wannabes
40 Biblical tower
41 Driftwood site
42 Conestogas
43 Bursting into flower
46 Proofreader's mark
47 "Little House on the Prairie" place
50 Letterman's turf
53 Present Persia
54 Martini garnish
55 "Star Wars" character
56 Alaska city
57 German sociologist Max
58 Redundant partner of "done with"
59 Black fly
60 Homes in the sticks?
61 Its eye is used in spooky recipes

DOWN
1 Colossal, moviewise
2 "As if that weren't enough . . ."
3 "Buffy the Vampire Slayer" place
4 N.J. time zone
5 Weasel-like carnivore
6 Standard of perfection
7 Wedding cake section
8 Nocturnal swimmers
9 5:00 p.m. occurrence
10 Showy flower
11 Heathen gods
12 Banking expert?
13 Burgoo and pepper pot
21 Bones partner
22 Surprising exclamations
24 Wherry equipment
26 Gymnast Korbut
27 Honest-to-goodness
28 Legion
29 Unnamed people or things
31 Slayer of Adonis
32 "Murder, She Wrote" place
33 Pizza maker's need
34 Coagulates
36 Clark Gable movie
37 Pet store purchase
39 You, of yore
40 Unadorned
41 Shakespearean offering
42 Vacillates
43 Knocking for a loop
44 Title for Munchhausen
45 Andean ruminant
46 A "shalt not"
48 Mirth
49 Some are prime
51 Squandered, as a lead
52 Work in the mailroom
55 Solomon, to David

WHAT'S THE BIG IDEA?

By Fran & Lou Sabin

ACROSS

1 Checks out, slyly
6 Move stealthily
10 Under the covers
14 Cause for a blessing
15 Enjoy "Buddenbrooks"
16 Emulate a critic
17 Thomas Edison's 1877 good idea
19 Pull an all-nighter
20 Get-up-and-go
21 It's good to meet them
22 Picasso or Casals
23 Social rejects, stereotypically
24 She ain't what she used to be
25 Punjab's capital city
28 Series segments
32 Double curve
33 Hasenpfeffer ingredients
34 Twain's talent
35 Hamlet
38 Where way-clearers may want you to move to
40 "My God," in the Scriptures
41 Word with "Peace" or "Job"
43 Ready for surgery
44 End-blown flute
46 Changes direction abruptly
48 Mine yields
49 Tried pot luck?
51 Tribe descended from the Anasazi
53 Small natural hill
54 Hardly one with stage fright
57 Certain chorister
58 Emile Berliner's 1877 good idea
60 Barn dance
61 Juarez whoopees
62 Has coming
63 Oliver's request
64 Plant opening
65 Units of force

DOWN

1 Dogpatch creator
2 Pain in the neck
3 Place of horrors, in film
4 Indefinable time
5 Oklahoman
6 Lost one's way
7 Israel-Jordan lake
8 Spaces between objects or points
9 "Th" in Old English
10 Whirlaway's Triple Crown jockey
11 Joseph Glidden's 1874 good idea
12 Substitute for the unnamed
13 Wannabe recording star's tape
18 "Bee Season" star
22 Like yesterday's news
23 Christmas card word, often
24 Countenance
25 Paramour
26 Gracefully athletic
27 Igor Ivan Sikorsky's 1939 good idea
29 Anti-antis?
30 Kinda down?
31 Procedure parts
33 "You are ___"
36 Smiley novel "A Thousand ___ "
37 Certain Olympians
39 Deserved a citation
42 Memorable team member
45 Cal Ripken, Jr., notably
46 Manche's capital city
47 Chipped in
50 Scandinavian
51 Detriment
52 Spreader's choice
53 Smuggler's amount
54 Rhino feature
55 British royal
56 Military fare
58 Deck cleaner
59 Filly fare

IN THE DISTANCE
By Carol Lachance

ACROSS
1 Dandy's scarf
6 Whale-seeker of note
10 Witty folks
14 Southern nickname
15 Nintendo's one-time rival
16 Land in water
17 Human gliders
19 Lender's recourse
20 A measure in Pennsylvania
22 Guru's title
23 Regarding grades K–12, for short
24 Dance if they're in your pants
27 Caps on the Clyde
30 Gulf War surveillance sys.
34 "The Bells" poet
35 Completed, in Caen
36 Like land with rich soil
37 A measure in Winnie-the-Pooh books
40 Bones of contention
41 They're there to welcome you
42 Nobelist and statesman Hammarskjold
43 Inventor of the steel plow
44 Valley in California
45 Flat-nosed pooch, briefly
46 Came down to earth
48 Restorative resort
50 A measure for Noah
58 Mountain range of southwest Kyrgyzstan
59 Bette Davis role in "Pocketful of Miracles"
60 Bubble-gum action hero Williams
61 Romantic corner
62 Officially sanctioned
63 The yoke's on them
64 Spanish crowd?
65 Part of room and board

DOWN
1 "This won't hurt ___!"
2 It may precede or follow "as"
3 Gabby truck driver
4 To be excessively preoccupied
5 One who makes a giver a giver
6 Italian wine center
7 Last slice of bread
8 Shakes hands on
9 Pesto ingredient
10 Gore Vidal's first novel
11 Cantonese is spoken here
12 Narrow valley
13 E-mail command
18 Peaceful relations between nations
21 Portfolio units
24 Ladybug's lunch
25 "___ crying over spilt milk"
26 High-strung
28 Not to mention
29 City known for its Heat
31 Place to hang your hat
32 Dagger companion
33 Everglades grass
35 With no strings attached
36 Not a run-of-the-mill entertainer
38 As long as it lasts
39 Hockey Hall of Famer Neely
44 Drunken daze
45 "Dances with Wolves" enemy
47 Pessimist's phrase
49 Sacred song
50 Baccarat alternative
51 Holly tree
52 Notoriety
53 Lodge letters
54 Kinds or sorts
55 She played Gretchen on "Benson"
56 "___ M for Murder"
57 Sinuous shockers

BRIDE'S PRIDE
By Billie Truitt

ACROSS
1 "Ben-___," Charlton Heston film
4 Like many radios
8 Hamm's sport
14 "Housewife" Longoria
15 Sub station?
16 Historic Harlem theater
17 Pool table success
18 M.D.'s diagnostic tools
19 Pistil-packing
20 Relatives of urban legends
23 Low point
24 Culinary directive
25 One of a sailor's seven
28 Chance to start again
32 Snake's greeting
35 Frenzy of publicity
36 Ice cream nut
37 It's only skin-deep
40 Bring into existence
41 German submarine
42 Lavish party
45 Guitar pioneer Paul
46 Period of reprieve
50 Pig's digs
51 Avatar of Vishnu
52 Was under the weather
56 Time to recognize achievements
60 Searches thoroughly
62 Way up a hill
63 Unrefined find
64 Examine
65 Garr of "Mr. Mom"
66 According to
67 Naive country folks
68 Bookmaker's concern
69 Commercials

DOWN
1 Frog-hunting bird
2 Back-of-the-mouth pendulum
3 New products div.
4 Look upon with favor
5 Game show creator Griffin
6 Goes quickly, as time
7 Blunder
8 Exotic expedition
9 Car manufacturer Fritz von
10 Command to Fido
11 Like Beethoven's music
12 Building extension
13 Lobster coral, e.g.
21 Take all the marbles
22 Buster Brown's dog
26 Related on the mother's side
27 Moorehead who played Endora
29 One of the five W's
30 Radio's PBS
31 Born, on the society page
32 Ticket parts
33 Wooden shoe
34 Type of happy ending
38 Petroleum product
39 Oklahoma tribe
40 Greek X
42 Stock market pessimist
43 Make a confession
44 Pierced
47 Takes by force
48 Early New Zealanders
49 "Ich bin ___ Berliner"
53 Parkinsonism treatment
54 Like some seals
55 Hairdressers, at times
57 Gospel author
58 Russian range
59 The ___ of Avon
60 He's had a Rocky career
61 Murmur amorously

UP A TREE
By Matthew J. Koceich

ACROSS
1 Patsies
6 Like a nursery rhyme cupboard
10 Cram into the overhead, e.g.
14 In the slightest degree
15 Most eligible, once
16 Burned up the road
17 Toronto team
19 Toll unit for trucks
20 Part of a clinical trial
21 School term
23 Be undecided
25 Lacking in resonance
26 "Elvira" group
32 Harvest
33 Use an extra-big spoon
34 Out of production
37 Count (on)
38 "To ___ own self be true"
40 Canal of renown
41 Clairvoyance
42 Tree offshoot
43 Let up
44 Southern dessert
47 Like organza or chiffon
50 Artist Rundgren
51 Railroader
54 Ludlum's "Identity" and "Ultimatum"
59 Ship in a historic 15th-century trip
60 Protection against moths
62 "Romeo Is Bleeding" star
63 It's sometimes certified
64 Display poor sportsmanship
65 Insect repellent
66 Formerly, formerly
67 Capital of Oregon

DOWN
1 Not all wet
2 Weber State University state
3 "___ Was a Rollin' Stone"
4 Some wings
5 Arise late on purpose
6 Plane manufacturer
7 RN's organization
8 Football officials
9 Smooth sailing
10 Inaction
11 Poisonous substance
12 Wrinkle-resistant synthetic
13 Teeny-___
18 Told a tale
22 Eyelid infection
24 Enchant
26 Shrek, for one
27 Fermented beverages
28 Brown seaweed
29 Kind of gun
30 Forbiddance
31 Lines of homage, collectively
34 Face-to-face exam
35 Dietary, in advertisements
36 Two or three bucks
38 Co. once owned by Howard Hughes
39 Sot's involuntary sound
40 Flow back
42 Glossary entry
43 Kidnaps
44 One who goes strictly by the book
45 Silver-white element
46 Something fishy?
47 Ecclesiastical assembly
48 Emperor Selassie
49 Sesame Street dweller
52 Highest point
53 In the neighborhood
55 Cassowary kin
56 Country singer McCoy
57 To be, in Latin 101
58 Bow to the ship?
61 Insult, slangily

WHAT'S NEW?
By Lynn Lempel

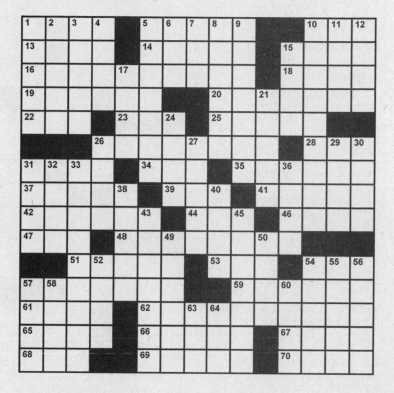

ACROSS

1 Oaf
5 Large weasel
10 Bases loaded situation, for the pitcher
13 Dude ranch prop
14 Tattoo's sighting
15 Really dry
16 What peers typically have in common
18 In boxing shape
19 Ancient Mexican
20 Gets by
22 Shaky start?
23 Bird bill
25 Really silly
26 Most-watched sports event
28 Lgths. of tape
31 Gwyneth title role of 1996
34 Be litigious
35 Coin of the realm
37 American frontiersman
39 Topsy's playmate
41 Singly
42 Not on the best of terms
44 Agcy. with not many happy returns
46 Dumbfounded
47 Foreign exchange option
48 Poker player's phrase
51 Verb in Morton Salt's slogan
53 Big expanse
54 HUD division
57 Like Snow White
59 Fireside treats
61 With cameras rolling
62 Catalog inclusion
65 It might come off the top of your head
66 Striker's demand
67 They have corners but still roll
68 Something to shoot for
69 Church assembly
70 Large quantity

DOWN

1 Old, rickety vehicle
2 Symbols of industry
3 Some German autos
4 Problem for the bottom line
5 Orthodontic aids
6 Comfort, briefly
7 Symbol of solidity
8 Not so red-blooded?
9 Infection needing an injection
10 Dairy denizen
11 Hardly suitable for farming
12 It may circulate in an office
15 WWII weapon
17 "___ 911!: Miami" (2007 film)
21 Letter for a scholar?
24 Spectrum component
26 Magician's prop
27 Theology figure
29 Eat in style
30 Progeny
31 "For Sale" site
32 Bit for the dust rag
33 Hit song from "Breakfast at Tiffany's"
36 Spiritedness
38 Foy with seven little ones
40 Munitions
43 Burglar alarm features
45 Becomes incensed
49 Off the right path
50 Two-syllable foot
52 Floor space, e.g.
54 Weak or delicate
55 Thus
56 Cockeyed
57 Saucy
58 Verdi heroine
60 Carmaker with a namesake car
63 Clamor
64 Paul Anka's "___ Beso"

SALUTE THE FLAG
By Carol Lachance

ACROSS

1 Did a doggy trick
6 Turkish jambalaya
11 School media depts.
14 Tampico pal
15 "The Baron in the Trees" author Calvino
16 In need of restocking
17 Card game that's smokin'?
19 Knock the socks off of
20 Unmeasured amount
21 ___ de coeur
22 Plain tuckered out
24 Handy evidence of being frightened?
28 Those in need of a change
31 Ship sunk in Havana harbor
32 Symbols of stubbornness
33 Monopoly avenue
37 Certain Plains native
38 Military nickname
39 Gardner of Hollywood
40 A word from Bart Simpson
43 Make blood boil
45 Greek island
46 D flat
47 Righteous Brothers' musical style
51 Famed root beer seller
52 Roman goddess of plenty
53 "Isn't ___ bit like you and me?" (Beatles lyric)
56 Pencil stump
57 Packed with celebs
62 To's reverse
63 Where Hawkeye served
64 Chipped in a chip
65 Type of office machine
66 "That angers me!"
67 Gets clean

DOWN

1 Teasdale of poetry
2 "You can say that again!"
3 Shipshape
4 Cry of revulsion
5 Some pets, informally
6 Meadow songbird
7 "What am ___ do?"
8 "Mighty ___ a Rose" (1901 song)
9 Capp's pub order
10 One million dollars, to some
11 Happy as ___
12 "Wheel of Fortune" purchase
13 Nobel or Garbo, e.g.
18 Speaker of baseball
23 Nails down just right
24 Golfer Michelle
25 Came forth
26 Roo's mom
27 Top baccarat score
28 Coll. hotshot
29 Lincoln or Ford, e.g.
30 Emulate Gabriel
33 Oncle's mate
34 Epic chronicle
35 Loving and lasting leader
36 Wild West lawman
38 Chop ___ (stir-fried dish)
41 Got 100 on, as a test
42 Cold one
43 Like always
44 Org. for Sharks and Penguins
46 Egyptian Christian
47 Canadian National Park site
48 First lady Bush
49 Take out to place on shelves, perhaps
50 Everly Brothers hit
53 Modern wall hanging
54 Rare shoebox marking
55 Foots a column
58 Jerry's cartoon foe
59 The law has a long one
60 Stephen of "The Crying Game"
61 Genetic evidence

OPEN ENDINGS
By Gail Grabowski

ACROSS

1 Supermarket sections
6 Geometry calculation
10 Ruin the secret
14 Synthetic fiber
15 Document with blanks
16 Wedding rental
17 Nutritious snack
19 Declare openly
20 Family member
21 Became threadbare
22 Review, as damage
24 Kuwait's peninsula
26 Colon components
27 Broadcasting
31 HBO rival
34 Annex, briefly
37 Movie genre
38 Standard product?
39 Hang down
41 "___ the Walrus"
42 New Mexico's state flower
44 No matter which
45 Sheen
48 Veer off course
49 Cattle call
50 Current
52 Mil. branch
54 Subtract
58 Food prep course
60 Long-necked bird
62 Damascus's land (Abbr.)
63 "Night" novelist Wiesel
64 Region beyond the Earth's atmosphere
67 Orange throwaway
68 Beat badly
69 Patriotic symbol
70 Brings to a halt
71 Recedes
72 Knight's horse

DOWN

1 Church doctrine
2 Proofreader's find
3 South American mammal
4 Charged particle
5 Isolate, due to a blizzard
6 Miles away
7 Judge's garment
8 Memorable time
9 Uncommon source of music nowadays
10 Dynamite
11 Farm animals
12 Famous cookie man
13 Gift decorations
18 Reluctant
23 Classic Parker Brothers game
25 '60s singer Sonny
28 Raise, as with a crane
29 Poetry muse
30 Ready for war
32 Blind trio of song
33 Cat's weapon
34 Actor Sandler
35 First 007 film
36 "Excuse me"
40 Fancy feather
43 Pre-owned
46 Requirement for a rebate, often
47 Control tower tracker
51 Past and present
53 Watermelon throwaways
55 Customary practice
56 Ride a bike
57 Cornered
58 Roll call response
59 Lena of "Chocolat"
60 Ticket remnant
61 Some fly traps
65 City area, briefly
66 Frisk (with "down")

BOING
By Fran & Lou Sabin

ACROSS
1 Lacking rain
5 Foot pound?
10 "Is that all right?"
14 Hitcher's hope
15 Type of wave or bore
16 Sermon subject
17 Does likewise
18 The end of ___ (legend's retirement)
19 Opening scene?
20 "Annie" exclamation
23 Medieval
24 Jacob's wife and namesakes
25 Hammett falcon
29 Enter slowly
33 OB/GYN's org.
34 "___ la Douce"
37 Coeur d'___, Idaho
38 Starting line
42 Wickerwork willow
43 October stone
44 Bovine mouthful
45 They ring some necks
47 "Do the Right Thing" extras
50 Peer
53 Slangy denial
54 Bursting out
60 Picador's victim
61 Present occasion
62 Croesus' desire
63 Sigher's word
64 Samantha of "The Phantom"
65 State forcefully
66 Site of the 1960 Summer Olympics
67 Some swingers?
68 Rank, in a way

DOWN
1 Sea near the Caspian
2 Ready for plucking
3 Sneaking suspicion
4 Idi Amin, notably
5 Faces the pitcher
6 Triangle tone
7 "Island of the Blue Dolphins" author
8 An Osmond
9 Public squares
10 Make exaggerated claims
11 Jason of the NBA
12 Pair split in Vegas
13 Hankering
21 Word on a French map
22 "You're in ___ of trouble!"
25 Baseball league designation
26 Cause laughter
27 Female vampire
28 Logician's conjunction
30 '60s greeting
31 Bring on oneself
32 Must-haves
35 Item in a bucket
36 Worshipper's locale, perhaps
39 Banned ballplayer
40 Baghdad native
41 Moundsmen, hurlers, pitchers, etc.
46 Caught some rays
48 Bumbler
49 Biblical doubter
51 "Disco" attachment
52 Shop talk?
54 Go it alone
55 Nanny's buggy
56 Neighbor of Tenn.
57 Be footloose
58 Ginkgo or baobab
59 Bunch of bison
60 Swabbie

BEST FRIENDS
By Eugene Newman

ACROSS

1 Lukas of "Rambling Rose" (1991)
5 Criticizes sharply
9 Fad
14 "___ It Romantic?"
15 Furnish with a false alibi, e.g.
16 Refuge
17 Canute II?
19 Change, as the Constitution
20 Babe Ruth's middle name
21 It dissolves in H2O
23 "The Omen" boy
25 Hammett's falcon
30 Sharp-billed wader
32 Complained bitterly
33 Buddhist scripture
36 Amtrak alternative
38 Inst. in Nashville
39 Birch and root, e.g.
40 ___ chi
41 Go-getter
44 Minoan culture site
46 Chekhov and Bruckner
47 Cowpoke's charge
49 Teacher's tool
51 Tiller attachment
54 Soul singer Redding
56 Dry red wine
58 Permanent place?
62 This puzzle's theme
64 Idolize
65 One of Pittsburgh's three rivers
66 Impertinent person
67 Community type
68 Makes indistinct
69 Word with "souci" or "serif"

DOWN

1 It's linked to mighty
2 Comparable to a beet
3 The end of ___ (legend's retirement)
4 Speak with involuntary pauses
5 Comic Gilda
6 Atty.'s gp.
7 Famous Quaker
8 Be angry
9 Egg-rich bread
10 He's after ewe?
11 Caesar's hail
12 Buddhist sect
13 Cease all action
18 Subarctic forest
22 Actors Grant and Elwes
24 Israeli desert
26 Uruguayan uncle
27 Wash out with solvent
28 French legislature
29 Singer Rabbitt
31 Trapped, in a way
33 Razor sharpener
34 "___ HOOKS" (crate instruction)
35 ___-frutti
37 Shortstop's bane
39 Attack from all sides
42 Director Howard
43 Performed a canticle, e.g.
44 Apple product
45 Make restitution for
48 Cajun concoctions
50 Free from
52 Actress Verdugo
53 Thinking man's sculptor?
55 London district
57 Three make a tbsp.
58 Droop
59 Nabokov heroine
60 Sodom refugee
61 Seamy matter?
63 Band date

SPIN CONTROL
By Fran & Lou Sabin

ACROSS
1 "___ and Soul" (1930 song)
5 Offshoot groups
10 Commiserator's word
14 U.S. Grant's home state
15 Sensing
16 Spy-in-hiding
17 Noted work?
18 Annapurna's country
19 Kind of sale
20 Start of a comic query
23 Mythical big bird
24 Coyote kin
25 Genteel
30 Noted Grandma
33 ___ Dhabi
34 Covent Garden highlight
36 Flexible
38 Middle of the comic query
42 "Drat!" and "Egad!"
43 "The Sopranos" Emmy
    winner Falco
44 Cincinnati threesome
45 Neophytes
47 Register signer
50 Flamenco accolades
52 Reagan's "Star Wars" plan
53 End of the comic query
61 Sheepherding areas
62 Small insect-eating bird
63 Like early television
64 Patrick's "Ghost" co-star
65 Cousteau milieu
66 Without walls
67 Adam's arboretum
68 Blackens
69 Took one's turn

DOWN
1 Springsteen's nickname
2 "That's trouble!"
3 Pet in Bedrock
4 Healthy snack
5 Shore scuttler
6 Flock members
7 Sadie Hawkins Day creator
8 Lag behind
9 Hardly every day

10 Food of the gods
11 Rich soil
12 ___-Seltzer
13 Detected
21 Piniella of baseball note
22 "Christ Stopped at ___"
25 Gangland biggie
26 WWII enemy sub
27 Full of vigor
28 Perry's penner
29 Part of LED
31 Memorable Merman
32 Rise partner
35 Once more, hillbilly-style
37 Being, to Caesar
39 Adds, offer-wise
40 Italian palace city
41 Windows XP, Windows NT,
   e.g.
46 Electronic control systems
48 Kind of duck
49 Stay in hiding
51 Wedge of pizza

53 Ye ___ Shoppe
54 Garden trespasser
55 Appellation
56 "Joey" cast member
   de Matteo
57 Day-to-day deterioration
58 Buff
59 Without advantage or
   disadvantage
60 Needing straightening

BON APPETIT
By Eugene Newman

ACROSS

1 Big-time celebration
5 Birthplace of Chang and Eng
9 Birch kin
14 Burgundy buddies
15 Sheriff Andy Taylor's boy
16 French GI
17 Champignons
19 Great reviews
20 Christmas time in NYC
21 Wind up
22 Epinards
24 Applicant's offering
26 Spot in the mer
27 Not total
31 Scandalous gossip
35 Superior of a monastery
38 Fictional Christie and Karenina
40 Expected to arrive
41 This puzzle's theme
44 Be less than 100 percent
45 Large herbivore
46 Is sibilantly challenged?
47 Learning method
49 Long-horned grasshopper
51 Rickenbacker, e.g.
53 Pleistocene epoch nickname
57 Huitres
61 Asian sash
62 Type of tank
63 Like most American films
64 Cotelettes de mouton
67 Soft palate resonance
68 Victim one of murder one
69 Specialty
70 Sanctions
71 Chromosome passenger
72 Knight's wife

DOWN

1 More courageous
2 Cause a chuckle
3 Tilts
4 Vesuvius debris
5 Oklahoman
6 Portable music player
7 Purpose
8 K.P.'s milieu
9 Its first is for fools
10 Like a library book
11 Prima donna
12 It's measured in kwh
13 Word with "hour" and "job"
18 Losing athlete's demand, sometimes
23 Rice dish (Var.)
25 Second word in many fairy tales
28 Sister city of St. Petersburg
29 Bungling
30 Irritate
32 Bad time for Julius
33 Type of roast
34 Ms. Truehart of "Dick Tracy"
35 Many miles away
36 Verve
37 Stiff drink
39 Pertaining to the second most common element in the Earth's crust
42 Backpacker, e.g.
43 Ocean phenomenon
48 Greasy spoon
50 Planting tool
54 Ancient mall
55 Was visibly awestruck
56 Virginia Woolf piece
57 Estimator's phrase
58 Sudden pull
59 Sheltered promenade
60 Smelting refuse
61 Straw in the wind
65 Supreme Court Justice Fortas
66 Holbrook of "The Firm"

SMALL TALK
By Fran & Lou Sabin

ACROSS
1 Half of the "Monday, Monday" singers
6 Cut off, as a branch
9 "Beat the Clock" activity
14 Political sphere
15 "___ had it up to here!"
16 Audio antiques
17 Louisa May Alcott novel
19 ___ Gay
20 Grimley and Norton
21 Self-centered
22 Old Faithful, famously
23 Sprightly
24 Marjoram, e.g.
25 Team from Los Angeles
28 Emulated a carpenter
32 Double curves
33 One with no capacity for veracity
34 "The Wolf Man" actor Lugosi
35 Opinion
36 Goes out of business
37 Bart Simpson, e.g.
38 Reese in "Legally Blonde"
39 Galoots
40 Dish of a dish
41 One on the run
43 Wailed in lamentation
44 Symbol of slimness
45 Pequod's crew, e.g.
46 Approach the summit
49 Beaut
50 Mustangs go nowhere without it
53 Tam's cousin
54 Alternative to hot pants
56 Remove graphite
57 Forum farewell
58 Like "Night Gallery" stories
59 Emulated a horse whisperer
60 For each
61 "Blowin' in the Wind" singer

DOWN
1 Kind of bonding
2 Hardly suitable for farming
3 They battle the Yankees for ink
4 Dirt excavator, at times
5 Food trays
6 Casino maximum
7 You might get your mitts on it
8 White House souvenir
9 Swerves
10 Don Ho's theme song
11 Abductors' crafts, some say
12 "Aida" backdrop
13 Boris Godunov, for one
18 Trophy handles
22 First, second et al.
23 Short shortstop?
24 Flip comment?
25 Was sweet on
26 Light-footed
27 Barks' bottoms
28 Roger Bannister, memorably
29 Aired anew
30 Make rhapsodic
31 Like a photo of you in bell-bottoms
33 Ran comfortably
36 Without a choice in the matter
40 Read with great care
42 Like many cars, houses, etc.
43 Shiva's wife
45 Audio signal receiver
46 Assist in malfeasance
47 Red Cross supplies
48 Stuff
49 Broadcast while happening
50 Funny one of film
51 "Brava!" elicitor at La Scala
52 British submachine gun
54 Direction finder?
55 Most important

LONG DIVISION
By Randall J. Hartman

ACROSS
1 Burns or Byron
5 Give everything away
9 Gives everything away
14 Too
15 Exclamation by Captain Jack Sparrow
16 "A Cooking Egg" writer
17 Ananias, for one
18 Target in the wild
19 In isolation
20 "Hello, Dolly!" Grammy winner
23 Bring to bear
24 No longer trendy
25 Sheiks' cliques, sometimes
29 Spelunker's light
31 Baseball iron man Ripken
34 Team building?
35 Turn toward
36 River under the Ponte Vecchio
37 Mr. Spock's forte
40 Surrounded by
41 Daily charge
42 Old MacDonald refrain
43 Stockholm flier
44 Give a ticket
45 Garden State city
46 Social worker?
47 Fritz or Felix
48 Fans
56 Jets and Sharks
57 Member of the first family
58 Hardly bumpy
59 When the script calls for it
60 Jets or Sharks
61 Dalai ___
62 Judges
63 Jane you may have read about
64 Group of toads

DOWN
1 Gloomy covering
2 Eclectic collection
3 Hairy one of Genesis
4 Spelling or doughnuts
5 Circumvent
6 Peter of "The Maltese Falcon"
7 "Um . . . excuse me"
8 Most Little Leaguers
9 Get weepy
10 Distribute
11 Share holder?
12 King of Skull Island
13 Sault ___ Marie
21 Tannin source
22 Marisa of "What Women Want"
25 Papa Bear of the NFL
26 Patisserie output
27 One-time partner of Kathie Lee
28 Camelot character
29 Starbucks order
30 Reason for an ice pack
31 Proclaimed aloud
32 Photographer Leibovitz
33 Open Windows?
35 Lacking effervescence
36 Actor Tamiroff
38 Shakespearean sprite
39 Old slangy word of enthusiasm
44 Discontinues
45 Parting words
46 Brit's emphatic phrase
47 Transparent
48 Space between Botts dots
49 Almost never
50 Kismet
51 Toe the line
52 Champagne music maestro
53 "Fathers and Sons" novelist Turgenev
54 Clown fish kids love
55 Bug-spray target
56 The Almighty

A VERY OLD HERO
By Frances Burton

ACROSS

1 Obie contender
6 Diogenes' prop
10 Pub brews
14 Treeless plain
15 Item in the dairy case
16 Something cons do
17 Start of a bio
20 Combination of dread and wonder
21 Brown coal
22 Shade tree
23 Opposite of adore
24 Actress Lotte
26 Fills cavities with mortar
29 Pink lady ingredient
30 Respond to stimuli
31 The stuff of legends
34 Asian desert
38 End of the bio
41 Symbol of prying
42 Makes a contribution
43 Gullible
44 Sign of a smash hit, briefly
46 Hamster or porcupine
47 Lightweight wood
50 Thin out
53 Exclamation of surprise
54 Barbary pirate
56 Not in operation
59 Subject of the bio
62 Hairless
63 Piece of fencing?
64 Foolish talk
65 Brainstorm
66 Famous loch
67 Spicy sauce

DOWN

1 Code word
2 Type of hammer
3 Unlikely to bite
4 Noted Japanese-American
5 Wheel used in a game of chance
6 File, as a complaint
7 Ladd and Alda
8 Deserve
9 Pablo Neruda, e.g.
10 "Thanks, I already ___"
11 Animate
12 Bronte sister
13 Alabama city
18 Rests for a moment
19 Sandwich shop
23 Duke's lady
25 Fencing stance
26 ___ and bear it
27 Split city?
28 Mare's morsels
29 Coagulate
31 Container top
32 Leftover
33 Map abbrs.
35 S-shaped molding
36 "___ there, done that!"
37 "___ it Romantic?"
39 Long March VIP
40 Self-aggrandizements
45 Indy, for one
46 Downfall

47 1942 Disney classic
48 Out front
49 Spoon-shaped utensil
50 Window dressing
51 Small land masses
52 Huron and Erie
55 Pizza maker's need
56 White House office
57 Singer Domino
58 Dog's bane
60 Actress Lupino
61 Special time in history

SEA HUNT
By Fran & Lou Sabin

ACROSS

1 Sit-down affairs
6 Obviously eager
10 Tapered tuck
14 Central courts
15 Sitarist Shankar
16 Its motto is "Industry"
17 Motown, for one
18 Sour fruit
20 Ivy Leaguer
21 Needing relief
23 Ballpark figures?
24 Bring under control
26 Gold holder
27 "A pocketful of ___ . . ."
28 Chevron weave
32 Caspian Sea feeder
33 It's tall when exaggerated
34 From Oslo
39 Chemical salt
41 Floor protector
42 Abject fear
43 Ugly public encounter
44 Naval assignment?
46 Boric, e.g.
47 Court-ordered responsibility
50 Stephen of "V for Vendetta"
53 "His ___ Is on the Sparrow"
54 Unwelcome expression
55 Fills space
57 Unloaded, in a way
59 TVA project
62 Breaded, fried nibble
64 Another 46-Across
66 First Lady of Scat
67 Small case for a lady
68 Jay Silverheels role
69 Mouthpiece attachment
70 Mechanical learning method
71 Moved stealthily

DOWN

1 Father, son, uncle, etc.
2 Lineup ender
3 Be a middle man?
4 "A ___ of the Mind," Shepard drama
5 Genoa export
6 Eyebrow shape
7 Larson of "The Far Side"
8 Potential progeny
9 Baseball great, Josh
10 Hornswoggle
11 Face-valued, as stocks
12 Political get-together
13 What we have here
19 Sit in
22 Part of a nickel
25 "Stormy Weather" composer
26 Kind of justice or license
28 Attila's faithful
29 Idle of Monty Python
30 It's not a sure thing
31 Earsplitting sound
35 Deliver a valedictory
36 Studio creation
37 Put into words?
38 Whirlpool
40 Falls back or springs forward, e.g.
45 Beach scavenger
48 Rock-clinging mollusk
49 Far from jumpy
50 Direct to a source
51 Napoleon's punishment
52 Supermarket section
56 Roe producer
57 Rabbit's tail
58 Dust Bowl figure
60 Kick in for a hand
61 Frame of mind
63 Ice queen Midori
65 Stylish

STRANGE BEAUTY PAGEANT

By Eugene Newman

ACROSS

1 Auctioneer's cry
5 "Beware the ___ of March"
9 Weight that sounds like a fruit
14 Higher in authority
15 Carnivore's diet
16 Atelier item
17 Embezzler's entrant?
20 Actors Norton and Harris
21 Turkey feature
22 Slugger's stats
23 Titanic message
24 Word on a matching towel
26 Fail to prevent
27 Sling mud at
31 Efficiency expert's goal
33 Prosecutor's entrant?
36 "Siegfried" solo
37 AP rival
38 It has three feet
42 Spin doctor's entrant?
47 Deserving of a slap
49 They get Shaq off his feet
50 Overly
51 Nothing more than
54 Gross minus tare
55 It's on tap in Mexico
57 Train unit
59 Song syllable
62 CPA's entrant?
65 Fictional rabbit
66 Tradition
67 Arsenal stock
68 Analyze
69 Individuals
70 Hammer part

DOWN

1 Not all
2 "Metamorphoses" author
3 Minus
4 Ph.D.s
5 Gridlock
6 Pt. of USDA
7 ___ Day, April 22
8 Filched
9 Each
10 Bestial hideaway
11 Functional
12 Forte
13 Sanctified with holy water (Var.)
18 "___ to the wise . . ."
19 Juan or Eva
23 TV street
25 Full house indicator, briefly
27 Doc's org.
28 How to address a baronet
29 The Beatles' "___ Love You"
30 Flightless birds
32 Timber decay
34 Prefix with "center" or "cycle"
35 "___ Misbehavin'" (1978 Tony winner)
39 Big name in bowling alleys
40 TKO decider
41 Oral surgeon's deg.
43 Doctrine
44 "Come Back, Little ___" (Inge)
45 They're sometimes grand
46 It may be light or grand
47 Fuddy-duddies
48 Awakens
50 St. Petersburg's sister city
52 Nancy's comic book friend
53 Parolee, for one
56 Bewildered
58 Permanent solution
59 It heals all wounds
60 The Tiber runs through it
61 Presently
63 Weep
64 Spigot

YES, SIRREE BOB
By Lynn Lempel

ACROSS

1 Middle East notable
5 Wolf gang
9 Just right
14 Actress Theda
15 Shampoo add-in
16 Freight
17 Eliminate any means of retreat
20 Subtraction word
21 Laundry challenge
22 Poem of praise
23 Not everyone
25 Peaty places
27 Stark economic choice
31 Current units
35 Building projection
36 Points put on paper
37 Cherish
38 URL ending
39 Difference between a lot and a little, maybe
42 Compete
43 Refers to
45 Best-selling novelist Roberts
46 Young prankster
47 It might be said to a dog
48 Walking skeleton
51 Pond hopper
53 Passed notes?
54 There's much of this in Shakespeare
57 Unreactive
60 Fast break?
62 Judy Garland-Mickey Rooney film
66 Jailhouse
67 Songster Celine
68 Stare at the stars
69 Run-down
70 About
71 They may be behind glasses

DOWN

1 Slacken
2 Manhandle
3 Indecisive
4 Forced fee for freedom
5 Deem unworthy
6 Heady brews
7 Outlay
8 Skewered chunks
9 Cake decorator's medium
10 Pop
11 Hence
12 Like wine and cheese
13 Take a beating
18 Singing sibs of the '70s
19 Mob gone wild
24 Port between Buffalo and Cleveland
26 Heartsick
27 Tree with smooth bark
28 Blast from the past
29 "Doctor Who" airer
30 Manipulating
32 Leaving the home front
33 Kind of rate or suspect
34 Slowly trickles
37 Heart of Dixie
40 Low in the lea
41 Samoyed syllables
44 Will Ferrell Christmas flick
48 U2 activist
49 Meeting guide
50 Jumpy
52 Fraught with uncertainty
54 Pre-K lessons
55 Motivational guru Carnegie
56 Village Voice theater award
58 Homecoming hits?
59 Brisk pace
61 Sit around
63 Call off
64 Lennon collaborator
65 "It's a go!"

PETTING ZOO
By Gail Grabowski

ACROSS
1 Sackcloth companion
6 Syrup source
11 Green shade
14 Command to Fido
15 Constellation in a night sky
16 Circus routine
17 Pet
19 Country club instructor
20 Spheres
21 Showed the way
22 Throw in the towel
24 Ward healers?
25 Moon Unit, to Dweezil
26 State with confidence
27 Pet
32 High-class tie
34 Self-image
35 You, biblically
36 Being hauled
37 Cribbage board insert
38 Upper management, loosely
39 British machine gun
40 Trusted one
41 Places to make bale?
42 Pet
45 Get an eyeful
46 Before, of yore
47 Meal opener?
50 Trifling
52 Caribou relative
53 Competent
54 "What an adorable baby!"
55 Pet
58 Meadowland
59 Expert, as in language
60 Modify, as a law
61 "___ to Remember"
62 Wipe the chalk from
63 Walk casually

DOWN
1 In reference to
2 Reject with contempt
3 Saucy seasonings?
4 Corn servings
5 Wild blue yonder
6 To a greater extent
7 Bone-dry
8 Bakery buy
9 Way back when
10 Salad vegetable, perhaps
11 Amazingly waferlike
12 Neutral shade
13 Perched on
18 Act like a coquette
23 Risk, as a guess
25 Put safely away
27 Candleholders
28 Naval bases?
29 Bacon contemporary?
30 Tennis replays
31 "By all means!"
32 Player's stake
33 Leave on the sly
36 Ideal ending?
37 It's 72 at Pebble Beach
38 Squirrel away
40 Annually
41 Doorbell responses,
    sometimes
43 Request for assistance
44 Panther or puma
47 Symphonic reeds
48 Single-handedly
49 Rough Rider nickname
50 Barley used in brewing
51 Ornamental jug
52 Chronological brinks
53 Armory supply, briefly
56 "Die Meistersinger von
    Nurnberg" heroine
57 Cured serving

PUT IT THERE!
By Fran & Lou Sabin

ACROSS

1 "Look out ___!"
6 Many of these went to Woodstock
10 "___ you don't!"
14 Turkish city on the Seyhan
15 Hollow out
16 Late-night snack attack
17 Precious items container
19 River to the Ligurian Sea
20 Landers of advice
21 A bit too intrusive
22 Music-lover's woe
24 Confers a title upon
25 Sharp sensation
26 Well-mannered
29 John, Bobby and Rose
33 Put together
34 Young equine
35 "Titanic" extras
36 Department store gift-wrapper, perhaps
37 Achy places
38 "Julius Caesar" setting
39 Equal, in France
40 Manitoba Indian
41 Hindu royalty
42 Gable-Harlow film
44 Like some fingerprints
45 It haunts the Himalayas
46 Hamlet or his father, e.g.
47 Armed bodies
50 Invoice stamp
51 Put this down on paper
54 "Norma" highlight
55 Dairy product container
58 Takes a break, in a way
59 Sphere of expertise
60 Take off
61 Great joy
62 In the wind
63 Hit TV legal drama, 1986–94

DOWN

1 ___ California
2 Opening scene?
3 Mower's expanse
4 What I may mean
5 Paulie of "The Sopranos"
6 Fathomless depth
7 Half a whale?
8 "Aye!" sayer
9 Astronomers' instruments
10 Certain fruit container
11 Bunny's kin
12 Famed Atlantic crosser
13 Floral attraction
18 Bench wear
23 Name on many a motel
24 Department store container
25 Martinique volcano
26 Classy spreads
27 Series ender
28 Harry Truman's birth city
29 Country partitioned in 1948
30 Unmanned aircraft
31 Republic on the Red Sea
32 "___ Hearts Dance" (1988)
34 Short-legged dog
37 Rob Roy, e.g.
41 Tony of "The Odd Couple"
43 Word with "shirt" or "ball"
44 Secular
46 Senegal capital
47 Venom carrier
48 Like courtroom testimony
49 Fit for picking
50 Court action
51 Off-center type, briefly
52 ___ Scotia
53 Recognized
56 Rage
57 "V for Vendetta" star Stephen

WHERE'S THE HAM?

By Amos Gould

ACROSS

1 Arrest
5 Goodyear icon
10 Domestic's word
14 Tilted tower town
15 Hawaiian island
16 Recognize the intentions of
17 "Nay!" sayer
18 Whittle away
19 Poetic foot
20 It may go with a beer budget
23 Nosh
24 Get a lode of this
25 Mathematician's highest degree?
26 Man of ___ (Superman)
28 One way to run
31 Organ of equilibrium
34 Extra dose of trouble
38 Gillette razor
41 Painter of big-eyed children
42 Entertainer Martha
43 What the Juilliard String Quartet plays
46 Vietnamese holiday
47 Concerning
48 Cause friction
52 Fireplace shelf
54 To's reverse
56 What boys will be
57 U.S. president, 1861–1865
62 Earth unit
63 Not silently
64 One of Jay Gould's railroads
65 First-class
66 Vampire vanquisher
67 Turner of "Madame X"
68 House of Lords member
69 Puts an edge on
70 It moves on a large white bed

DOWN

1 Word separators
2 Dorothy's woodsman wore one
3 Mansion and grounds
4 Cause serious injury to
5 Make dim
6 Above average in size
7 Look ___ (visit briefly)
8 Whipped up
9 Painter Mondrian
10 Like fresh brownies
11 Solemn denunciation
12 "Hey, Mom! Look ___!"
13 Type of scene
21 Game divided into chukkers
22 Egyptian symbol of life
27 Mild cheese
28 Remember this!
29 It's read at the table
30 Carries a mortgage
32 Pulitzer poet Lowell
33 Pastrami partner
35 Picked-on instruments, briefly
36 Host Convy or Parks
37 Sight on the Champs-Elysees
38 Word with "riot" or "class"
39 "We ___ People . . ."
40 Basil with a magnifying glass
44 ___ au rhum
45 Screen symbol
49 Indifferent to ethical standards
50 Like a leopard
51 Group of nine
53 Efficiency expert's goal
54 Bit of serendipity
55 Takes the bus
57 Shampoo ingredient, perhaps
58 Kind of house
59 Cumulus lead-in
60 Distress indicator
61 Animation frames
62 Commencement wear

FEELING DEFEATED

By James E. Buell

ACROSS

1 Cell-nuclei substances
5 Dredged matter
9 Oscar-winning best film
14 "Rent-___" (1987 film)
15 Have down cold
16 Strong cotton thread
17 Defeat convincingly
20 Public places for walking
21 "Uh-Oh!" cookie
22 "Hogwash!"
23 Blockhead
25 Can openers
27 Hard-and-fast rules
30 Pained reactions
32 When repeated, a guitar effect
33 Public order?
34 Catch fish, in a primitive way
36 Sibyl's deck
40 Defeat convincingly
43 Microbiologist's dish
44 Florida gulf city
45 By way of
46 Get off the fence
48 Aberdeen's river
49 Kid around
50 Shell purchase
54 Draft status
56 Reflux
57 They're good for tricks
59 Acute anxieties
63 Defeat convincingly
66 First name in cosmetics
67 Salon selection
68 ___ Romeo
69 West Yorkshire city
70 Fashionable resorts
71 Thickening mixture

DOWN

1 Somewhat moist
2 Some ESPN coverage
3 NASA affirmatives
4 Bicyclist's choices
5 It may run down a mountain
6 It's kept by a keeper
7 Out in left field
8 Cousin of a nerd or wimp
9 Shakespeare or Shaw character
10 Narrow inlet
11 Houston Colt .45, today
12 Single-masted sailer
13 Lifts
18 Jersey word
19 Siamese "Please?"
24 Shrinkage, to a retailer
26 Grow genial
27 End table item
28 Moisturizer ingredient
29 What Carroll's walrus did it
31 Bar preparation
34 Fellow bluejackets
35 Star-crossed lover
37 Tear violently
38 Elevator innovator
39 Just one of those things?
41 Stomp all over
42 Nonverbal welcome
47 RPM indicator
49 XKE, for one
50 Resist authority
51 Corpulent
52 Diminish
53 Sounds from a brood
55 Music producer Brian
58 "___ right up!"
60 D-Day invasion town
61 Soybean milk product
62 Tunisian seaport
64 "The Hawk in the Rain" poet Hughes
65 First name in college coaching legends

BIG DEALS
By Fran & Lou Sabin

ACROSS
1 Corduroy ridge
5 Grazing matter
10 Darting stinger
14 Jet black
15 Adjust, as a timer
16 Facial cream addition
17 Sicilian attraction
18 Admittance
19 In a foul mood
20 Marvel Comics creature
23 Vietnamese observance
24 Red Cross supplies
25 From Katmandu
30 Carpenters, at times
34 Words with "roll" or "diet"
35 ___ Ridge, Kentucky Derby winner, 1972
37 Fortune-teller's card
38 In-body film experience
42 Military elite
43 Wrap for a rani
44 Darn it
45 Person with many bills
47 They fit together snugly
50 Grandson of Adam
52 Nest egg consideration
53 Popular video game
60 "Schindler's ___"
61 Wine purveyors Julio and Ernest
62 Inadvisable action
64 Yearn painfully
65 Take the bolt off
66 "Titanic" extras
67 Closing document
68 Challenging years
69 Place for a run

DOWN
1 Cause for weeping
2 Not in favor of
3 One of the Redgraves
4 Two-horse bet
5 Some Wal-Mart employees
6 Tear apart
7 ___ Spumante
8 Belgrade citizens
9 Works with hair
10 Remove by cleaning
11 Baseball family name
12 Aretha's specialty
13 Businessman's bonus
21 Meth. or Prot., e.g.
22 Sister of Calliope
25 "Jack Sprat could eat ___"
26 Related on Mom's side
27 Discussion group
28 Chairs a meeting?
29 Designer water source
31 Scrub
32 Wilco's partner
33 Mulligan and Irish, e.g.
36 6,272,640 square inches
39 Gifted
40 Change for the better
41 Cons welcome them
46 Hooch
48 Singer's syllable
49 Cape Canaveral event
51 Classic Western
53 Pleased as Punch
54 Arroz con pollo ingredient
55 U.S. Open champ, Arthur
56 River to the North Sea
57 Caramel-custard sweet
58 Picador's target
59 Wad builders
63 Have a mortgage

F-STOPS
By Lynn Lempel

ACROSS
1 Vatican-related
6 Non-picker-uppers
11 Duck foot feature
14 Strasbourg school
15 House with a smoke hole
16 Dory propeller
17 Revolutionary in the kitchen?
19 GPS display
20 Highway hulk
21 Milk mishap
22 Distort
23 Repetitious sound
25 Tot tenders
27 Nile menace
30 Farm cacklers
32 Powerful Norse god
33 Mongrel dog
34 Large lake named after a tribe
35 Dead-to-the-world type
38 Abrade
40 First of a game trio
42 Tip over
43 Puts off
45 Layered do
47 Cake leavener
48 Mosquito-induced fever
49 Butterfly impersonator
50 Service charge
51 Before-dinner nibbles
54 Mil. precursor
56 Bookie's offer
57 Hymn of praise
59 Family rec facility
63 Pol's funder
64 Combat accessory?
66 Sense of self
67 Onyx relative
68 End of a bridal path
69 Scout pack
70 Biology grouping
71 Start

DOWN
1 Bodybuilding targets
2 Throbbing
3 "To Autumn," for one
4 Best Actor-nominated role for Michael Caine
5 Trip segment
6 "Hurry!"
7 Strauss with the denim inventory
8 Sydney gems
9 Big purveyor of language lessons
10 Chantey subject
11 Union complaint?
12 Partygoer, usually
13 Pub picks
18 Wedding attendant
22 Trample
24 "Don't look so glum!"
26 Brainy output
27 Passed easily
28 Inevitable
29 Criminology odd couple?
31 Big quake
36 "The Dark at the Top of the Stairs" playwright
37 Upper hand
39 "Prima Ballerina" artist
41 Church melodies
44 Loss due to leaks
46 Make retribution
51 Dealt with adversity successfully
52 Simple saying
53 Evil incarnate
55 Recurring period
58 Words to Brutus
60 "The Simpsons" cartoonist Groening
61 Steep rock
62 High-profile hairdo
64 Place for lunch
65 Sofa problem

GONE!

By Carol Lachance

ACROSS

 1 Oriental delicacy
 6 Agrippina, to Nero
 11 Big wine holder
 14 Writer Chekhov
 15 Memorable 1836 battle site
 16 Old Clay
 17 What to hazard
 18 It was instant, according to Lennon
 19 Worm container
 20 Coed's parent, maybe
 22 Pest with "high hopes"
 23 Moves stealthily
 24 A ring doesn't have them
 25 LAPD alert
 28 Jolt, e.g.
 29 Tapered tuck
 31 Musket missile
 33 Home to the Komodo dragon
 37 Family way up north
 40 Ovum
 41 Fife player
 43 Mouse appendage
 44 Curly-leafed greens
 45 Damien's film (with "The")
 48 Steeped beverage
 49 Wet-dry machines
 51 Nanook's outerwear
 53 Mr. Kabibble
 54 Evolutionary mystery
 59 Little piggy
 60 For a joke
 61 Football film "Any ___ Sunday"
 62 Parenthesis, essentially
 63 Bete ___
 64 Related maternally
 65 100 qintars
 66 Pre-deal payments
 67 Overgrown

DOWN

 1 Word for the wise?
 2 E pluribus ___
 3 Put one's foot down
 4 Legions
 5 Jibing
 6 Prepare to shop
 7 Nome native
 8 Fruit desserts
 9 Plus-sized model Aronson
 10 Big laugh
 11 Bus-rider's bonanza
 12 ". . . unto ___ flowing with milk and honey"
 13 Beautician's stock
 21 Classic opener?
 24 Posture-perfect
 25 Opening run
 26 ___ Alto, Calif.
 27 Carte blanche
 29 Every one has its day
 30 Filmmaker Lee
 32 "Witness" actor Haas
 34 "State Fair" setting
 35 Rival of Bjorn in 1976
 36 ". . . and to ___ good-night!"
 38 Late-night TV fare since 1975
 39 Want ad letters
 42 Monk's trademark
 46 East end?
 47 Bugged
 49 All-important
 50 Stick out like ___ thumb
 51 ___ as a fiddle
 52 "In & Out" star, 1997
 54 "Dracula" girl
 55 Get ___ a good thing
 56 Infamous czar
 57 New Jersey hoopsters
 58 Mini revelation

ASLEEP AT THE SWITCH
By Raymond Hamel

ACROSS

1 Agronomists' study
6 Diner serving
10 Heavy reading
14 "Song of ___" (Rimsky-Korsakov)
15 This and that
16 Wished undone
17 Asleep at the switch
20 "Murder in the Cathedral" monogram
21 Natives, by suffix
22 Out of practice
23 Crime-solving factors
24 Close with a bang
26 Asleep at the switch
32 Broadway turkeys
33 "Closed" or "Open"
34 Thurman of "Kill Bill"
35 San ___ Obispo, Calif.
36 Moistly permeates
38 Hoover's staff
39 Incipient chick
40 Palindromic comics dog
41 Palm leaf
42 Asleep at the switch
46 Opening day site?
47 Highland miss
48 Put on
51 Swabbies
52 Computer problem
55 Asleep at the switch
59 Server's edge
60 Pastrami order
61 "Shane" or "Stagecoach"
62 Kiss or ABBA, e.g.
63 Dessert choice
64 1,000 large calories

DOWN

1 Pan for gold
2 Burden or responsibility
3 Type of chatter
4 Small, in Dogpatch
5 Words from the wise
6 Trustworthy
7 Mont Blanc's range
8 Base address
9 Furrow maker
10 Shock to the system
11 Sharing word
12 Gather in the boardroom
13 Whirling current
18 Jazz site
19 Shrimp's kin
23 Makes tracks?
24 Sassy sort
25 Falls behind
26 It may accompany "Ahem!"
27 Pamplona pal
28 Make ___ (employ)
29 It might be true . . . or not
30 Make revisions
31 Shorefront?
32 Exploded, as a tire
36 Ocular distress
37 Harrow rival
38 Pate de foie ___
40 Ancient
41 Nitpicker
43 Paul Bunyan, e.g.
44 Show off
45 Teri of "Tootsie"
48 Pierce with a knife
49 "How about that!"
50 Like kissing cousins
51 Peter the Great, for one
52 Orthodontist's concern
53 ___-friendly
54 Disinfectant's target
56 Short order, often with mayo
57 Congressional vote
58 Team booster

NEW WRINKLE
By Raymond Hamel

ACROSS
1 Agcy. with an eagle logo
5 Theater section
9 Street urchin
14 Ill-fated German admiral
15 "My Life as ___" (1985 film)
16 Arledge of ABC
17 Pillaging
19 Find pleasure in
20 Auto safety feature
22 Sean Lennon's mom
23 Brewery output
24 Like some cold beverages
26 Former airline name
30 American state
34 "___ Spock" (Leonard Nimoy book)
35 U.S.-Mexico border town ___ Laredo
38 Alimony collectors
39 Diner side
43 Counting-out starter
44 Due process proceeding
45 ". . . man ___ mouse?"
46 They frequent outlets
49 Restrained, as a flow
51 Popular Internet site
54 Seesaw necessity
55 Modifying wd.
58 Give in to pressure
63 Quash, as opposition
65 Rogaine alternative
66 Remove a knot
67 Fencing weapon
68 Precollege level
69 Michaelmas daisy
70 Watermelon discard
71 Canadian singer Celine

DOWN
1 "Semper Fi" org.
2 Practice pugilism
3 Country in the Andean highlands
4 Able-bodied one
5 Soup serving
6 Slobbering comics dog
7 Muppet with blue fur
8 Encourage
9 Where Athenians live
10 "I got an ___ my test!" (student's cry of achievement)
11 Austin Powers' asset
12 Party to
13 "Because of You" singer
18 Router connection
21 "Ladders to Fire" novelist Anais
25 From here to eternity
26 Arm muscle, familiarly
27 Less common
28 Type of acid
29 Sock inserts
31 Bit of wisdom
32 Name on some green tractors
33 Syrian leader
36 TiVo predecessor
37 French affirmatives
40 The Big Apple, initially
41 In shreds
42 Went into the air
47 Ibsen's Hedda
48 Moo ___ pork
50 Well-to-do (Var.)
52 Fall shade
53 Animal with zebra-striped legs
55 ___ Velva
56 Hits up for payment
57 Joan of rock
59 Credit report blot
60 Sandwich shop
61 Reverberated cry
62 Jockey's handful
64 Commit perjury

LIFE FORMS
By Fran & Lou Sabin

ACROSS

1 Rich supply
5 Deep drink
9 Blockheads
14 Club in a bag
15 Typical reply to "Que pasa?"
16 First name on a WWII bomber
17 One of Cristoforo Colombo's three
18 Not one, but two and four
19 Attractiveness
20 Three under par
23 ___ Gatos, California
24 Bullwinkle's rack
25 Haitian summers
27 Printer's measures
28 En masse
32 Tea holder
35 Casa component
36 Syndicate bigwig
37 Buckeyes' school letters
38 Driveway material
41 Hupmobile contemporary
42 A Christmas in "A Christmas Carol"
44 Horseshoe holder
45 "No questions ___"
47 Precede in time
49 Zoom on runners
50 Wall Street skeptic
51 Jacks or better, e.g.
55 It might give you chills
57 Grade school contest
60 Type of counter
62 Octopus home
63 Hang in the hammock
64 "Easy Street" musical
65 Part of T.A.E.
66 Nobel-winning author Wiesel
67 Ossie Davis role in "Do the Right Thing"
68 Christmas season
69 Human quirks

DOWN

1 Singer/photographer McCartney
2 Pleiades pursuer
3 Dunker's delight, informally
4 Made possible
5 Looks from film villains
6 They break on shore
7 Content of cognition
8 Turf occupier
9 Computer key
10 Singer/artist Yoko
11 Minnesota Fats, famously
12 Nevada city on the Humboldt
13 Contents of snippy retorts
21 Lotte of "The Threepenny Opera"
22 Word with "pad" or "tender"
26 List finish
28 Calif.-Nev. lake
29 Norwegian saint
30 Olympics event
31 Chancel cross
32 Barry Manilow's club
33 Straight-arrow link
34 Vacuum's target
35 Lady Macbeth's bane
39 Like some wits or cheeses
40 Like some seats
43 It's used in kicking off some events
46 Runner's jersey
48 Dancer's colleague
49 Notebook type
51 She likes a little salt
52 Literary Italian town
53 Museum artifact
54 Four-time Australian Open queen
55 Double-note drumbeat
56 Moon goddess
58 Assured vigor
59 Composer Schifrin
61 AFL offshoot

CUBICLE WISDOM
By Dave A. Bell

ACROSS
1 Taj Mahal locale
5 Calling company?
9 Western wanderer
14 Spool
15 Bean town?
16 Grads
17 "Gorillas in the ___"
18 Germany, Italy and Japan, once
19 Homies
20 Start of a Scott Adams quip
23 Singer Shannon
24 Seemingly forever
25 Like some inspections
28 Elizabeth of cosmetics fame
30 Party offering
33 More than fail to prevent
34 N, S, E or W
36 A musical Turner
37 First name among the "30 Rock" cast
38 Middle of the quip
42 Facts and figures
43 Pear-shaped fruit
44 It's like kissing your sister, to sports fans
45 Elite league
46 In search of
48 Kind of macaroni
52 Official language in Katmandu
54 Water clasher
56 It'll close your kimono
57 End of the quip
61 Kitchen gadget
63 Formerly, once
64 Last write?
65 Show flexibility
66 Not e'en once
67 "Tommyrot!"
68 Lightning units
69 Numskull
70 Breathalyzer test flunkers

DOWN
1 Warship fleet
2 Type of counter
3 Flipped
4 Voice above tenor
5 San Antonio landmark
6 Foxy ladies?
7 Leave out
8 John Glenn's org.
9 Nymph loved by Apollo
10 Sticks in the fridge?
11 Irregular fighter (Var.)
12 Prankish pipsqueak
13 Slalom curve
21 It's often blue
22 Packing a wallop
26 Set to drive (with "up")
27 Brief way to indicate "and so on"
29 Poet St. Vincent Millay
31 Loyal subject
32 Rap sheet letters
35 Basket-making fiber
37 First victim
38 Give in
39 Outside the norm
40 Caboodle colleague
41 Triangular road sign
42 Kipling's "Gunga ___"
46 Gives a heads up
47 Stirred up
49 Yogi Bear's pal
50 Certain member of the wind section
51 Lateral measurements
53 Expert
55 Opening remarks
58 E-mail command
59 Double Stuf cookie
60 Lots and lots
61 Apply gently
62 Bachelor's last words

ONE PLUS ONE
By Fran & Lou Sabin

ACROSS

 1 Wharton alums, perhaps
 5 Seaweed
 9 Kid stuff
13 Bern's river
14 Find contemptible
15 Swing around
16 Winged thing + winged thing = English club
18 Verb for 27-Down
19 Intensify
20 Architects' products
22 ___ bodkins
23 Applies, in a way
25 Mindy's mate's home
26 Kirk's helmsman
27 Broke a contract
31 Just a mo.
34 Boss of old NYC
36 Lacto-___ vegetarian
37 This puzzle's theme
41 Vacuum's lack
42 Tabasco ta-ta
43 Wait at the light
44 Collected abundantly
46 Lira's replacement
49 School beginner
50 Gentle, as a horse
51 Sneak's shout
54 Divide into two camps
58 Turn down
60 "That's not good!"
61 Vegetable + vegetable = spice
63 Easy partner
64 Mountain nymph
65 Pot builder
66 Leaves
67 Active type
68 Rimrock neighbor

DOWN

 1 "___ Man" (Village People hit)
 2 Showed all
 3 Three Tenors selections
 4 Splinter group
 5 Legal instrument
 6 Studs' placements
 7 Small school?
 8 Knock intro
 9 Have high hopes
10 Color + color = oil
11 Treat wisely, and well
12 Court divisions
14 Calyx leaf
17 Corkscrew-horned antelope
21 Dipper's dish (Var.)
24 Intrude
26 Porker's pad
27 Biblical miracle site
28 Job seeker's protector since 1964
29 Big name in daredeviltry
30 Rx recommendation
31 Boom, e.g.
32 Lamb, once
33 Put + put = Monopoly property
35 Doctor of sci-fi
38 Adult in the kiddie pool, perhaps
39 Ugandan baddie
40 Short life?
45 An antonym for "restores"
47 Announced strikes, e.g.
48 Back of the line
50 Conical home
51 En masse
52 Wrongs
53 Nighttime breathing problem
54 It gets you right here
55 Musical medley
56 Personal music source
57 Nada
59 Con job
62 ___ excellence

G-WHIZ
By Fred Jackson III

ACROSS
1 File drawer abbr.
5 Split seconds
10 Not fer
14 Mater lead-in
15 Cop ___ (negotiate for a lighter sentence)
16 Centers of activity
17 Holier-than-thou type
19 Oddball
20 Mary Kay rival
21 Latin deity
22 Green Gables girl
23 Recognized to be
25 Thread units
27 Nursery purchase
29 Provoke, as interest
32 Latest thing
35 Kitchen formula
39 Final resting place, for some
40 It may need a boost
41 Like a ruby
42 "... ___ in a galaxy far, far away..."
43 Liberal leader?
44 Wreckage
45 Time to beware
46 River feature
48 Wineglass part
50 Tom, Dick or Harry
54 Fish hawk
58 NASA failure
60 Tomato type
62 One way to lie
63 Gazillions
64 Flirtatious looks
66 Russo of "Outbreak"
67 Daisylike bloom
68 Bar order (with "the")
69 Gear teeth
70 They may be pressing
71 Stallone and Stone

DOWN
1 Wizards
2 Words of concession
3 Belted, biblically
4 Metronome indication
5 Bender
6 Modern music player
7 Arctic sights
8 Sick and tired
9 Final authority
10 Acid neutralizer
11 Hired thugs
12 Tiny trash can, e.g.
13 Greek goddess of victory
18 Wine label info
24 "No ___, Bob!" (Var.)
26 Columnists' page
28 The ___ ("Fawlty Towers" network, informally)
30 More than suggest
31 Grandson of Eve
32 Rip apart
33 Pulitzer writer James
34 Tennis champ Evonne
36 Lifesaving course
37 Tennessee's state flower
38 Tortellini topping
41 WWII turning point
45 Awe
47 Govt. securities
49 Hockey great Phil, familiarly
51 You'll hear it at the ballpark
52 Symbol of Wild West justice
53 Go over the top on Broadway
55 Kind of pain
56 A Hatfield, to a McCoy
57 Some Twenty Questions replies
58 Undercover worker, perhaps
59 It may be on a roll
61 Like some ports
65 Surgery sites, for short

SALOON SOLILOQUY

By Randall J. Hartman

ACROSS

1 High point
5 ___ Jima
8 Word that brings a smile?
14 Norse god of thunder
15 Farm female
16 "Whoopee!"
17 Prepare for takeoff
18 Appropriate first name for an attorney
19 Cancun compadres
20 Start of a quip
23 Capital of Canada?
24 Word with "October" or "rover"
25 Half and half
26 Sooner State city
29 Ground cover
30 Perfumes
32 Egghead
35 Pro ___
36 Polly, to Tom
37 Middle of the quip
40 Tel ___
41 "Tank Girl" actor
42 Villain's expression
43 Sorrowful through loss
45 Not a picky specification
46 Sault ___ Marie
47 Male youngster
48 12/31, e.g.
49 Home of 300 million plus
52 End of the quip
55 Garden shelter
58 Reading room
59 Olympian's quest
60 Like many Rod Serling works
61 Nonprofit Web site suffix
62 The good life
63 ___ Pointe, Michigan
64 White alternative
65 Lee of Marvel Comics fame

DOWN

1 Cobwebby place
2 Make sore by rubbing
3 Chutzpa
4 Bana of "Munich"
5 Put out
6 "Who ___ have thought?"
7 Was in debt
8 Logger's tool
9 Desert Storm vehicle
10 War of 1812 lake
11 Piece of work
12 ___ Paulo, Brazil
13 Puzzled reactions
21 Home of the University of Maine
22 Snapped
26 Intense
27 Al ___ (pasta order)
28 Mary of "The Maltese Falcon"
29 It's full of holes
30 Dog-___
31 Mary Poppins, e.g.
32 Spills the beans
33 Metal fastener
34 Burning up
35 Move away
38 Orally
39 WJM's Mr. Grant
44 "The dog ate my homework" and the like
45 Exact restitution
48 "God bless us ___ one"
49 Depth charge target
50 Burrito covering, perhaps
51 Elizabeth of cosmetics
52 Camera-bag item
53 Fish market feature
54 Piles on birthdays
55 Jazz combo's date
56 LAX posting
57 Central Park attraction

PLACES, EVERYONE
By Matthew J. Koceich

ACROSS
1 Be in stitches
6 A lot of a drill sergeant's drill
10 Comb creation
14 Follow immediately
15 Neutral color
16 Away from the wind
17 Traveling by boat
18 Panache
19 Coniferous tree
20 Preferential plane seating
22 What feuding families seek to get
23 Moo ___ pork
24 Book after Philemon
26 "Hee ___"
29 Minor encounter
32 Part of OOO
33 Son of Haakon VII
35 Nails down just right
37 Distribute proportionately
41 2003 film with Caine, Duvall & Osment
44 School for Francois
45 Arabian ruler
46 Edible pocket
47 Spot for a napkin
49 Polish companion?
51 Neither partner
52 One that's armed and dangerous?
56 Immeasurably long period of time
58 Farm implement
59 NBC's Peabody Award winning drama
65 It's yellow in NYC
66 Kind of list
67 Love intensely
68 Ireland, poetically
69 Greek god of love
70 Hardship
71 "Shucks!"
72 Have confidence or faith in (with "on")
73 Depicts, in a way

DOWN
1 Little photosynthesis factory
2 Proposal opponent
3 Country dissolved Dec. 8, 1991
4 Marcianos' label
5 Tracts of wasteland
6 It might be said to a dog
7 Abdul-Jabbar's alma mater
8 Carryout item?
9 Evening event
10 Office staple, ironically
11 Well partner
12 Regenerate
13 Harry Potter and friends, in book three
21 Amorous archer
25 Elijah went up against his prophets
26 Word with "fire" or "garden"
27 Baldwin in "The Getaway"
28 Title name of a Howard Keel Western
30 Motivation to keep a doctor's appointment
31 Some may or may not be in your league
34 In hot pursuit
36 Make paper dolls, e.g.
38 Filet mignon source
39 Aware of
40 Old monarch
42 Tide classification
43 Made raisins or beef jerky
48 Provider of little strokes
50 In the direction of
52 Chose
53 Barton of the Red Cross
54 Poisonous substance
55 Water's edge
57 Lowest point
60 Someone who's looked up to
61 "The Ghost of ___ Taylor"
62 Roman cloak
63 Unpleasant thing to eat
64 His towel partner?

JUST ROUTINE
By Diane C. Baldwin

ACROSS

1 Herd youngster
5 Check the bar code
9 Thumper's pal
14 Laos locale
15 State or river name
16 Homer classic
17 Secluded valley
18 Microscope attachment
19 Boom box component
20 "No explanation necessary"
23 Affirmative response
24 Zero in
25 Observe
29 Whitecap
31 Sixth sense
34 Poetry muse
35 Bit of gossip
36 Blue-green shade
37 Normal procedures
40 Acts on a preference
41 Informs on
42 Unsophisticated
43 School org.
44 Hardly looking good
45 Moved right along
46 Facial twitch
47 Land parcel
48 More of the same
57 Archie Bunker's wife
58 Feed bag fodder
59 Muddy the waters
60 Engage in ransacking
61 Eight for Caesar
62 Poet Pound
63 Smile of contempt
64 Sicilian spouter
65 Blubber

DOWN

1 Shrewd (Var.)
2 Capital by a fjord
3 Stead
4 Go down the tubes
5 Performed an aria, maybe
6 Ponders (with "on")
7 "___ She Sweet?"
8 Snack
9 Shuttlecock
10 Wake-up call
11 Longish skirt
12 Empty the bilge
13 Fan mail recipient
21 Stocking fiber
22 One place to find icicles
25 Jazz genre
26 Flare up
27 "___ la vista!"
28 Elevator man
29 Fritter away
30 Word of woe
31 Fit out
32 Debonair
33 Blanched
35 Peter or Ivan, historically
36 Stat equivalent
38 Novelist Jong
39 Army groups
44 Tizzy
45 Grass variety
46 Proof of ownership
47 Vulgate's language
48 Pronoun on a towel
49 Valhalla VIP
50 Talese's "Thy Neighbor's ___"
51 Wimbledon's zero
52 Twiddle one's thumbs
53 Expanded
54 Slimy stuff
55 Land of shamrocks
56 Response to a masher

A LITTLE PERSPECTIVE

By Roger Coburn

ACROSS

1 Rooster, at the store
6 Doc of the bay?
9 Carnivorous aquatic mammal
14 Positive post
15 League name
16 "Cheers" waitress
17 Start of a bonding moment
20 Finales
21 Seed-bearing pine
22 Waggoner, of "Wonder Woman"
23 Words with "precedent" or "good example"
25 Buddhist on the Mekong
27 Bonding moment (Part 2)
35 Solar god
36 Sagacious
37 Hogan's or Klink's rank, briefly
38 Nestling hawk
39 The Fourth Estate
41 Old chair bottom material
42 Key with Ctrl and Delete in a computer operation
43 Ice mass
44 Some are supporting
45 Bonding moment (Part 3)
49 You like yours fresh
50 Ascended
51 Popular contraction
54 ___ costs (by any means)
57 Droops
61 End of the bonding moment
64 Long-necked bird
65 Criticize
66 Palatal lobe
67 "Back Street" writer Fannie
68 "Able was I ___ . . ."
69 Muscular

DOWN

1 It may be upper or lower
2 Ever and ___
3 Setting for ducks
4 Greek hero
5 Recent prefix
6 Vance or Blaine
7 Flush
8 Hard-copy error
9 U.N. Day month
10 Twelfth president
11 Kind of weight
12 Ecclesiastical month
13 Steakhouse order
18 "What are you ___?"
19 Except when
24 Double curve
26 Reverence
27 Collection
28 Card game authority
29 Pontificate
30 Former New York boss
31 Partner of hers
32 Florida city
33 Set of nine voices
34 Sharon of "Cagney & Lacey"
39 Like mice and geese
40 "Applesauce!"
41 Sticking
43 Org. for some feds
44 Some QB protectors
46 Claws
47 Dahl or Francis
48 Charity
51 This needs to be scratched
52 "No ___ traffic"
53 A king or a jet
55 Genre
56 At a distance
58 Shivering fit
59 Course activity
60 Whalebone, once
62 Information highway
63 Movie popcorn unit

NOT REALLY
By Fran & Lou Sabin

ACROSS
1 Stylish haircut or stylish carpet
5 Balthazar, e.g.
10 One of Marmee's girls
14 ___ Alto, Calif.
15 Expand the family, in a way
16 To ___ (perfectly)
17 H.G. Wells tribe
18 Tex-Mex sauce
19 "___, Britannia" (Thomas Arne classic)
20 Bad note?
23 Glue for feathers
24 Family lineage diagram
25 Hitchcock thriller
30 Quit a union
34 "___ Haw"
35 U follower
37 Charlie et al.
38 Jarvik creation
42 William's mother
43 French military cap
44 Woods' wood item
45 Private agreement?
47 Mental stability
50 Cholers
52 ___-mo camera
53 Legal cause for appeal
61 Get off the stage
62 Going up in smoke
63 Kind of page
64 Fake out
65 Fatty compound
66 One-armed pitcher?
67 Downhill racer?
68 Makes it from start to finish
69 It may be shifting

DOWN
1 An unsolicited script, e.g.
2 Sacred circle
3 Baseball's Matty or Moises
4 Describe more fully
5 Auto designer Ernesto
6 Month before Nisan
7 Course sport
8 Drive into a tizzy
9 They tie stories together
10 Hot dogs, ribs, steak, etc.
11 Carrier for needles and pins
12 Poker player's giveaway
13 Crumbum
21 Create knotted lace
22 Jaw line?
25 Not to be trusted
26 Condor's digs
27 Sorority letters
28 Sticky stuff
29 Early Iroquois foes
31 Mom's brother, perhaps
32 Has the guts
33 "Ginger Pye" author Eleanor
36 Golden State wine city
39 Demanded obedience
40 Laissez-___ (freedom of action)
41 Some oil producers
46 Amnesiac's lack
48 Ernie of 7-Down
49 Grabs a bite
51 Oprah's "The Color Purple" role
53 Ness' crew
54 Rink leap
55 Word with "crazy" or "clockwork"
56 Spin backward?
57 Glassmaker's material
58 "State Fair" state
59 Black cat, e.g.
60 Computer geek

LIE LOW
By Lynn Lempel

ACROSS
1 Winged wonders of myth
5 "Car Talk" home
8 Wild West peacekeepers
13 "Serves you right!"
14 Tony winner Wallach
15 Kind of kitchen
16 "Messiah," for one
18 Future tiny worker, maybe
19 "Still Me" autobiographer Christopher
20 Media letters since 1980
21 Singer DiFranco
22 Maurice Ravel favorite
24 Imaginary scarer of tots
26 Lady who rings a bell?
27 Common practice
29 With the wherewithal
30 Lay it down in Vegas
31 Cinder-covered
32 Popular prom rental
34 Twist together
36 Wood-cutting tools
39 Oscar Wilde's homeland
40 Quaff with cannelloni
41 Sock section
42 Pan
44 Inca's pack animal
46 "Damn Yankees" actress Verdon
47 Paine's revolutionary booklet, e.g.
49 Legal scholar
51 GP's group
52 911 request
53 Destroy an automobile or add up the damage?
54 Be empathetic
56 Salad in shreds
59 Deboner, e.g.
60 Permission in Paris
61 Kind of dream
62 Editorial overrides
63 Driller's discovery
64 Crop starter

DOWN
1 Sigma preceder
2 One of 170 on a trireme
3 Caribbean capital
4 Shiny cotton
5 Worrywart
6 Ballet bend
7 Brazilian hot spot, briefly
8 Pasta variety
9 Granola morsel
10 Disney trailblazing cartoon
11 Cue
12 Wankel's wonder
17 Lazy poet's above?
18 Oscar-winning U.N. Goodwill Ambassador
20 Tooth that won't bite
22 Chatty porker of film
23 Witch killer in "Hansel and Gretel"
24 Aircraft compartment
25 Turkey side dish
28 "Thar ___ blows"
31 Make public
33 Intro to Wall St.?
35 Big baby
36 It's inside the tire
37 Troubles
38 Transported
40 Dye holder
42 Electrical flashes
43 Bemoan
45 Headed up
46 Gets
48 Finds intolerable
50 Reservation dweller near Durango
53 Soldier's period of deployment
55 Sailor's rear end?
56 Dovish sound
57 Hairy anthropoid
58 Form a union

THREE CCs, STAT!
By Fran & Lou Sabin

ACROSS
1 "___ Howdy Doody time!"
4 From a time
9 Church aisle finishers
14 Beer source
15 Foot the bill
16 Duplicate copy
17 Board game with marbles
20 Walker in a liquor cabinet
21 Gingerbread house visitor
22 Coup d'___
23 Throw money around, so to speak
25 Lucy of "Kill Bill"
28 Twilled fabric
30 They may come a-wooing
33 Out of order
36 Shutter attachment
37 Bank assessments
42 Double curves
43 Word with "case" or "well"
44 Studio 54 and The Limelight, e.g.
46 Nyet or nah, e.g.
51 Formic acid source
52 Tattler's supply
55 Flit about
56 Mind duller
59 They're hard on the joints
60 New Mexico national park
64 "Paper Moon" star
65 Way to go?
66 Psych subject
67 River to the Seine
68 ___ alia
69 Simba's retreat

DOWN
1 Yearnings
2 "Mutiny on the Bounty" island
3 Football's flight
4 Pipe part
5 Agcy. with many schedules
6 Family name preceder, at times
7 Stockpile
8 Wharton's Frome
9 Circles, in part?
10 Silky-haired pooch
11 Grade school focus
12 Fluff a line
13 ...---...
18 Archibald of NBA fame
19 Calls off
23 ___ Valley (Reagan Library site)
24 Downsides of childbirth
26 Playwright William
27 Puts to work
29 Command decision
31 Mooring site
32 Key factor in inflation?
34 The Beatles' Pepper, briefly
35 10/31 sensation
37 Final passage
38 Opposed, in Dogpatch
39 Art museum specialist
40 Button on a camcorder
41 Skedaddles
45 Guess
47 Encourage
48 Turned bad
49 Get back for
50 Moral, generally
53 Games specialist
54 Played the vamp
57 Look ahead
58 ___ of Palms, S.C.
59 Declare
60 . follower
61 Santa trailer
62 Director's cry
63 Downed

GETTING A HEAD IN HOLLYWOOD?

By Sefton Boyars

ACROSS

1 Native-born Israeli
6 A door that's not a door?
10 Holiday weekend event, often
14 Like weather without clouds
15 Be overly sentimental
16 Beseeched
17 Andy Griffith's movie debut
20 Win for Fischer
21 Winning sign
22 Galileo's muse
23 Place to park at church
24 Mental conceptions
25 Celeb's accessory
29 "It's ___ to Tell a Lie"
30 Dobie Gillis had many
31 Domed church recess
32 Jason's vessel
36 Faye Dunaway/Tommy Lee Jones thriller
39 The "good" chocolate
40 Great receiver
41 Early copters
42 Don't tempt it
43 Guadalupe grocery
44 Sawbones
47 Word with "feed" or "grab"
48 Word in a Christmas carol title
49 Animal house?
50 The Edsel was one
54 Stephen Frears biopic about playwright Joe Orton
57 James, the blues singer
58 Stink
59 Bicolor predators
60 Curds partner
61 Relaxation
62 Showed great respect

DOWN

1 Nigerian e-mail, sometimes
2 ___ Romeo (imported auto)
3 Tuckered out
4 Word with "arms" or "drag"
5 Violets-blue connector
6 Veep after Humphrey
7 Cordage fiber
8 Volcano detritus
9 More affected by a cold
10 Wedge placed beneath a wheel
11 Going stag
12 Martin's partner, once
13 Scandinavian sagas
18 Oscar winner Burl
19 Some Ocean Spray drink starters
23 Money in Acapulco
24 Discussion point
25 Rosebud was one
26 Georgetown athlete
27 Assert
28 City or copy at a newspaper
29 At full tilt
31 Colleague of Thomas and Roberts
32 Surrounded by
33 One in a million
34 Swab's swig
35 Peak in Greece's Olympus Mountains
37 Hairline problem?
38 Thunderstruck
42 "Barton ___"
43 Capital on the Caspian
44 Gloom's opposite
45 Upper crust
46 Tooth trouble
47 If it ain't this, don't fix it
48 Release, as lava
49 Votes for
50 Nonflowering plant
51 Fine fabric
52 Of the mouth
53 "Over here"
55 Whistle part
56 Korean War soldier

HELP!
By Matthew J. Koceich

ACROSS

1 Precursor to duke or bishop
5 Aluminum potassium sulfate
9 Mentally responsive
14 Coffee shop
15 Rig
16 Cobalt or copper
17 South American empire
18 Depletes
19 Type of Greek column
20 SOS
23 Where you are
24 Double-reed instrument
25 Pack to capacity
28 Jeans guru Levi
30 Rotating mechanism
33 Come together
35 Prefix with "Columbian"
36 Criminal game?
37 SOS
41 Cape fox
42 Circular band of foliage
43 Desert watering hole
44 "Watch it, buster!"
45 Term used to describe tension between U.S. and Russia
48 Pigpen
49 Complaint
50 Seeks permisison
52 SOS
58 Web journals
59 Additional
60 NYSE's colleague
61 Topic of dispute
62 Leo or Aslan
63 Window unit
64 Petty officers, briefly
65 Breathe noisily
66 Conclusions

DOWN

1 Carbolic and sulphuric ender
2 Hindu princess
3 Ozone no-nos
4 Uncultivated land
5 Affirm solemnly
6 One who owns rental property
7 K callers
8 Show-Me State
9 Spanish buddies
10 Sierra ___
11 Active volcano in Sicily
12 Train track
13 "Waterfalls" trio
21 Stitch again
22 "Ghosts" dramatist
25 Fourth son of Jacob
26 Liquorice-flavored seed
27 Young woman
29 Small plant-sucking insect
30 What a truant skips
31 Accounting inspection
32 Like many kids' rooms
34 Common article
36 One who is good with nos.
38 Succulent plants
39 Bookstore section
40 Park in Moscow (Var.)
45 Stops
46 Holmes' cohort
47 Agree
49 Small air rifle
51 Hogwarts professor
52 As well
53 Bruce Springsteen's nickname
54 Hip bones
55 FBI agent
56 Contribute
57 Former mates
58 Baby accessory

REVERSALS
By Fran & Lou Sabin

ACROSS

1 Brighton buggy
5 It may get rattled
10 Fictional captain
14 Lovers' destination
15 Yucca family
16 Received wisdom
17 Disregarded
19 "The Bridge of San ___ Rey"
20 Turkey's wattle
21 "Idylls of the King" character
23 "Told you!"
24 "This ___ fine how-do-you-do!"
25 Most desolate
27 Enrolls
31 Street vernacular
32 Buckeyes, briefly
33 Norwegian king, 995–1000 A.D.
35 "From your ___ to God's ear!"
38 Head for the hills
40 Nitrous ___ (laughing gas)
43 "The Way We ___"
44 Edison rival
46 Tipster
48 Blue whale's kin
49 Oklahoma university city
52 Con artist
54 Like runners, swimmers et al.
57 Silver source
58 Shocking sound
59 Jamie of "M*A*S*H"
60 Strict teacher
64 Beethoven's Ninth, e.g.
66 Checked out
68 Steep-sided land formation
69 Donizetti's "___ di Lammermoor"
70 American beauty, e.g.
71 Bucket of suds
72 Hardhearted
73 Aardvark fare

DOWN

1 Walk laboriously
2 Maniacal act
3 From square one
4 Mythical magician
5 Brazil's biggest city
6 Past
7 Sits in the sun
8 Major openings, e.g.
9 Ring twice
10 Barring none
11 Weekend visitor
12 Pisces successor
13 Put pressure on
18 Cow catcher
22 Pub shot
26 Be aware of
27 Easygoing
28 Antigua, e.g.
29 Where 11-Down may stay
30 ___ Romana (state of peace)
34 Jigsaw puzzle success
36 Wren's occasional roost
37 Designated recipient
39 Month after Av
41 "Every ___ has his day"
42 From Italy, Spain, France et al.
45 First Hebrew letter
47 Sick partner
50 Book fair booths
51 Clear of odors, in a way
53 Sardou play for which a hat was named
54 Bikini blaster
55 AA candidate
56 "Time in a Bottle" singer
61 Bard's river
62 Snug spot
63 "___ bien!"
65 Words of wisdom
67 Royale drink

FOREVER AND EVER

By Matthew J. Koceich

ACROSS

1 Brass instruments
6 Go with the flow
11 Small quantity?
14 "The Marriage of Figaro," for one
15 Addams family manservant
16 Super Bowl ___ (Dallas over Denver)
17 Rome moniker
19 Under the weather
20 Piece of furniture
21 Iota
22 Steak sauce brand
23 1974 Beach Boys album
28 American and National
30 Fail to keep
31 Played a part
32 Bowl-shaped strainer
36 Wrath
37 Did livery work
39 Pitcher's stat
40 Time period
43 Oliver Twist, for one
45 Ralph Lauren line
46 Dealing a mighty blow
48 Fastest way from here to way over there
52 Soothing plant
53 Campaigned
54 Scientific workplaces
57 Energy
58 All integers or real numbers
62 Actress Longoria
63 Elaborate banquet, e.g.
64 Totally befuddled
65 Was in charge of
66 Drenches
67 Itsy-bitsy

DOWN

1 Some are big, some are little
2 Capable
3 Yeoman of the English royal guard
4 Order flowers
5 ___ Antonio Spurs
6 Friendly nations
7 "Air" and "tear" enders
8 Onassis who married Jackie
9 Tipper's 15, briefly
10 "___ kingdom come . . ."
11 Widely accepted saying
12 Creator of Rabbit and Piglet
13 Ceramic layer
18 Fit to perform
22 Prayer ending
24 Misfire
25 Blackthorn
26 Realtor's sign
27 Dream Team letters
28 Put down, as carpet
29 Designer shade
32 Pro partner
33 Small coffee cup
34 Ms. Brockovich
35 Reverberated
37 Farm tower
38 Basket some shoot at
41 Church section
42 Young child
43 Booking for musicians
44 Wheaties box adorner
46 Lies obliquely
47 Cooper car
48 Orange feature
49 Popeye's "goyl"
50 One with wanderlust
51 Pat down
55 "Life's ___ Good" (Joe Walsh tune)
56 Remain in place
58 "No ___, ands or buts"
59 Prefix with "Catholic" or "classic"
60 Org. that keeps an eye on pilots
61 Make lacework

JAILED IN THE END
By Randall J. Hartman

ACROSS
1 Guitarist Joe of the Eagles
6 Swimmer's routine
10 Captain of the Pequod
14 In reserve
15 Creole vegetable
16 Bonkers
17 Basketball and TV star from LSU
18 Ukraine's capital
19 Blows it
20 Calligraphy aid
23 Leader of Denmark?
24 ___ Aviv
25 Stuck by a thorn
27 ___ tai
30 Come from behind
33 Something picked up at the beach
34 Forearm bone
36 Actor Stephen
37 Film detective played by Peter Lorre
40 2002 Tom Hanks/Leonardo DiCaprio movie
43 Break in the action
44 Stutz contemporary
45 Burlesque bit
46 "Delta of Venus" author Anaïs
47 Showing expertise
49 ___-mo
50 Like some modern cameras
53 Bug
55 Ring rhymer
56 Air conditioner alternative
62 Calligrapher's fine points?
64 On the Red or Yellow
65 Speak from a soapbox
66 Chaucer piece
67 Feature of a birthday suit
68 Use an Exercycle
69 Paradise from the beginning
70 Also-ran in an Aesop fable
71 "Sorry to say . . ."

DOWN
1 Chesapeake bay?
2 ___ Domini
3 Place
4 Barely enough
5 Skelter head
6 Norse troublemaker of myth
7 Analogous
8 Ivy League-ish
9 401(k) participant
10 One thing candles represent
11 Adversity
12 Come to terms
13 Headquartered
21 Eye openers
22 Big bang producer
26 "The Stranger" writer Albert
27 A whole bunch
28 Jai ___
29 Difficult to grasp
31 Food Network host Sandra
32 '70s defense secretary Melvin
35 When Juliet says "Parting is such sweet sorrow"
37 Shortsighted
38 Whippet wagger
39 Not fooled by
41 Fox-and-hound forays
42 Membership charge
47 1867 purchase for a little over $7 million
48 Boy Scout groups
50 Infernal author?
51 Old war story
52 Flooded
54 1950s battleground
57 Former Israeli prime minister Golda
58 You can see right through it
59 Alan of "Shane"
60 List shortener
61 Trust (with "on")
63 Japanese coin

NONFINANCIAL AID

By Sefton Boyars

ACROSS

1 War game played on a board
5 Soft stuff
9 Like a celebrity
14 Arthur of the courts
15 Its icon is a light bulb
16 Gaucho locale
17 Net thoughts
18 Box springs support
19 College Station student
20 Help category for gamblers?
23 "___ Now or Never"
24 Bruins great
25 Die, for example
26 Second half of a cocktail
27 Safe place?
28 Bookcase locale, often
31 Cricket segments
34 Lara Croft location
35 Dough in Dusseldorf
36 Help category for some marchers?
39 Pans in reverse?
40 Thousandths of an inch
41 Gives the eye
42 Burns or Jennings
43 Word with "high" or "jerk"
44 Hadrian's "Hail!"
45 Piece of eight, for one
46 Wharton achievement
47 Gov. purchaser
50 Help category for classic comedy bits?
54 Germany has had three of them
55 Scrap
56 Topic of gossip, sometimes
57 Birchbark transport
58 Fired, informally
59 Strauss of denim
60 Parson's place
61 Ancient Greek instrument
62 Famous apple site

DOWN

1 Akiba, e.g.
2 Caribbean key, e.g.
3 Word with "long" or "warning"
4 Frat supply
5 Time of Rosh Hashanah
6 Freud colleague Alfred
7 Canadian flag feature
8 Early cemeteries
9 Like some hot entrees?
10 Primitive aquatic organisms
11 Gift-bearing kings
12 OK place?
13 She brings in the bucks?
21 Warm comparative
22 Cuban dance
26 Type of wire
27 He rules often
28 Having two parts
29 Canal of Rome
30 Dozes
31 Russian industrial center
32 Tuscany plant
33 Distinctive style
34 Occurring every third year
35 Win by a nose
37 Test for the expecting one
38 Old Chevy models
43 Like food fit for 1-Down
44 Use a file, e.g.
45 Hot drink
46 Top hat in the church
47 Type of community with guards
48 Kitchen filter
49 Pt. of NASA
50 Prosperity
51 Inkling
52 Calculating
53 Bathroom floor material, perhaps
54 Nipper's co.

ORIGINAL EQUIPMENT

By Eugene Newman

ACROSS

1 Latin American music
6 Brooklyn Dodgers nickname
10 Equal partner's cut
14 Ridley Scott film
15 Jacob's twin
16 Code type
17 Proceed easily
18 Old garbage disposal?
20 They're sometimes drawn
22 Generic dog?
23 Invasion craft, briefly
24 Apportion (with "out")
26 Faithfulness
28 Old ATV?
32 "The Hairy ___" (O'Neill play)
33 Jury member
34 Word with "shoulder" or "spaghetti"
38 Come down in buckets
40 Lithograph, e.g.
43 Shakespearean villain
44 Scrawny one
46 Tenure
48 Sal of song
49 Old price scanner?
53 Spielberg's favorite state?
56 Random number generators
57 A Thai language
58 Invigorates (with "up")
60 Lobs
64 Old copier?
67 Accepted practice
68 Teen affliction
69 It was once thought to be indivisible
70 Director Polanski
71 Venetian magistrate
72 Huey Lewis sings with them
73 16th century church council site

DOWN

1 Anatomical pouches
2 Quite often or quite a bit
3 "Billy ___" (Waterhouse book)
4 Bagel type
5 Port of Belgium
6 Oscar winner Kingsley
7 Mil. branch since 1947
8 Durable paper
9 Solar phenomenon
10 Crone
11 On ___ (hot)
12 Minimum
13 Old film star Arbuckle
19 Fluctuates
21 Expensive
25 Battenberg's river
27 Nay voter
28 Webber musical
29 Vienna-based cartel
30 Change course
31 Compose prose
35 Fashion or passion
36 Petri dish contents, perhaps
37 11th U.S. president
39 Star witnesses?
41 Pocket-protected one of stereotypes
42 Mom's urging to a picky eater
45 Sales chart, e.g.
47 "'Tis" author
50 Type of show or band
51 "The Grass Harp" author
52 Landlord
53 Achilles vs. Hector epic
54 Anti-drug cop
55 "Nothing ___!"
59 Type of shoe or storm
61 Identical
62 "Magnet and Steel" singer Walter
63 Shipped
65 Realize
66 Units of length equal to 1,000 meters, briefly

NO BIG DEAL
By Sefton Boyars

ACROSS

1 Pare
5 Daily section
9 Coagulates
14 Corn Belt state
15 Record, in a way
16 Pi, for instance
17 Amplify
18 Bearded flower
19 Confusion descriptor
20 Act like a bear?
23 One way to have gotten home
24 Tucked it away
25 Omelette ingredients for Julius
28 Places of safety
31 Good times
34 Washroom tub
36 First woman to land a triple axel in competition
37 Word with "dining" or "restricted"
38 It could be a dangerous thing
42 Beatles-era Brits
43 The dead-ball ___
44 Ludicrous
45 Is plural?
46 Some vessels used for boiled breakfast items
49 The Pointer Sisters' "___ So Shy"
50 ___ juris
51 ". . . not always what they ___"
53 Woody Allen 2000 release
61 Bit part for a big star
62 Lady of Spain
63 Archaic pronoun
64 Clear the cribbage board
65 Roasting chamber
66 Many a game piece
67 Cantankerous
68 Rents
69 Clumsy cry

DOWN

1 Newton fruits
2 Old stories
3 Off base?
4 Vessels that sound like Southern pronouns
5 Ear infection
6 Monty Python bit, e.g.
7 Big story
8 Schoolroom fixture
9 Pie parts
10 Wood shaper
11 Bart Simpson's bus driver
12 Seating level
13 Kind
21 Viewpoint
22 South Pacific island group
25 Clinton rival
26 Mettle that earns a medal
27 Comment to the audience
29 Flower in a Noyes poem
30 All-around truck
31 Mr. Heep
32 Trattoria tubes
33 Pundits
35 "___ in the bag"
37 Raggedy redhead
39 Proper
40 Work unit
41 Flight segment?
46 Antony gave one for Caesar
47 Online discussion group
48 Southern nuts
50 Frozen rain
52 Slogan
53 Bambi's tail
54 Horse hair
55 Rock blasters
56 Target of fawning
57 Change residences
58 State of Xenia
59 Underwater forest plant
60 Understands

BEAT THE ODDS
By Mark Milhet

ACROSS
1 State with the motto "Industry"
5 Beat bigtime
9 Latin clarifier
14 "Hey, mate!"
15 Skyrocket
16 Circumference
17 Boat trailer?
18 Check out
19 Bert's buddy
20 Beats the odds
23 Broke bread
24 Disregard
25 Extract used in perfumes
30 Wall Street buys
34 Pen resident
35 Middle of three black keys
37 Kind of surgery
38 Beat the odds
42 Words with "fever" or "tight ship"
43 Be of use to
44 Navigator's need
45 Lack of vigor
48 Weapons
50 Creep
52 Ambient music composer Brian
53 Beats the odds
60 Words after "bend" or "lend"
61 Forbidden thing
62 Loafer or sneaker
64 Heart chambers
65 Dressed
66 DOS alternative
67 Motown's Berry
68 Kitchen addition?
69 Gondolier's need

DOWN
1 Motor City gp.
2 Defrost
3 PGA Tour player Isao
4 "Laughing" critters
5 Cancelled a debt
6 Exorbitant, as prices
7 Man, but not woman
8 Skins
9 "No need to explain"
10 Flat broke
11 Sea eagle
12 Brouhaha
13 He and she
21 Iron output
22 Gives the nod to
25 Capital of Ghana
26 Fireballer Ryan
27 Harebrained
28 Dorsal bones
29 Insect stage
31 Battery, for one
32 "On the Waterfront" director
33 Reposed
36 Old despot
39 1971 Neil Diamond hit
40 Salma Hayek film of 2000
41 Pirate ship feature
46 Paper collector on one's desk
47 Rhine whine
49 Swabs
51 For that reason
53 Den ___ Dutch city
54 Fond of
55 HI before statehood
56 Shock
57 Biol. subject
58 "How awful!"
59 Wearisome work
63 Common filename extension

I BELIEVE IN. . .
By Fran & Lou Sabin

ACROSS
1 Funny guys
5 Old enough to vote
10 "___ It Romantic?" (Rodgers & Hart)
14 Up to the job
15 Bedouin
16 Scott of "I Love N.Y."
17 Nighttime gift-giver
19 Sicily's Castrogiovanni, since 1927
20 Fertile surface layers
21 Arranged by type
23 Bellicose Greek god
24 Narrow inlet
25 Developed, as a player
29 Royal digs
33 World peace
34 Word with "funny" or "interesting"
35 Fond du ___, Wis.
36 Highway marker
37 Freudian focus
39 "Little House on the Prairie," e.g.
40 Place for the first couples cruise
41 Soup ingredient, sometimes
42 "___ be sorry!"
43 Military pass time
45 Put the squeeze on
47 Stephen of "Bloom"
48 Indonesian outrigger
49 Cavalry issues
52 Turns tail
57 Black cat, to some
58 Sleepy time visitor
60 Certain driver
61 Islamic prince (Var.)
62 Crib call
63 Maintained
64 "The Full ___" (1997 film)
65 "Tout de suite!" (briefly)

DOWN
1 Power unit
2 "Peek" follower
3 Hardly five-star fare
4 Bridge defeats
5 Hot as a pistol
6 Had a colt
7 Not quite right
8 Needle-toothed swimmer
9 Big name in ice cream
10 Spain and Portugal
11 Roly-poly gift-giver
12 "A stitch in time saves ___"
13 His pad's the pond
18 Old as the hills
22 Air France destination
25 Long-tailed parrot
26 Ligurian love
27 Julia Roberts role in "Hook"
28 Numic dialect speaker
29 Kid's ammo
30 Extension
31 Golfer's delight
32 Bring to a near boil
34 Check out
37 Leo's place?
38 Like 41-Across
39 "Mayday!" relative
41 Bull's counterpart
42 Want like mad
44 Wailed
45 Fixed in advance
46 Community club
48 Dress up
49 Last year's beginner, briefly
50 Caen friend
51 Banana stalk
53 Icelandic opus
54 Second of a Latin trio
55 "And there it is!"
56 Go off the deep end
59 Plan for millions, briefly

OFF THE CHARTS
By Norm Guggenbiller

ACROSS
1 Drawer oddments
6 Moderator
10 Lummoxes
14 Kipling's pack leader
15 Conception
16 Teapot ___ scandal
17 Became fainter
18 Clears out, slangily
19 Bandy words
20 Casino surveillance camera
23 Smoke, informally
24 A way to drink whiskey
25 Ordinarily
27 Beach bottle letters
30 Long-legged wading bird
32 Chat room abbr.
33 Bad beginning?
34 Changeless
35 Steam source, at times
38 Sister of Ares
40 Rock music genre
42 Ecru and taupe
43 Rockies denizen
45 ___ B'rith
47 He sings to the man
48 Growth chart nos.
49 Greek consonants
50 Get done with
51 Tiny margin
54 "___ have to do"
56 Cyberspace initials
57 Huge asset in Hollywood
62 Use a surgical beam
64 Biblical pronoun
65 Sierra ___
66 They can be big in Hollywood
67 Former Revlon model
68 "That is to say"
69 Fit the sound to the action
70 Gullible ones
71 Army bases

DOWN
1 Kind of cracker
2 "Fine by me"
3 Give up
4 Big name in fashion
5 Dysphoria
6 Noon?
7 Jim Davis' pup
8 Attacks
9 Pieces of work
10 Newspaper revenue sources
11 Celebrities are a part of it
12 Net receipt?
13 Suitable material?
21 Japanese straw mat
22 University founded in 1701
26 "Goodbye, Columbus" author
27 Merganser relative
28 Lead-in for "graph" or "legal"
29 Comedian who played Geraldine Jones
31 Not interfere with
35 Alien in "The Day the Earth Stood Still"
36 Like some ground chuck
37 Founded, on town signs (Abbr.)
39 Parks in a pew
41 Heirlooms, often
44 Sounds of disapproval
46 Like mullahs
49 Rodeo bull
51 United Kingdom land
52 Sub (Var.)
53 Kitchen add-ons?
55 Andean beast
58 Play around
59 Same as before
60 Gridiron play
61 Hankerings
63 Emergency PC key

WHAT A PAYNE
By Randall J. Hartman

ACROSS

1 Pedestal part
5 Billiards shot
10 Volcano near Messina
14 They're a part of history
15 Former name of Hagatna
16 Ten Commandments word
17 Give off
18 Big apes
19 Something to check
20 Window component
23 Sweater letter
24 Joan Rivers' "___ Talking"
25 Pizzeria purchase
26 Nile reptile
27 Put down, in slang
28 Film composer Schifrin
32 Free-for-all
34 Nabokov novel
36 Like many a marathon
   runner
37 Pest
41 Hard to fluster
42 "Time flies," with "fugit"
43 Woolly fabric
46 Bring up
47 "What's the Frequency,
   Kenneth?" band
50 Worn-frazzle link
51 Bernese mount
53 It doesn't hold water
55 Pouch
56 Former stockbrokerage
60 Ballet bend
62 Result of converting the 7-10
   split
63 Told all to an interrogator
64 "___ cost to you!"
65 Oft-linked Bacon
66 Suffix with "Rock" or "disk"
67 Tries to win over
68 "___ you ashamed of
   yourself?"
69 Alleged monster's loch

DOWN

1 Tooted the horn
2 Stylish suit brand
3 Peter and Paul
4 Cosmetician Lauder
5 A little lower?
6 All worked up
7 Julia of "Kiss of the Spider
   Woman"
8 Draft status?
9 Mountain range's backbone
10 And so on, briefly
11 Kind of artery
12 Biblical vessel
13 Final checkup?
21 Synthetic fabric brand
22 Sun. speech
29 Wepner whipper
30 Navel buildup?
31 Flounder's frat brother in
   "Animal House"
33 Stuns, in a good way
34 South American capital
35 "Alas!"
37 Stanford neighbor
38 Best Actor winner of 1992
39 Eco-friendly org.
40 Florence Nightingale,
   notably
41 Person used by another to
   gain an end
44 Tube top
45 Site of the Iditarod
47 Sales enticement
48 World Series and the Super
   Bowl, e.g.
49 Comes together
52 Hamelin musician
54 "Ghosts" playwright Henrik
57 Center of a cathedral
58 Ireland alias
59 "They ___ thataway!"
61 Goddess of the dawn

LOGIC

The next few pages have all the instructions you'll need to tackle all the logic puzzles in this book. They may look a little complicated but you'll soon get the hang of things.

Solving Tips

With each standard problem we provide a chart that takes into account every possibility to be considered in the solution. First, you carefully read the statement of the problem in the introduction, and then consider the clues. Next, you enter in the chart all the information immediately apparent from the clues, using an **X** to show a definite **no** and a ✓ to show a definite **yes**. You'll find that this narrows down the possibilities and might even reveal some new definite information. So now you re-read the clues with these new facts in mind to discover further positive/negative relationships. Be sure to enter information in all the relevant places in the chart, and to transfer newly discovered information from one part of the chart to all the other relevant parts. The smaller grid at the end of each problem is simply a quick-reference chart for all your findings.

Now try your hand at working through the example below—you'll soon get the hang of it.

Example
Three children live on the same street. From the two clues given below, can you discover each child's full name and age?

Clues
1. Miss Brown is three years older than Mary.
2. The child whose surname is White is 9 years old.

Solution

Miss Brown (clue 1) cannot be Brian, so you can place an **X** in the Brian/Brown box. Clue 1 tells us that she is not Mary either, so you can put an **X** in the Mary/Brown box. Miss Brown is therefore Anne, the only possibility remaining. Now place a ✔ in that box in the chart, with corresponding **X**s against the other possible surnames for Anne.

If Anne Brown is three years older than Mary (clue 1), she must be 10 and Mary, 7. So place ✔s in the Anne/10, Brown/10 and Mary/7 boxes, and **X**s in all the empty boxes in each row and column containing these ✔s. The chart now reveals Brian's age as 9, so you can place a ✔ in the Brian/9 box. Clue 2 tells us that White is 9 years old too, so he must be Brian. Place a ✔ in the White/9 box and **X**s in the remaining empty boxes in that row and column, then place a ✔ in the Brian/White box and **X**s in all the remaining empty boxes in that row and column. You can see now that the remaining unfilled boxes in the chart must contain ✔s, since their rows and columns contain only **X**s, so they reveal Green as the surname of 7-year-old Mary.

Anne Brown, 10.
Brian White, 9.
Mary Green, 7.

	Brown	Green	White	7	9	10
Anne	✔	X	X	X	X	✔
Brian	X			X		X
Mary	X			✔	X	X
7	X					
9	X					
10	✔	X	X			

	Brown	Green	White	7	9	10
Anne	✔	X	X	X	X	✔
Brian	X	X	✔	X	✔	X
Mary	X		X	✔	X	X
7	X		X			
9	X	X	✔			
10	✔	X	X			

The solving system for the puzzles that don't have grids is very similar. Read through the clues and insert any positive information onto the diagram. Then read through the clues again and use a process of elimination to start positioning the remaining elements of the puzzle. You may find it easier to make a few notes about which elements of the puzzle you know are linked but that cannot yet be entered on the diagram. These can be positioned once the other examples of those elements are positioned. If you find it difficult to know where to begin, use the starting tip printed upside down at the foot of the page.

Battleships

Before you look at the numbers around the grid, there are a number of squares you can fill in from the starter pieces given. If an end piece of a ship is given then the square next to it, in the direction indicated by the end must also be part of a ship. If a middle piece is given then the pieces either side must also be ship parts; in this instance, you need some more information before you can decide which way the ship runs. Also, any square that is adjacent to an end piece (apart from those squares in the direction of the rest of the ship), any square touching the corners of a middle piece, and all squares around destroyers (one-square ships) must be sea.

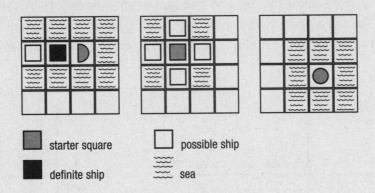

■ starter square   □ possible ship

■ definite ship   〰 sea

Now, look at the numbers around the grid and identify rows and columns in which the large aircraft carrier might be. Either from this or by looking at the next consequences of the remaining possibilities, you should be able to position this ship. Now fill in the sea squares around the carrier and move on to the smaller ships.

Cell Blocks

Fill the grid by drawing blocks along the grid lines. Each block must contain the number of squares indicated by the digit inside it. Each block must contain only one digit. Blocks must be four-sided squares or rectangles, no "L" shapes, etc.

Codewords

This puzzle has no clues in the conventional sense. Instead, every different number printed in the main grid represents a different letter (with the same number always representing the same letter, of course). For example, if 7 turns out to be a "V," you can write in V wherever a square contains 7.

Wordwheel

Using only the letters in the Wordwheel, you have ten minutes to find as many words as possible, none of which may be plurals, foreign words, or proper nouns. Each word must be of three letters or more, all must contain the central letter, and letters can only be used once in every word. There is at least one nine-letter word in the wheel.

Add Up

If the number in each circle is the sum of the two below it, how quickly can you figure out the top number?

San Guinari Border Post

There are four cells in the border post on the San Guinari side of that small South American republic's border with Bananaria, and today all four are occupied by dissidents who have been caught trying to smuggle themselves out of San Guinari. From the clues below, can you work out the name and occupation of the man in each cell, and how he tried—and failed—to get over the border?

Clues

1. Both schoolteacher Carlos Ortiz and the man who was caught trying to cross into Bananaria disguised as an American tourist (a female American tourist) have been locked in even-numbered cells.

2. The priest who was found hiding in a shipping crate on its way to Bananaria City, who is not Diego Valdez, isn't in either the highest-numbered or lowest-numbered cell.

3. Juan Rivera, who was found clinging under a railway car on a cross-border train, is not the physician nor is he in the cell next to the one where the physician has been incarcerated.

Cell	Prisoner

	Carlos Ortiz	Diego Valdez	Juan Rivera	Ramon Gomez	Journalist	Physician	Priest	Teacher	Disguised as tourist	In back of truck	In shipping crate	Under railway car
Cell 1												
Cell 2												
Cell 3												
Cell 4												
Disguised as tourist												
In back of truck												
In shipping crate												
Under railway car												
Journalist												
Physician												
Priest												
Teacher												

Occupation	Attempt

Add Up

If the number in each circle is the sum of the two below it, how quickly can you figure out the top number? Try solving in your head before writing anything down.

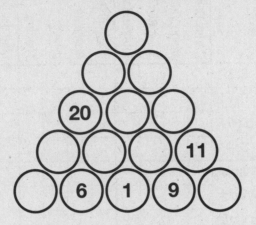

Add Up

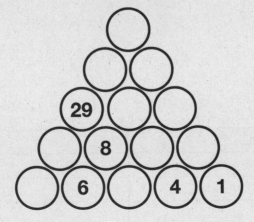

Wordwheel

Using only the letters in the Wordwheel, you have ten minutes to find as many words as possible, none of which may be plurals, foreign words, or proper nouns. Each word must be of three letters or more, all must contain the central letter, and letters can only be used once in every word. There is at least one nine-letter word in the wheel.

Codewords

Every number in the grid represents a different letter of the alphabet. Three letters have been filled in to give you a start.

13	11	3	16	5		14	11	3	25	6	2	22
11		8		3		11		12		25		3 **A**
16	3	12	21	8	11	25		25	3	4	11	13 **D**
8		5		2			26					22 **G**
13	25	6	24	5	11	13		18	25	3	7	11
11		26				3		3		16		5
	6	2	15	23	6	25	3	5	6	26	2	
24		11		25		11				2		25
25	3	13	6	26		15	1	8	22	22	16	11
6				17			25		15			1
11	16	3	5	11		20	11	18	15	6	5	11
10		25		12		11		3		13		13
11	19	12	6	5	11	13		2	11	11	13	9

A̸ B C D̸ E F G̸ H I J K L M N O P Q R S T U V W X Y Z

1	2	3 **A**	4	5	6	7	8	9	10	11	12	13 **D**
14	15	16	17	18	19	20	21	22 **G**	23	24	25	26

Grandmother's Pride

A proud grandma was showing photos of her four teenage grandchildren to a visitor. The group photo shown here pictures all four. From the clues given, can you name the girls in positions 1 to 4, say which musical instrument each plays, and what sport she enjoys taking part in?

Clues

1. As you look at the photo, Judith is farther to the left than her sister who plays tennis.

2. The girl whose instrument is the guitar is an excellent distance runner; she is not number 1 in the photo, and her name is not Michelle.

3. The squash player is sandwiched between Sonya and the girl who plays the cello, who isn't in position 2.

4. Katherine, who is a keen member of a local basketball team, is depicted next but one to the piano player.

Names: Judith; Katherine; Michelle; Sonya
Instruments: cello; clarinet; guitar; piano
Sports: running; basketball; squash; tennis

	1	2	3	4
Name:	_____	_____	_____	_____
Instrument:	_____	_____	_____	_____
Sport:	_____	_____	_____	_____

Starting tip: Work out first the sport favored by girl number 1.

On the Leash

Five youngsters who live on the same street all have dogs nearly as big as themselves and regularly exercise them. From the clues given, can you say who lives at which number on the street, identify the breed of his or her canine friend, and work out the latter's name?

Clues

1. Aaron lives on the same side of the street as the dog named Rex.

2. Collie-owner Susie lives in a house with a two-digit street number.

3. Danny is the dog Julie takes for walks, or is it the other way around?

4. Titan's owner is the same sex as the walker of the Labrador, whose house bears a lower number.

5. Francesca's house is number 15.

6. Butch lives at number 8, which is not on the same side of the street as Joel's house.

7. Arthur lives at a house with a higher number than the Alsatian, but a lower number than the retriever.

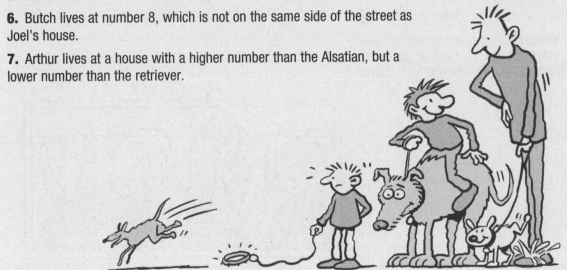

Number	Child

	Aaron	Francesca	Joel	Julie	Susie	Alsatian	Collie	Dalmatian	Labrador	Retriever	Arthur	Butch	Danny	Rex	Titan
Number 3															
Number 8															
Number 15															
Number 20															
Number 27															
Arthur															
Butch															
Danny															
Rex															
Titan															
Alsatian															
Collie															
Dalmatian															
Labrador															
Retriever															

Breed	Pet's name

Cell Blocks

Fill the grid by drawing blocks along the grid lines. Each block must contain the number of squares indicated by the digit inside it. Each block must contain only one digit. Blocks must be four-sided squares or rectangles, no "L" shapes, etc.

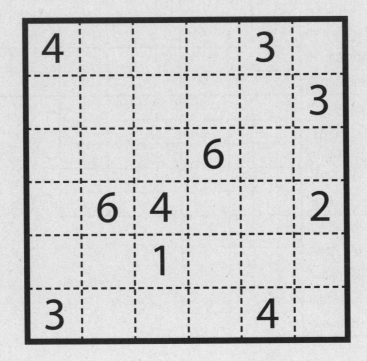

Battleships

Do you remember the old game of battleships? These puzzles are based on that idea. Your task is to find the vessels in the diagram. Some parts of boats or sea squares have already been filled in, and a number next to a row or column refers to the number of occupied squares in that row or column. The boats may be positioned horizontally or vertically, but no two boats or parts of boats are in adjacent squares—horizontally, vertically, or diagonally.

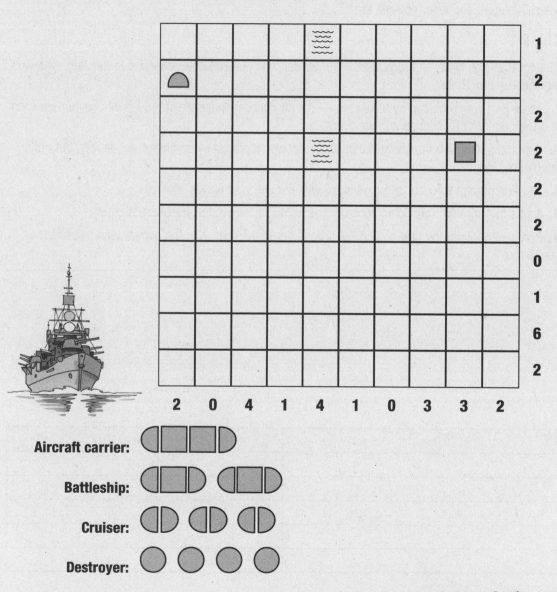

Replacement Polvonis

The Polvonis is a popular TV series for the very young, featuring five cuddly, pink creatures who engage in activities calculated to entertain and educate its target age-group; since it's a live-action series, the Polvonis are also five young dancers in ungainly costumes. But the job comes with a very restrictive contract, and since the show began last year, all five Polvonis have quit and been replaced. From the clues below, can you work out which Polvoni each of the original quintet played, when they quit, and who replaced them?

Clues

1. Gary Hurst quit later in the year than the dancer who played Sese (pronounced Seesee), who was replaced by Sue Ridley.

2. Annie Bird was replaced by Mike Lamb—the all-concealing nature of the Polvoni costume means that the gender of its occupant is irrelevant.

3. Nick Oaks, who left the show in July last year, was replaced by another male dancer, but not in the role of Dudu.

4. The first person who had to be replaced was the one who played Momo.

5. It was in April that Kate Johns took over as a Polvoni; she didn't replace Cathy Day.

6. Pete Olsen joined the cast of *The Polvonis* earlier in the year than the person who became the new Baba.

Original	Role

	Baba	Dudu	Momo	Sese	Vivi	March	April	July	September	October	Danny Crane	Kate Johns	Mike Lamb	Pete Olsen	Sue Ridley
Annie Bird															
Cathy Day															
Gary Hurst															
Nick Oaks															
Todd Usher															
Danny Crane															
Kate Johns															
Mike Lamb															
Pete Olsen															
Sue Ridley															
March															
April															
July															
September															
October															

Month	Replacement

Wordwheel

Using only the letters in the Wordwheel, you have ten minutes to find as many words as possible, none of which may be plurals, foreign words, or proper nouns. Each word must be of three letters or more, all must contain the central letter, and letters can only be used once in every word. There is at least one nine-letter word in the wheel.

Cell Blocks

Fill the grid by drawing blocks along the grid lines. Each block must contain the number of squares indicated by the digit inside it. Each block must contain only one digit. Blocks must be four-sided squares or rectangles, no "L" shapes, etc.

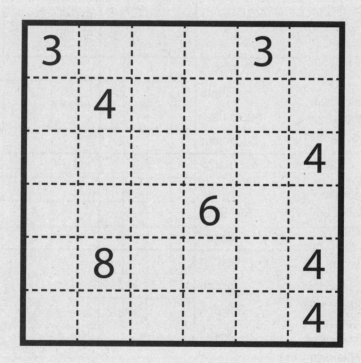

Classic Mystery

Classic Mystery is a quarterly magazine for lovers of "hard-boiled" detective stories, and its editor, Michael Hamner, is a friend of mine; we met yesterday, and he was telling me all about the "headliner" stories that will be featured in next year's issues. From the clues below, can you work out which will be the lead story in each issue, and the full name of its author?

Clues

1. Darby's story, "Eye Witness," features a tough Philadelphia private eye hunting for his partner's killer—his business partner, that is.

2. Wayne, who has written the leading story for the June issue of *Classic Mystery*, isn't McMillan.

3. The March story, "Memento Mori," tells the story of a tough Atlantic City private eye hunting for his best friend's killer; it isn't by the man named Sheldon.

4. Joseph's story will appear in the issue immediately after "Point of Honor"—which features a tough Los Angeles private eye hunting the man who killed his brother—and immediately before the story by Knapp.

	"Eye Witness"	"Memento Mori"	"Night Work"	"Point of Honor"	Gordon	Joseph	Sheldon	Wayne	Darby	Knapp	McMillan	Saxon
March												
June												
September												
December												
Darby												
Knapp												
McMillan												
Saxon												
Gordon												
Joseph												
Sheldon												
Wayne												

Issue	Story	First name	Surname

Codewords

Every number in the grid represents a different letter of the alphabet. Three letters have been filled in to give you a start.

1		1		1				23		1		14
26	13	18	26	26	25		5	7	7	3	26	25
18		6		14		17		6		15		12
6	14	22	8	1	4	7	6	3		20	8	15
26		11		16		18						1
4	14	11	10	26	23	14	6	26		18	14	4
		10		10		10		25 D		10		
19	7	26		10	26	22	1	15 U	6	26	10	9
14						5		18 C		6		14
1	14	24		26	10	26	17	14	4	22	7	8
4		7		14		25		4		18		21
26	2	15	14	4	26		25	26	11	14	4	26
8		4		1				25		10		25

A B Ⓑ Ⓓ E F G H I J K L M N O P Q R S T Ⓤ V W X Y Z

1	2	3	4	5	6	7	8	9	10	11	12	13
14	15 U	16	17	18 C	19	20	21	22	23	24	25 D	26

Spring Color

Last autumn we planted a lot of bulbs in the garden, and are looking forward to them appearing in the spring. From the information given below, can you discover which variety of which type of bulb we planted, the number, and where they were put?

Clues

1. We planted more than 50 narcissus bulbs, but not the "Sky Queen" variety; neither the daffodils, which weren't "Sky Queen," nor the bulbs planted along the hedge numbered 35.

2. We didn't plant 35 tulips, but 55 "Misty Morn" bulbs went in.

3. The "Golden Beauty" bulbs were planted in the island bed, but neither they nor the "Sky Queen" variety numbered 45.

4. Sixty bulbs of one variety were planted in the terraced bed.

5. The "Midas" crocuses were not planted in the lawn.

6. We planted 20 hyacinths.

Bulb	Variety

	"Fanfare"	"Golden Beauty"	"Midas"	"Misty Morn"	"Sky Queen"	20	35	45	55	60	Along hedge	In lawn	Island bed	Terraced bed	Under apple tree
Crocus															
Daffodil															
Hyacinth															
Narcissus															
Tulip															
Along hedge															
In lawn															
Island bed															
Terraced bed															
Under apple tree															
20															
35															
45															
55															
60															

Number	Location

Battleships

Do you remember the old game of battleships? These puzzles are based on that idea. Your task is to find the vessels in the diagram. Some parts of boats or sea squares have already been filled in, and a number next to a row or column refers to the number of occupied squares in that row or column. The boats may be positioned horizontally or vertically, but no two boats or parts of boats are in adjacent squares—horizontally, vertically, or diagonally.

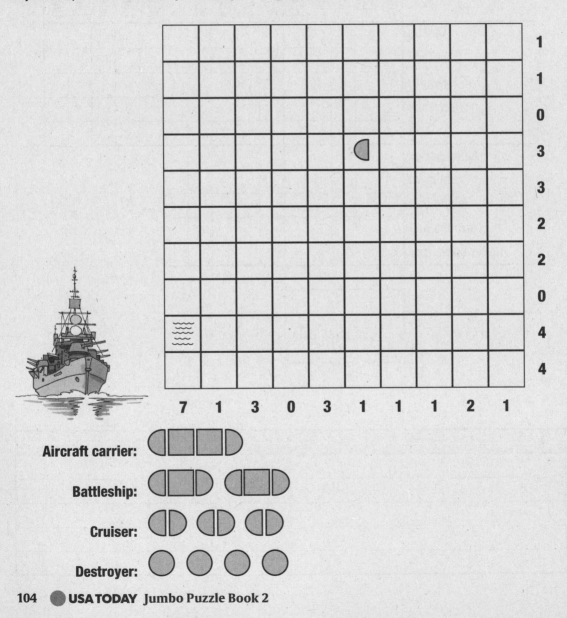

Cell Blocks

Fill the grid by drawing blocks along the grid lines. Each block must contain the number of squares indicated by the digit inside it. Each block must contain only one digit. Blocks must be four-sided squares or rectangles, no "L" shapes, etc.

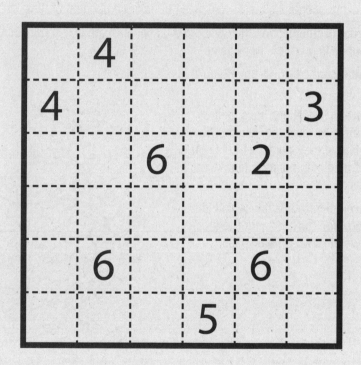

Colonies

The star MWQBH-24352, otherwise known as Lik, has four planets, all fertile but uninhabited, each of which has now been colonized by a different space-going race. From the clues below, can you work out the name of each planet, the name of the race that has colonized it, the name of their main settlement, and what they do there?

Clues

1. The race that has colonized the planet Darlik, officially designated MWQBH-24352(3), has set up large-scale coal-mining operations there, coal being a major component of their diet.

2. The Melisari's main settlement on their colonized planet is Orspi, which translates into Terran (or English, as it was once known) as "Newcastle."

3. The colonial settlement called Ul-Boc (Redhill) is not on the planet Frolik.

4. The planet where the Zastrians have built up enormous beetle farms to meet the demand from the hungry population of their home world is not the one where the main community is known as Effraj (Palm Springs).

5. The Quirrigi have colonized Saltlik, which is not the planet where the lizard farmers live in and around the town of Avwasil (Blackpool).

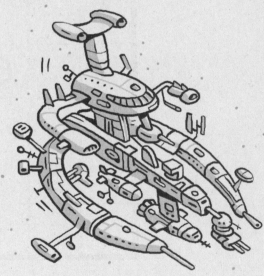

Planet	Colonizing race

	Corians	Melisari	Quirrigi	Zastrians	Avwasil	Effraj	Orspi	Ul-Boc	Beetle farming	Coal mining	Lizard farming	Nut farming
Darlik												
Frolik												
Garlik												
Saltlik												
Beetle farming												
Coal mining												
Lizard farming												
Nut farming												
Avwasil												
Effraj												
Orspi												
Ul-Boc												

Settlement	Industries

Add Up

If the number in each circle is the sum of the two below it, how quickly can you figure out the top number? Try solving in your head before writing anything down.

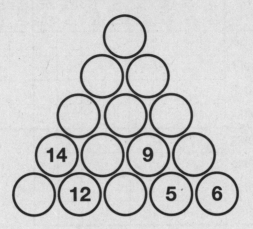

Add Up

Wordwheel

Using only the letters in the Wordwheel, you have ten minutes to find as many words as possible, none of which may be plurals, foreign words, or proper nouns. Each word must be of three letters or more, all must contain the central letter, and letters can only be used once in every word. There is at least one nine-letter word in the wheel.

Codewords

Every number in the grid represents a different letter of the alphabet. Three letters have been filled in to give you a start.

10	15	12	14	17	1	■	10	14	18	14	4	17
25	■	8 L		22		6		18	■	1	■	11
18	16	4 I	5	18	14	12		26	22	12	10	10
15	■	14 T		23		26		12		5	■	14
■	3	4	22	12		14	25	22	26	12	6	25
22	■	10	■			1		12	■			5
12	19	14	12	16	14	■	18	6	1	12	22	12
26	■			12		20				24		22
12	16	21	22	18	2	12		9	8	11	22	■
8	■	22		22		13		22	■	18		12
8	25	25	10	12	■	12	19	18	17	14	12	6
12	■	13	■	10		8	■	13	■	12		21
6	25	16	18	14	12	■	21	8	18	6	8	7

A B C D E F G H J̸ J K L̸ M N O P Q R S T̸ U V W X Y Z

1	2	3	4 I	5	6	7	8 L	9	10	11	12	13
14 T	15	16	17	18	19	20	21	22	23	24	25	26

Healthy Occupations

Eight people, who all work in town and have occupations concerned with keeping us healthy, live in the houses numbered 1 to 8 on the plan. From the clues given, can you name the occupant of each house, and describe his or her occupation?

Clues

1. Jim, Lily, and the ambulance driver live in houses that form a straight line on the plan, the latter's home being indicated by an odd number.

2. Martin's house is numbered two higher than that of the health-food store owner, but they are not in direct alignment.

3. Hester's house is due north of the dentist's.

4. Lily's house has a number on the plan twice that of the chemist, who lives due west of the osteopath.

5. One of the men owns house 4.

6. Iris lives in house number 5.

7. Neil, who is a physiotherapist, lives in an odd-numbered house.

8. The radiographer's house is number 8.

9. Graham lives somewhere to the south of the town, but the home of the nurse is somewhere to the north.

Names: Graham; Hester; Iris; Jim; Kath; Lily; Martin; Neil

Occupations: ambulance driver; chemist; dentist; health-food store owner; nurse; osteopath; physiotherapist; radiographer

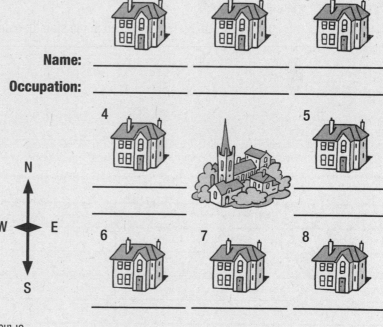

Name: _____

Occupation: _____

N

W — E

S

Starting tip: Work out first the occupation of the owner of house 6.

A Gentleman in America

Sir Emmett Gentle, Bart, went to the United States in 1859, at the age of 20, and promptly vanished. In 1901, he returned to England, and, after a court case to prove his identity, resumed his place in society. New research has produced some details of what he did during the missing years. From the clues, can you work out what facts have come out about each of the listed years—what name Sir Emmett was using, where he was located, and what he was doing for a living?

Clues

1. In 1865, Sir Emmett was, it seems, calling himself Joe Stone; he wasn't known as Sam Nails in either Arizona or Montana.

2. In 1872, Sir Emmett was pursuing a successful career as a stagecoach robber, while when he lived in Arizona he was a rustler.

3. Sir Emmett wasn't living in Texas in 1879, nor when he was using the name Matt Flint; he became a bank robber some time after he had left Texas (closely pursued by the Rangers) but some time before adopting the pseudonym Dan Leathers.

4. Sir Emmett was robbing trains seven years after he was known to be calling himself Matt Flint.

5. Sir Emmett was known as Jack Steel in New Mexico seven years before he was involved in a large-scale arms smuggling racket.

6. In 1893, the regrettably criminal baronet surfaced in the state of Montana.

Year	Pseudonym

	Dan Leathers	Jack Steel	Joe Stone	Matt Flint	Sam Nails	Arizona	California	Montana	New Mexico	Texas	Bank robbery	Rustling	Smuggling	Stagecoach robbery	Train robbery
1865															
1872															
1879															
1886															
1893															
Bank robbery															
Rustling															
Smuggling															
Stagecoach robbery															
Train robbery															
Arizona															
California															
Montana															
New Mexico															
Texas															

State	Crime

Cell Blocks

Fill the grid by drawing blocks along the grid lines. Each block must contain the number of squares indicated by the digit inside it. Each block must contain only one digit. Blocks must be four-sided squares or rectangles, no "L" shapes, etc.

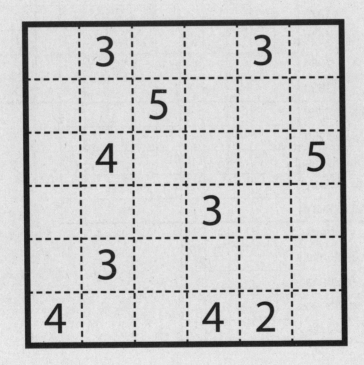

Battleships

Do you remember the old game of battleships? These puzzles are based on that idea. Your task is to find the vessels in the diagram. Some parts of boats or sea squares have already been filled in, and a number next to a row or column refers to the number of occupied squares in that row or column. The boats may be positioned horizontally or vertically, but no two boats or parts of boats are in adjacent squares—horizontally, vertically, or diagonally.

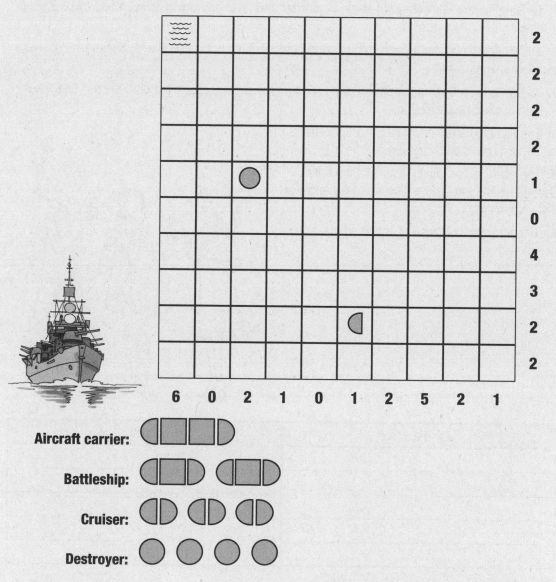

Scent Packing

Five perfume manufacturers have recently launched new products. From the following information, can you discover the name of each manufacturer's scent, the distinctive shape of the bottle, and the color of the packaging?

Clues

1. La Luna, in its stylish crescent-shaped bottle but not silver packaging, is not made by De Klein or Hicoste.

2. The La Roma perfume is sold in a spherical bottle, but it's not called Sirène; Sirène isn't sold in a teardrop-shaped bottle.

3. Infatuation is a Giveninch perfume, but is neither the scent sold in a teardrop-shaped bottle nor the one in ice-blue packaging.

4. The Hicoste perfume, which is not Coquette, is sold in distinctive black packaging.

5. The ice-blue packaging is not employed by Christophe Eor and does not contain a spherical or a square bottle.

6. The spherical bottle is not contained in a silver or yellow box.

Manufacturer	Scent

	Coquette	Craving	Infatuation	La Luna	Sirène	Crescent	Sphere	Square	Tall and thin	Teardrop	Black	Ice-blue	Red and gold	Silver	Yellow
De Klein															
Christophe Eor															
Giveninch															
Hicoste															
La Roma															
Black															
Ice-blue															
Red and gold															
Silver															
Yellow															
Crescent															
Sphere															
Square															
Tall and thin															
Teardrop															

Shape	Color

Wordwheel

Using only the letters in the Wordwheel, you have ten minutes to find as many words as possible, none of which may be plurals, foreign words, or proper nouns. Each word must be of three letters or more, all must contain the central letter, and letters can only be used once in every word. There is at least one nine-letter word in the wheel.

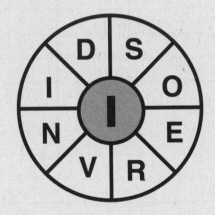

Battleships

Do you remember the old game of battleships? These puzzles are based on that idea. Your task is to find the vessels in the diagram. Some parts of boats or sea squares have already been filled in, and a number next to a row or column refers to the number of occupied squares in that row or column. The boats may be positioned horizontally or vertically, but no two boats or parts of boats are in adjacent squares—horizontally, vertically, or diagonally.

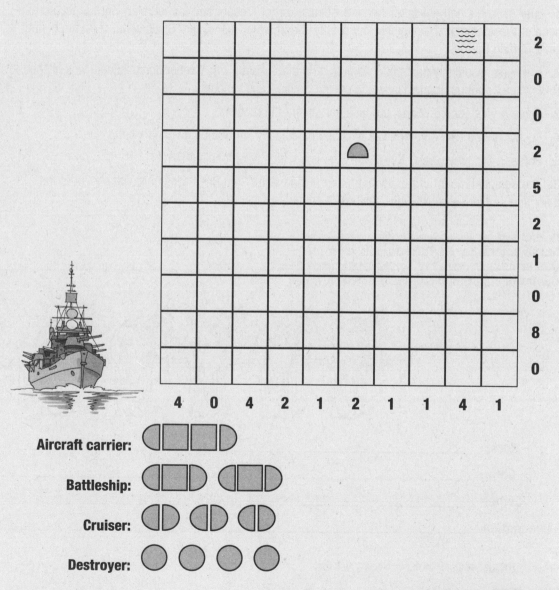

Outside the Silver Dollar

Five horses were hitched outside the Silver Dollar Saloon in the town of Sweetwater, Arizona, one day back in 1878, while their owners were inside enjoying a drink. From the clues below, can you fill in the name and color of each horse, and the name and occupation of the man to whom it belonged?

Clues

1. Lute Judson's horse was hitched immediately left of Trooper and immediately right of the sorrel; none of these animals belonged to the county sheriff, who was visiting Sweetwater from the county seat, Buffalo Springs.

2. The horse insultingly named Crowbait (a term that meant a very inferior horse indeed) was hitched somewhere—but not immediately—to the left of Ollie Lane's mount.

3. Horse 4 was named Windy, but let's not go into the reason.

4. Bucky, Hondo Pike's horse, was hitched immediately left of the cowhand's pinto.

5. Horse 3, the gray wasn't Key Moffit's mount, which wasn't called Hero.

6. The personal mount of the horse breaker, who wasn't Sam Riley, was immediately left of the palomino, but wasn't next to the trailboss's animal.

Horse names: Bucky; Crowbait; Hero; Trooper; Windy
Horse colors: bay; gray; palomino; pinto; sorrel
Owner names: Hondo Pike; Key Moffit; Lute Judson; Ollie Lane; Sam Riley
Owner occupations: cowhand; horse breaker; rancher; sheriff; trail-boss

Horse: _____ _____ _____ _____ _____

Color: _____ _____ _____ _____ _____

Owner: _____ _____ _____ _____ _____

Occupation: _____ _____ _____ _____ _____

Starting tip: Begin by positioning the sorrel horse.

Codewords

Every number in the grid represents a different letter of the alphabet. Three letters have been filled in to give you a start.

A B C̸ D E F G H̸ I J K L̸ M N O P Q R S T U V W X Y Z

1	2	3	4	5	6	7	8	9	10	11	12	13
	L			**C**							**I**	
14	15	16	17	18	19	20	21	22	23	24	25	26

Not-So-Merry Men

Not all of the outlaws in Sherwood Forest were as merry as is supposed. Some joined Robin Hood's band but quickly changed their minds when they experienced the privations of the great outdoors. Here are five who didn't last the course; from the information given, can you discover the name and former job of each, the number of days they lasted in the forest, and their main complaint?

Clues

1. Cedric Grumbell complained of the monotonous food in the forest and returned to Nottingham more quickly than the cowherd.

2. Dickon Grype lasted only 5 days as an outlaw, but not because of the lack of privacy; the outlaw who complained of that lasted fewer days than Barney Crabb.

3. Jethro Growse was a blacksmith, while Billy Akins wasn't the outlaw who gave it up after 6 days.

4. One of the five complained he was cold at night and gave up after just 4 days—it wasn't the potter.

5. The thatcher hated having constantly wet feet.

6. The mason returned to normal life after 7 days in the forest.

Name	Job

	Blacksmith	Cowherd	Mason	Potter	Thatcher	4	5	6	7	8	Cold at night	Constantly wet feet	Hard ground	Monotonous food	No privacy
Billy Akins															
Barney Crabb															
Jethro Growse															
Cedric Grumbell															
Dickon Grype															
Cold at night															
Constantly wet feet															
Hard ground															
Monotonous food															
No privacy															
4															
5															
6															
7															
8															

Days	Complaint

Battleships

Do you remember the old game of battleships? These puzzles are based on that idea. Your task is to find the vessels in the diagram. Some parts of boats or sea squares have already been filled in, and a number next to a row or column refers to the number of occupied squares in that row or column. The boats may be positioned horizontally or vertically, but no two boats or parts of boats are in adjacent squares—horizontally, vertically, or diagonally.

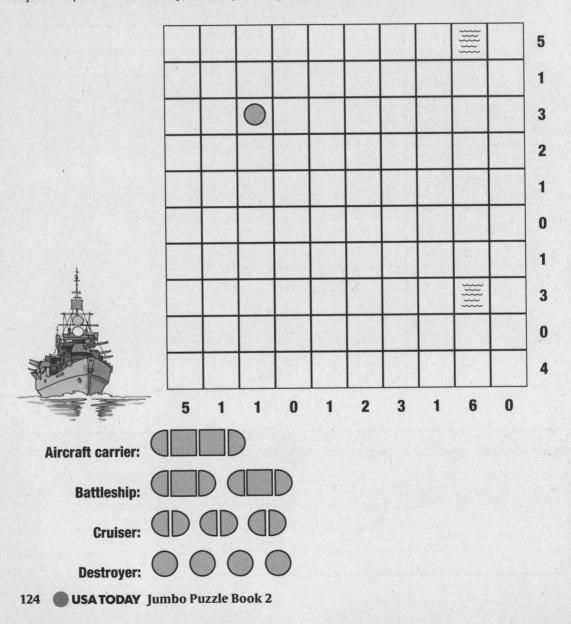

Aircraft carrier:

Battleship:

Cruiser:

Destroyer:

Cell Blocks

Fill the grid by drawing blocks along the grid lines. Each block must contain the number of squares indicated by the digit inside it. Each block must contain only one digit. Blocks must be four-sided squares or rectangles, no "L" shapes, etc.

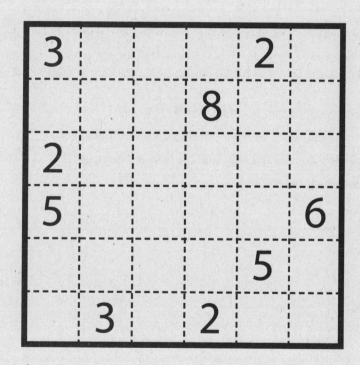

Mugs Game

The local radio station's morning music program includes a daily general knowledge quiz where listeners can phone in with their answers for the pleasure of receiving a coffee mug bearing the station's logo. From the clues given below, can you name all of last week's winners, and match them with their occupations and their mug-winning answers?

Clues

1. John Sage, the builder, phoned in the morning before the provider of the winning answer "the magpie."

2. The unemployed listener won a mug earlier in the week than Graham Nozett, but later than the secretary.

3. "Saturn" was the answer that won a mug for the sales manager two days after Joyce Brainey won hers.

4. The answer to Wednesday's quiz question was "Plutonium."

5. It was a woman who phoned in with the correct answer on Thursday.

6. Mary Wise succeeded in winning a mug with the answer "Venezuela."

7. The Tuesday winner was the student.

Day	Name

	Graham Nozett	John Sage	Joyce Brainey	Mary Wise	Sandra Smart	Builder	Sales manager	Secretary	Student	Unemployed	"Charles Dickens"	"Plutonium"	"Saturn"	"The magpie"	"Venezuela"
Monday															
Tuesday															
Wednesday															
Thursday															
Friday															
"Charles Dickens"															
"Plutonium"															
"Saturn"															
"The magpie"															
"Venezuela"															
Builder															
Sales manager															
Secretary															
Student															
Unemployed															

Occupation	Answer

Add Up

If the number in each circle is the sum of the two below it, how quickly can you figure out the top number? Try solving in your head before writing anything down.

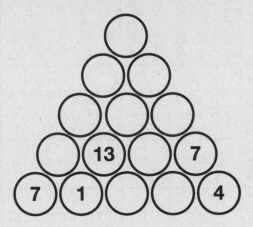

Add Up

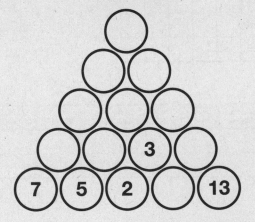

Wordwheel

Using only the letters in the Wordwheel, you have ten minutes to find as many words as possible, none of which may be plurals, foreign words, or proper nouns. Each word must be of three letters or more, all must contain the central letter, and letters can only be used once in every word. There is at least one nine-letter word in the wheel.

Massaging the Figures

The five osteopaths in our local practice are busy with five patients. From the information given below, can you work out in which room each is working, his or her patient, and the part of the body being treated in each case?

Clues

1. Osteopath Anne Culpayne is in the room numbered one higher than the one where Mr. Aiken is the patient, and one lower than the one where the leg is being treated.

2. German osteopath Gunther Hertzum is in Room 4, but he's not treating Mrs. Smart, who does not have a problem with her hand.

3. Amy Leggerts is not the osteopath dealing with the arm in Room 1.

4. Rick Yorbach's patient is Mr. Twist.

5. Mr. Crick is being treated in Room 3.

6. Ms. Sharp has a neck problem.

Room	Osteopath

	Anne Culpayne	Gunther Hertzum	Amy Leggerts	Paul de Muselle	Rick Yorbach	Mr. Aiken	Mr. Crick	Ms. Sharp	Mrs. Smart	Mr. Twist	Arm	Back	Hand	Leg	Neck
1															
2															
3															
4															
5															
Arm															
Back															
Hand															
Leg															
Neck															
Mr. Aiken															
Mr. Crick															
Ms. Sharp															
Mrs. Smart															
Mr. Twist															

Patient	Part of body

120

Codewords

Every number in the grid represents a different letter of the alphabet. Three letters have been filled in to give you a start.

15	5	15	22	12	14		19	13	15	15	6	15
5		5		4				25		9		25
12	17	12	25	23		22	17	3 **S**	14	2	20	8
4		4		2		15		4 **O**		24		26
3	10	17	2	13	15	24		14 **T**	18	15	15	14
15		20				25		14				26
	24	15	23	25	7	25	4	17	3			
13				11		25			15		2
15	20	14	15	13		20	15	8	2	14	15	24
21		25		25		2		23		14		16
4	12	14	25	7	2	23		25	8	23	4	4
13		23		2				24		15		25
22	15	15	1	23	11		14	15	20	24	4	20

A B C D E F G H I J K L M N Ø P Q R Ø Ø U V W X Y Z

1	2	3 **S**	4 **O**	5	6	7	8	9	10	11	12	13
14 **T**	15	16	17	18	19	20	21	22	23	24	25	26

132 ● **USA TODAY** *Jumbo Puzzle Book 2*

Heading West

On sale on an Internet auction site is a poster for the 1948 movie *Heading West*, the story of a pioneer wagon train in the 1870s, which shows the four male stars in character. From the clues below, can you fill in on the drawing the name of each actor and the name of the man he played in the film?

Clues

1. The picture of the man who played wagon train scout Duke Logan is diagonally adjacent to the photograph of Grant Leopold and horizontally adjacent to that of Kenny Van Ern.

2. The portrait of the man who played treacherous landowner Joe Whitney is horizontally adjacent to the picture of actor Matt Rideau, which is not photograph C.

3. The picture of ex-cavalry officer Captain Gus Hayden is on the upper half of the poster.

4. Picture D shows movie star Ross Benmore, who went on to play private eye Nick Cleaver in a dozen film hits in the fifties.

Actors: Grant Leopold; Kenny Van Ern; Matt Rideau; Ross Benmore
Characters: Duke Logan; Gus Hayden; Joe Whitney; Seth Barry

Actor: _____

Character: _____

Starting tip: Decide who played Gus Hayden.

Poster Parade

Back in the 1950s it was common in towns to see a row of billboards advertising products of all kinds. A typical example is shown in our diagram. From the clues given, can you name the manufacturer of the product featured on each of posters 1 to 6, describe the product itself, and name the designer responsible for the content and layout of each?

Clues

1. The cigarette poster, acceptable in those days, was sandwiched between the one for Logan's product and the one designed by Dick Sellett.

2. Hogan's is the name of the firm that makes the soap powder.

3. Wogan's is the company whose product is featured on poster 1, while the one advertising the product made by Deacon's is farther left than the one designed by Phil Craven.

4. The poster advertising fridges, then becoming a more common household item, is in position 5 on the billboards.

5. The Regan's poster designed by Walter Cokes is next but one to the one recommending a locally brewed beer.

6. Tim Flogham designed the poster extolling the virtues of a new breakfast cereal, which is separated by two others from the poster paid for by Logan's.

7. Anna Peel was responsible for poster 3, while Jack Kidham's work is on display immediately to the left of the canned soup poster.

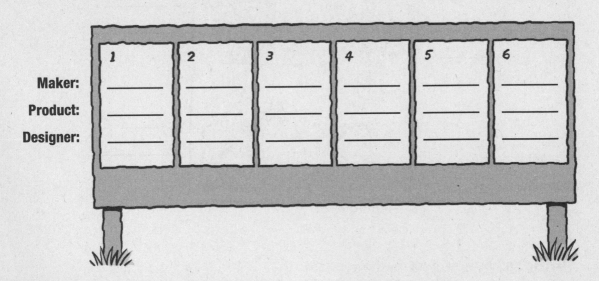

Maker:
Product:
Designer:

	Deacon's	Fagan's	Hogan's	Logan's	Regan's	Wogan's	Beer	Cereal	Cigarettes	Fridges	Soap powder	Canned soup	Anna Peel	Dick Sellett	Jack Kidham	Phil Craven	Tim Flogham	Walter Cokes
1																		
2																		
3																		
4																		
5																		
6																		
Anna Peel																		
Dick Sellett																		
Jack Kidham																		
Phil Craven																		
Tim Flogham																		
Walter Cokes																		
Beer																		
Cereal																		
Cigarettes																		
Fridges																		
Soap powder																		
Canned soup																		

123

Cell Blocks

Fill the grid by drawing blocks along the grid lines. Each block must contain the number of squares indicated by the digit inside it. Each block must contain only one digit. Blocks must be four-sided squares or rectangles, no "L" shapes, etc.

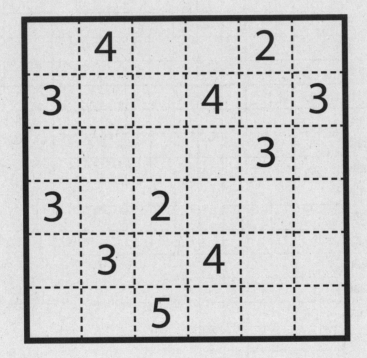

Battleships

Do you remember the old game of battleships? These puzzles are based on that idea. Your task is to find the vessels in the diagram. Some parts of boats or sea squares have already been filled in, and a number next to a row or column refers to the number of occupied squares in that row or column. The boats may be positioned horizontally or vertically, but no two boats or parts of boats are in adjacent squares—horizontally, vertically, or diagonally.

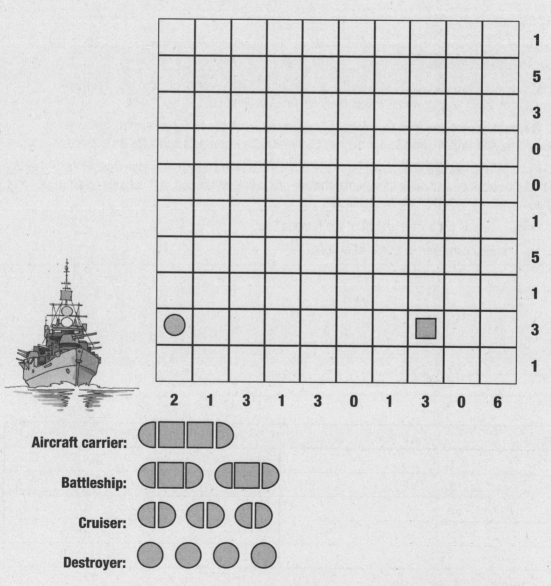

Aircraft carrier:

Battleship:

Cruiser:

Destroyer:

Independence Day

Mack and Mabel Washington have lived in London for almost thirty years, working for an international TV corporation, but they're still proud of their American citizenship and every July 4th they invite a group of other U.S. expatriates to dinner. From the clues below, can you work out the full name of each of their five male guests this year, where he came from, and the profession or occupation that brought him to England?

Clues

1. Earl comes from Anchorage in Alaska—which, he jokes, is the best thing to do with it; his surname isn't Jefferson.

2. Mr. De Kalb is a cartoonist who works on the comic book—sorry, graphic novel series—*Timestalkers*; his hometown isn't Anchorage or Orlando, Florida.

3. Wayne doesn't come from Indianapolis, Indiana, and isn't the historian who has been doing research at the British Museum for the last two years; the historian's surname isn't Hancock.

4. Lewis is a junior diplomat assigned to the U.S. Embassy in London; the man from El Paso, Texas, is an actor working with an experimental theater group in East London, but actually earning his living by doing voice-overs for TV advertisements.

5. Ches Revere is not a descendant of the famous Paul.

6. Mr. Steuben comes from Utica, New York.

First name	Surname

	De Kalb	Hancock	Jefferson	Revere	Steuben	Anchorage	El Paso	Indianapolis	Orlando	Utica	Actor	Aero engineer	Diplomat	Cartoonist	Historian
Ches															
Earl															
Lewis															
Ross															
Wayne															
Actor															
Aero engineer															
Diplomat															
Cartoonist															
Historian															
Anchorage															
El Paso															
Indianapolis															
Orlando															
Utica															

Town	Occupation

Wordwheel

Using only the letters in the Wordwheel, you have ten minutes to find as many words as possible, none of which may be plurals, foreign words, or proper nouns. Each word must be of three letters or more, all must contain the central letter, and letters can only be used once in every word. There is at least one nine-letter word in the wheel.

127

Battleships

Do you remember the old game of battleships? These puzzles are based on that idea. Your task is to find the vessels in the diagram. Some parts of boats or sea squares have already been filled in, and a number next to a row or column refers to the number of occupied squares in that row or column. The boats may be positioned horizontally or vertically, but no two boats or parts of boats are in adjacent squares—horizontally, vertically, or diagonally.

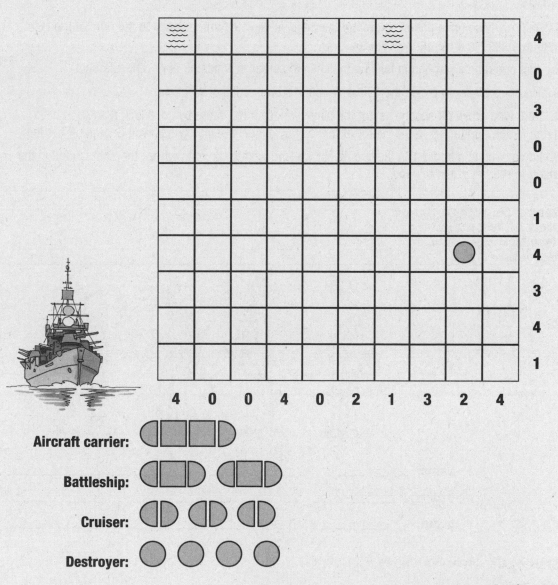

Unlucky for Some

The 13th hole at our local golf course is, like all the other 17, it must be said, given the varied abilities of the membership, unlucky for some. Our diagram shows a foursome, having completed the 12th, making their way to the 13th tee. From the clues given, can you identify players 1 to 4 in the line, and say in what order they made their shots off the 13th tee, and with what results?

Clues

1. Ralph, whose drive ended up among the trees, is depicted immediately to the right of the last man to make his drive off the 13th tee.

2. Just one man's position in the line matches the order in which he played his tee-shot.

3. The third player to tackle the 13th hole found a bunker full of wet sand.

4. Don, who drove off second, is not the player whose drive, more by good luck than good management, ended up in the center of the fairway, who immediately followed George off the tee.

5. Eddie, who is number 1 in the line, is not walking next to the man whose tee-shot landed in the rough to the left of the fairway.

Names: Don; Eddie; George; Ralph
Order off tee: first; second; third; fourth
Results: in rough; in sand; in trees; on fairway

Name: _____ _____ _____ _____

Order: _____ _____ _____ _____

Result: _____ _____ _____ _____

Starting tip: First work out where Don's drive landed.

Codewords

Every number in the grid represents a different letter of the alphabet. Three letters have been filled in to give you a start.

4	10	10	17	■	2	25	21	10	7	7	10	19
16	■	26	■	18	■	14	■	26	■	23	■	16
14	15	23	2	1	10	21	■	2	21	25	18	3
■	■	21	■	10	■	15	■	10	■	23 **T**	■	3
7	17	25	21	10	■	17	15	3	17	12 **I**	23	■
25	■	13	■	6	■	23	■	■	■	7 **S**	■	25
11	10	25	21	10	19	■	3	12	23	23	10	21
20	■	24	■	■	■	10	■	11	■	12	■	12
■	8	25	3	2	16	11	■	8	25	2	10	19
22	■	11	■	25	■	19	■	3	■	25	■	■
25	2	23	16	21	■	10	5	15	25	3	3	9
7	■	3	■	24	■	25	■	26	■	3	■	10
20	10	9	14	16	25	21	19	■	1	9	22	11

A B C D E F G H ̸I J K L M N O P Q R ̸S ̸T U V W X Y Z

1	2	3	4	5	6	7 **S**	8	9	10	11	12 **I**	13
14	15	16	17	18	19	20	21	22	23 **T**	24	25	26

Around the Course

The Freshton Green Golf Club, near Storbury, has introduced a new way for its members to go around the course; there's now a fitness track around the edge of their 18-hole course, so those who wish can walk or jog around it. And they've even provided seats at half-mile intervals, for those who need a rest; coincidentally, each is adjacent to a particular landmark on the course. This morning, five members tried it out; from the clues below, can you work out each one's full name, where they stopped to rest, and which course feature they stopped by?

Clues

1. Terry took a rest at the 2-mile marker, 1 mile beyond the one where Stride, who isn't Jane or Nicholas, stopped for a breather.

2. March, who reached the marker alongside the 16th tee before having to rest, has a first name one letter shorter than that of the person who needed a sit-down after jogging 1.5-mile; the .5 marker is adjacent to the green keeper's hut.

3. Neither the golfer surnamed Pace nor Donald rested on the seat by the lake.

4. Nicholas isn't Toddell, and didn't rest on the seat beside the driving range.

5. Amanda Foote has been a member of the Freshton Green club since she was a teenager.

6. Jane took a rest on the seat by the 8th green, which is prudently provided with a protective screen.

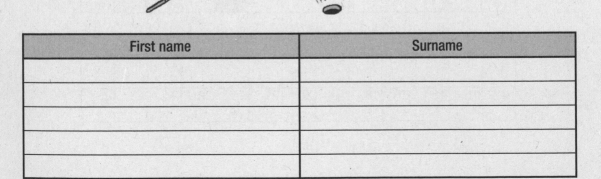

First name	Surname

	Foote	March	Pace	Stride	Toddell	.5 mile	1 mile	1.5 miles	2 miles	3 miles	Driving range	8th green	Green keeper's hut	Lake	16th tee
Amanda															
Donald															
Jane															
Nicholas															
Terry															
Driving range															
8th green															
Green keeper's hut															
Lake															
16th tee															
.5 mile															
1 mile															
1.5 miles															
2 miles															
3 miles															

Distance	Landmark

Battleships

Do you remember the old game of battleships? These puzzles are based on that idea. Your task is to find the vessels in the diagram. Some parts of boats or sea squares have already been filled in, and a number next to a row or column refers to the number of occupied squares in that row or column. The boats may be positioned horizontally or vertically, but no two boats or parts of boats are in adjacent squares—horizontally, vertically, or diagonally.

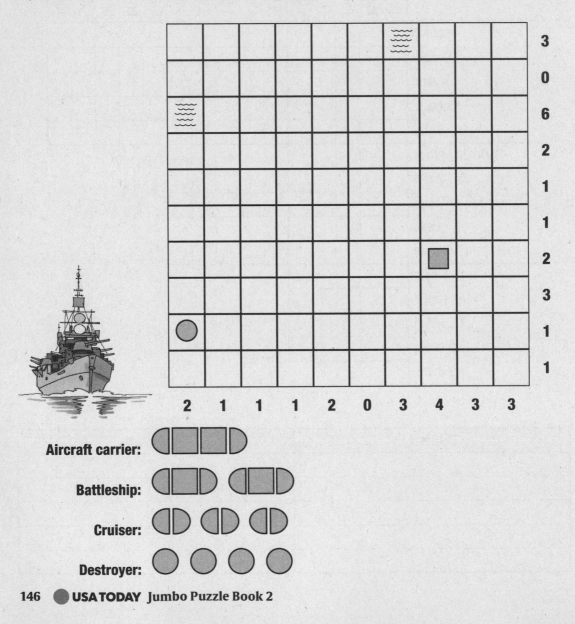

Cell Blocks

Fill the grid by drawing blocks along the grid lines. Each block must contain the number of squares indicated by the digit inside it. Each block must contain only one digit. Blocks must be four-sided squares or rectangles, no "L" shapes, etc.

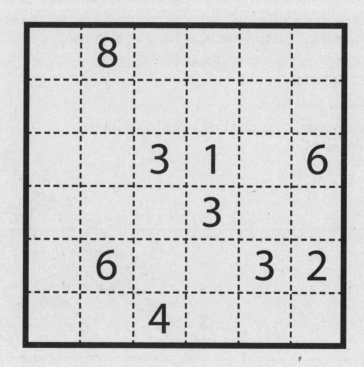

Let's Squirm Again

The 1960s was very much the decade for new dance crazes, and below are details of five of them. From the following information, can you discover the year of each craze, the name of the dance, the artist whose record launched the dance, and the highest position each reached in the Hit Parade?

Clues

1. The "Jetplane" record reached No. 3 in the charts earlier than Lola Powers's 1964 hit.

2. The "Jack-in-the-Box" was a dance craze the year before the "Whirligig" displaced it.

3. Neither the 1961 dance nor the one popularized by Gary Eden began with the letter "J," and both got higher in the charts than the record introducing the "Jack-in-the-Box."

4. Jessie Fisher didn't get as high in the charts with her dance record as the singer of the "Corkscrew."

5. Eddie Lewis's record got to No. 8.

6. One of the releases topped the charts in 1963, while Scott Dillon's hit was "Let's Squirm Again."

Year	Dance

	"Corkscrew"	"Jack-in-the-Box"	"Jetplane"	"Squirm"	"Whirligig"	Scott Dillon	Gary Eden	Jessie Fisher	Eddie Lewis	Lola Powers	1	3	5	6	8
1961															
1962															
1963															
1964															
1965															
1															
3															
5															
6															
8															
Scott Dillon															
Gary Eden															
Jessie Fisher															
Eddie Lewis															
Lola Powers															

Artist	Position

134

Add Up

If the number in each circle is the sum of the two below it, how quickly can you figure out the top number? Try solving in your head before writing anything down.

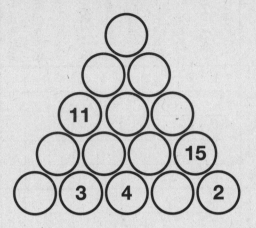

135

Add Up

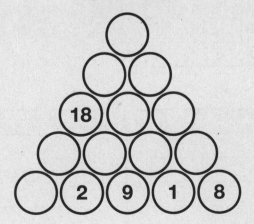

Wordwheel

Using only the letters in the Wordwheel, you have ten minutes to find as many words as possible, none of which may be plurals, foreign words, or proper nouns. Each word must be of three letters or more, all must contain the central letter, and letters can only be used once in every word. There is at least one nine-letter word in the wheel.

Codewords

Every number in the grid represents a different letter of the alphabet. Three letters have been filled in to give you a start.

■	8	7	6	18	11	8	1	■	5	6	7	18
11	■	6	■	6	■	7	■	■	11	■	■	7
10	15	25	25	7	6	1	■	5	11	22	2	3
23	■	11	■	20	■	2	■	13	■	8	■	11
15	20	5	13	5	■	15	20	10	7	13	5	■
13	■	■	22	■	■	3	■	2	■	9	■	22
6	7	10	9	7	8	■	7	26	8	7	14	11
11	■	15	■	6	■	21	■	11	■	■	■	20 **N**
■	18	6	13	11	24	11	■	5	13	9	11	5 **D**
16	■	4	■	20	■	13	■	13	■	11	■	7 **A**
11	17	7	9	3	■	18	6	11	25	8	13	20
6	■	9	■	■	■	12	■	20	■	8	■	3
19	20	11	11	■	10	3	7	3	13	2	20	■

A̷ B C D̷ E F G H I J K L M N̷ O P Q R S T U V W X Y Z

1	2	3	4	5 **D**	6	7 **A**	8	9	10	11	12	13
14	15	16	17	18	19	20 **N**	21	22	23	24	25	26

American Sportsmen

Four sportsmen from the United States are visiting Britain to promote a new airline; the picture below shows them at London's Heathwick Airport, posing for photographers. From the clues below, can you fill in each man's name, which state he originates from, and the sport in which he has achieved fame?

Clues

1. Nick Flint hails from Connecticut; he's playing ball with the football player, whose home state is not Nebraska.

2. Figure B is the ice hockey player.

3. Basketball star Roy Lowell—who's actually seven feet tall, but if we showed that, it would make the problem too easy—isn't playing ball with Carey Troy.

4. Figure D is the man from Akron, Ohio.

5. Figure A isn't the sports star from Chicago, Illinois.

Names: Carey Troy; Nick Flint; Roy Lowell; Val Denver
States: Connecticut; Illinois; Nebraska; Ohio
Sports: baseball; basketball; football; ice hockey

Name:	_____	_____	_____	_____
State:	_____	_____	_____	_____
Sport:	_____	_____	_____	_____

Starting tip: Work out the home of figure A.

Lunch Hour

One of the advantages of working for a small company is that you get to know the other workers really well; another is that you can operate from a small suite of offices over a shop right in the middle of the town. The Starr Model Agency in Storbury is a company like that, and at lunchtime yesterday most of the staff popped out for various reasons, taking advantage of their position. From the clues below, can you work out the role each of the listed workers fills at the agency, where they went at lunchtime yesterday, and what they had for lunch?

Clues

1. Neither Claire, who is the MD's secretary (and, to be truthful, everybody else's), nor the person who popped down to the garden center to pick up some grass seed had meat for lunch.

2. Ellen decided just to go for a walk during the lunch hour, stopping briefly on a park bench to consume her lunch.

3. The one person who didn't go out but stayed in the office doing problems in a puzzle book, who wasn't the contracts manager, holds a position in the agency that appears in the alphabetical list immediately ahead of the one held by the person who had a corned beef sandwich for lunch.

4. The unfortunate individual who had to pay a visit to the dentist only had a cup of lukewarm tomato soup for lunch—for obvious reasons.

5. It was the receptionist, who is trying to lose a little weight, who lunched on a cheese and pasta salad.

6. The agency's managing director visited a shoe shop (for window shopping purposes only) during lunch.

7. Jason wasn't the person who ate the ham salad.

8. Paul had just a bar of chocolate—quite a large one—for lunch.

9. Val isn't the agency's one and only accounts clerk.

Name	Position

	Accounts clerk	Contracts manager	Managing director	Receptionist	Secretary	Dentist	Puzzle book	Garden center	Shoe shop	Walk	Cheese and pasta	Chocolate	Corned beef	Ham salad	Tomato soup
Claire															
Ellen															
Jason															
Paul															
Val															
Cheese and pasta															
Chocolate															
Corned beef															
Ham salad															
Tomato soup															
Dentist															
Puzzle book															
Garden center															
Shoe shop															
Walk															

Activity	Lunch

Cell Blocks

Fill the grid by drawing blocks along the grid lines. Each block must contain the number of squares indicated by the digit inside it. Each block must contain only one digit. Blocks must be four-sided squares or rectangles, no "L" shapes, etc.

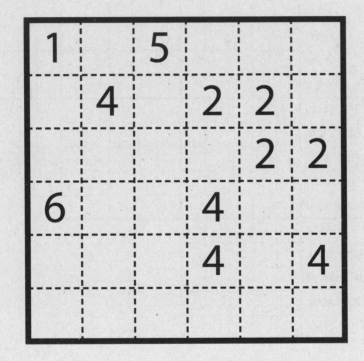

Battleships

Do you remember the old game of battleships? These puzzles are based on that idea. Your task is to find the vessels in the diagram. Some parts of boats or sea squares have already been filled in, and a number next to a row or column refers to the number of occupied squares in that row or column. The boats may be positioned horizontally or vertically, but no two boats or parts of boats are in adjacent squares—horizontally, vertically, or diagonally.

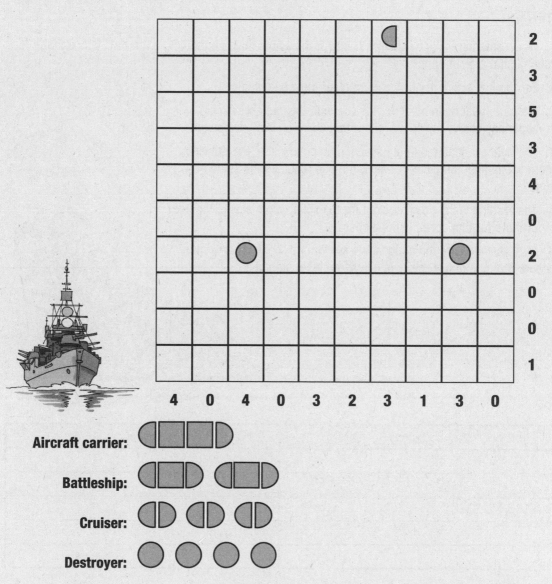

Setting the Scenes

Assistant stage manager Audrey Torium has very important jobs to do before each scene during the current production. Before each scene she must ensure that a particular piece of furniture is set, and that one of the actors has a particular prop before entering. From the following information, can you discover the setting of each scene, and the piece of furniture and prop for which Audrey is responsible in each?

Clues

1. When entering for Act 1, Scene 1, one of the actors must be carrying a tea tray, although the scene is not a restaurant.

2. For the last scene of Act 1, an armchair must be on stage.

3. A statue must be in place for the scene in the garden, which immediately follows the scene where the vital prop is a newspaper.

4. The suitcase features in the scene immediately after the drawing room scene and immediately before the one requiring the standard lamp.

5. The knitting is the prop required for the sitting room scene; the item of furniture for that scene is not a chair.

6. After making sure the cupboard is set for one scene, Audrey must ensure that one of the actors in it is carrying an umbrella.

Scene	Setting

	Bedroom	Drawing room	Garden	Restaurant	Sitting room	Armchair	Cupboard	Standard lamp	Statue	Wicker chair	Knitting	Newspaper	Suitcase	Tea tray	Umbrella
Act 1, Scene 1															
Act 1, Scene 2															
Act 1, Scene 3															
Act 2, Scene 1															
Act 2, Scene 2															
Knitting															
Newspaper															
Suitcase															
Tea tray															
Umbrella															
Armchair															
Cupboard															
Standard lamp															
Statue															
Wicker chair															

Furniture	Prop

Wordwheel

Using only the letters in the Wordwheel, you have ten minutes to find as many words as possible, none of which may be plurals, foreign words, or proper nouns. Each word must be of three letters or more, all must contain the central letter, and letters can only be used once in every word. There is at least one nine-letter word in the wheel.

Cell Blocks

Fill the grid by drawing blocks along the grid lines. Each block must contain the number of squares indicated by the digit inside it. Each block must contain only one digit. Blocks must be four-sided squares or rectangles, no "L" shapes, etc.

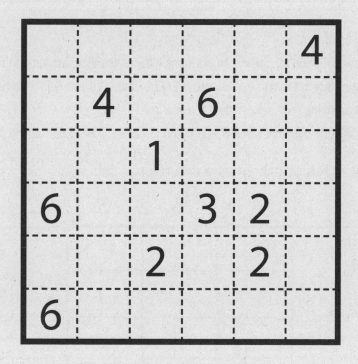

Looking for Gold

Each of the twelve boxes forming the large rectangle contains a word that may be preceded by the word GOLD. From the clues given, can you place the correct word in each of the twelve boxes?

Clues

1. Only one corner box contains a four-letter word.

2. MEDAL is in the same horizontal row as FINCH, but they are not in adjoining boxes.

3. RUSH is in the row below WATCH and the row above CREST, though not necessarily in the same column as either.

4. SMITH is not in column A.

5. The words in boxes A4 and B2 begin with the same letter of the alphabet, as do those in A3 and C4.

6. FISH is in a higher box in the same column as LEAF; neither of these is in a corner box.

7. The word in C3 contains more letters than the one in A1.

8. FINGER is immediately diagonally below and to the left of the RING that may be put on it.

Words: Crest; Digger; Finch; Finger; Fish; Leaf; Medal; Miner; Ring; Rush; Smith; Watch

Starting tip: Begin by identifying and placing the word referred to in clue 1.

Codewords

Every number in the grid represents a different letter of the alphabet. Three letters have been filled in to give you a start.

19	8	9	12	18	20	■	9	10	5	19	19	10
26	■	13	■	15	■	14	■	3 **A**	■	26	■	25
10	15	12	7	3	23	20	■	14 **S**	9	19	2	19
12	■	25	■	4	■	1	■	18 **T**	■	15	■	18
15	19	13	3	1	■	10	1	3	18	18	19	15
19	■	■	■	19	■	24	■	■	■	19	■	20
■	21	19	11	15	3	■	11	1	3	2	19	■
25	■	10	■	■	■	3	■	25	■	■	■	1
11	25	12	1	12	13	6	■	18	3	14	18	19
22	■	14	■	2	■	15	■	18	■	24	■	13
19	11	25	13	20	■	19	1	19	17	19	13	18
23	■	2	■	1	■	19	■	15	■	3	■	12
18	15	19	11	1	19	■	19	20	19	16	9	1

A~~A~~ B C D E F G H I J K L M N O P Q R ~~S~~ ~~T~~ U V W X Y Z

1	2	3 **A**	4	5	6	7	8	9	10	11	12	13
14 **S**	15	16	17	18 **T**	19	20	21	22	23	24	25	26

Hall Earmarked

Our local village hall has five regular bookings each week for a variety of activities. From the following information, can you work out which activity takes place on which day, the time, and the contact name for each group?

Clues

1. Monday's booking is for the drama group, but their contact is not Ms. Owen, while Mr. Hughes is the contact for the Tuesday booking.

2. One of the groups has booked the hall for 11 o'clock on Thursdays, and Ms. Douglas's group has it at 7:30 one evening each week.

3. The keep-fit class uses the hall two days before Mr. Dobson's group.

4. The painting class is held in the hall the day after the 10:30 booking.

5. Line dancing commences at 4:30 each week.

6. Mrs. Muir is the contact for the upholstery class.

Day	Activity

	Drama group	Keep-fit	Line dancing	Painting	Upholstery	10:30	11:00	2:30	4:30	7:30	Mr. Dobson	Ms. Douglas	Mr. Hughes	Mrs. Muir	Ms. Owen
Monday															
Tuesday															
Thursday															
Friday															
Saturday															
Mr. Dobson															
Ms. Douglas															
Mr. Hughes															
Mrs. Muir															
Ms. Owen															
10:30															
11:00															
2:30															
4:30															
7:30															

Time	Contact

Battleships

Do you remember the old game of battleships? These puzzles are based on that idea. Your task is to find the vessels in the diagram. Some parts of boats or sea squares have already been filled in, and a number next to a row or column refers to the number of occupied squares in that row or column. The boats may be positioned horizontally or vertically, but no two boats or parts of boats are in adjacent squares—horizontally, vertically, or diagonally.

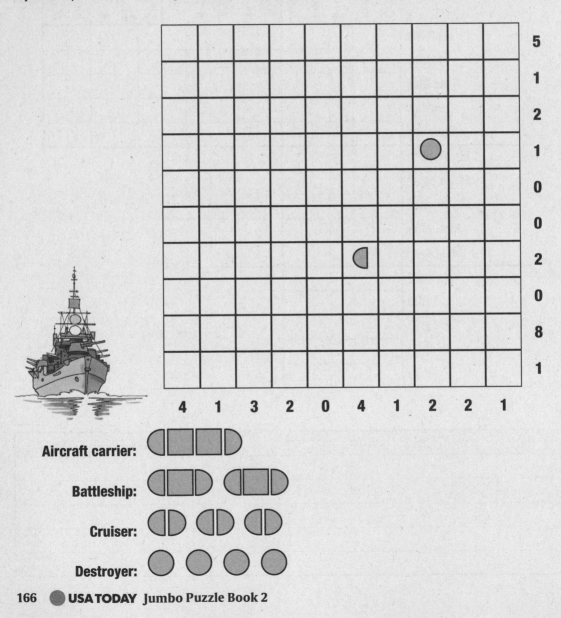

Aircraft carrier:

Battleship:

Cruiser:

Destroyer:

Cell Blocks

Fill the grid by drawing blocks along the grid lines. Each block must contain the number of squares indicated by the digit inside it. Each block must contain only one digit. Blocks must be four-sided squares or rectangles, no "L" shapes, etc.

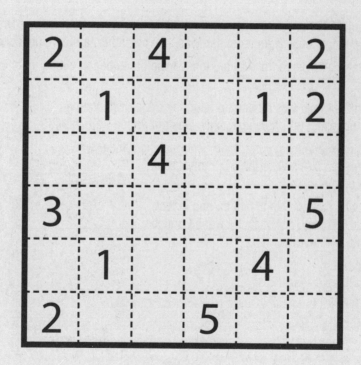

Sofie's Choice

Back in the year 1667, Princess Sofie's father, King Siegfried of the little German kingdom of Mittelerde, provided her with a list of five eligible princes from surrounding realms and instructions to pick one of them as her husband. But there were factors for and against each man; from the clues given, can you work out each young man's name, the name of his father's kingdom, and the good and bad things Sofie had to consider before making her choice? (Which incidentally was to elope with an Irish mercenary soldier, one Captain Dominic Desmond—but that's another problem.)

Clues

1. The extremely charming and well-mannered Prince Lorenz came from neither Drakenraupe nor the kingdom whose king's only (legitimate) son was, like his father, a notorious lecher.

2. Prince Archimbald, who came from a kingdom whose name began with a letter in the second half of the alphabet, wasn't the lecher.

3. The prince from Lohringia was a talented poet; the prince who was a war hero but also, unfortunately, hideously ugly, was not Prince Archimbald.

4. Prince Patrizius of Hochenberg wasn't the good-looking prince, who wasn't the one who—well, his Victorian biographer said that he had no interest in women.

5. Prince Crispus was cursed with ill health, and in fact died before his 21st birthday; obviously he wasn't athletic, and he wasn't good-looking either.

6. It was the prince from Schwabenz who was poor—as, indeed, was everyone from Schwabenz.

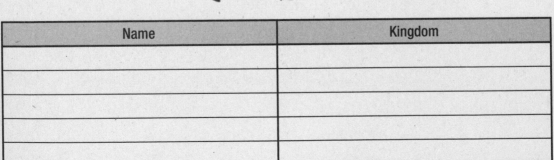

Name	Kingdom

	Drakenraupe	Hochenberg	Lohringia	Schwabenz	Westerfelsen	Athletic	Charming	Good-looking	Poet	War hero	Ill health	Lecher	No interest	Poor	Ugly
Archimbald															
Crispus															
Gotthart															
Lorenz															
Patrizius															
Ill health															
Lecher															
No interest															
Poor															
Ugly															
Athletic															
Charming															
Good-looking															
Poet															
War hero															

Good	Bad

Add Up

If the number in each circle is the sum of the two below it, how quickly can you figure out the top number? Try solving in your head before writing anything down.

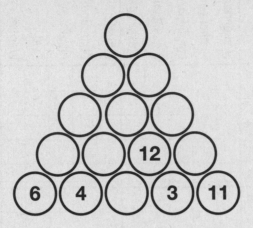

Add Up

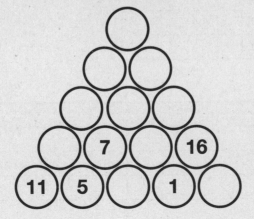

Wordwheel

Using only the letters in the Wordwheel, you have ten minutes to find as many words as possible, none of which may be plurals, foreign words, or proper nouns. Each word must be of three letters or more, all must contain the central letter, and letters can only be used once in every word. There is at least one nine-letter word in the wheel.

Intellectual Pursuits

Among the many lecturers at the University of Goatsferry, you can find people with all sorts of leisure-time interests—literature and languages, philosophy and philately, music and—well, you get the idea; but there are some whose hobbies are a little more unusual. From the clues below, can you work out the full names of each of these people, the subject in which they lecture, and what they do in their time off?

Clues

1. Oliver lectures in media studies.

2. Dr. Strangelove, who is a member of the Physics Department, isn't Ursula, and has no interest in cryptology—the study of codes and ciphers.

3. Irving isn't the lecturer who collects cola memorabilia—we can't name the brand, of course, nor can we explain why anyone would want to collect it.

4. Neither Dr. Aubrey Jekyll nor the lecturer in German literature have a hobby that has a name beginning with a "c."

5. Dr. Dolittle took up juggling as therapy after an accident, then became hooked.

6. The law lecturer, who is studying the Eldarin tongues—the Elvish languages devised by J. R. R. Tolkien for *The Lord of the Rings*—has a longer surname than Ursula, who isn't Dr. Kildare.

First name	Surname

	Dolittle	Frankenstein	Jekyll	Kildare	Strangelove	Economics	German literature	Law	Media studies	Physics	Building rockets	Cola memorabilia	Cryptology	Elvish	Juggling
Aubrey															
Evangeline															
Irving															
Oliver															
Ursula															
Building rockets															
Cola memorabilia															
Cryptology															
Elvish															
Juggling															
Economics															
German literature															
Law															
Media studies															
Physics															

Subject	Hobby

Codewords

Every number in the grid represents a different letter of the alphabet. Three letters have been filled in to give you a start.

18	1	3	3	16	24	13	■	24	26	8	14	19
3	■	6	■	11	■	24	■	10	■	25	■	24
12	6	13	26	6	■	18	4	24	24	5	24	13
6	■	■	■	16	■	8	■	14	■	■	■	13
13	24	6	9	8	1	7	■	19	8	6	13	6
■	■	2	■	■	■	1	■	24	■	12 L	■	14
18	17	23	6	18	11	■	6	9	25	8 I	13	24
23	■	13	■	6	■	20	■	■	■	16 K	■	■
20	12	24	6	19	■	13	24	15	13	24	18	11
18	■	■	■	8	■	8	■	12	■	■	■	6
8	25	5	3	18	24	9	■	24	6	18	24	12
9	■	8	■	15	■	7	■	24	■	23	■	26
24	1	24	25	21	■	24	22	19	13	24	25	24

A B C D E F G H I̸ J I̸ L̸ M N O P Q R S T U V W X Y Z

1	2	3	4	5	6	7	8 I	9	10	11	12 L	13
14	15	16 K	17	18	19	20	21	22	23	24	25	26

In Training

The horses who occupy the stalls numbered 1 to 7 at a training stable are all due to perform on the racetrack next week, and are being exercised today by the "lad" (or, in some cases, lass) allocated to look after their welfare. From the clues given, can you name the horse in each stall, and the "lad" who is exercising it?

Clues

1. The horse in stall 3 is called Nimbus.

2. Kevin's mount is separated from Milton by one other stall; the latter is not in stall 1.

3. Alan's charge has a stall numbered two lower than Sally Lunn's, which is not number 7.

4. Charlotte's horse in stall 6 has a two-word name, as does its immediate neighbor in stall 5.

5. Steffie is exercising the horse in the stall next left to that of Scotch Mist as you look at the row.

6. Jerry will be riding Al Capone as the horses exercise this morning; the latter's stall is farther left than Yeoman Warder's, which is adjacent to the one occupied by Ray's mount.

7. Maria is responsible for a horse in an odd-numbered stall, which is next door to Jetstream's.

Horses: Al Capone; Jetstream; Milton; Nimbus; Sally Lunn; Scotch Mist; Yeoman Warder
Lads: Alan; Charlotte; Jerry; Kevin; Maria; Ray; Steffie

Horse: _____ _____ _____ _____ _____ _____ _____

Lad: _____ _____ _____ _____ _____ _____ _____

Starting tip: Identify first the horse in stall 1.

Hyperman

In these days of hype, what with hyperinflation and supermarkets becoming hypermarkets, it is no surprise that Superman has finally been superseded by Hyperman. Hyperman's story has been told in five episodes by the *Daily Cosmos*, as allegedly reported by everyday onlookers (all, in fact, aliases used by Hyperman himself, seeking to avoid the limelight). From the clues given, can you put the feats in order, say which planet of the solar system played a role in each incident, and work out the name under which each report was submitted?

Clues

1. Hyperman's sole act on Earth was to repair the San Andreas Fault, saving the future lives of several millions in California.

2. In the last article (submitted in advance), Hyperman describes how he collected all the diseases in the world into his own body allowing himself just sufficient time to take them to another planet, where he (and they) expired.

3. Tom Matthews told the tale of how Hyperman gathered together every lethal weapon in the world, and "decommissioned" them.

4. Hyperman's tinkering with the solar system, so that another planet's gravity pulled the Earth away from the Sun to put an end to global warming, was described in the account next after the one involving Saturn, and the one before the one written by Chuck Lomas.

5. The planet involved in the first Hyperman feat described in the *Daily Cosmos* was Jupiter.

6. Al Smith was the name under which Hyperman sent in his account of his fourth endeavor, which did not feature the planet Pluto.

7. Hyperman's feat of transferring the Earth's carbon footprint by making one himself in another area of the solar system immediately preceded the one reported by Jim Robinson.

Order	Feat

	Carbon footprint	Diseases	Global warming	Lethal weapons	San Andreas Fault	Earth	Jupiter	Mars	Pluto	Saturn	Al Smith	Chuck Lomas	Jim Robinson	Sam Miller	Tom Matthews
First															
Second															
Third															
Fourth															
Fifth															
Al Smith															
Chuck Lomas															
Jim Robinson															
Sam Miller															
Tom Matthews															
Earth															
Jupiter															
Mars															
Pluto															
Saturn															

Planet	Reporter

Wordwheel

Using only the letters in the Wordwheel, you have ten minutes to find as many words as possible, none of which may be plurals, foreign words, or proper nouns. Each word must be of three letters or more, all must contain the central letter, and letters can only be used once in every word. There is at least one nine-letter word in the wheel.

Codewords

Every number in the grid represents a different letter of the alphabet. Three letters have been filled in to give you a start.

A B C D E F G H I J K L M N O P Q R S T U V W X Y Z

1	2	3	4	5 M	6	7	8	9	10	11	12	13
14	15	16	17	18	19 P	20	21	22	23	24	25	26 O

Wide-Awake Club

Many people suffer dreadfully from insomnia, like the five dealt with in this puzzle. From the information given below, can you work out each person's bedtime last night, the remedy to which each resorted when sleep wouldn't come, and the time each finally drifted off to sleep?

Clues

1. One of the five went to bed at midnight and used his or her herbal pillow before getting to sleep as the clock struck half-past; this was not Jeff or Maria.

2. Debbie went to bed at 11:30 and fell asleep on the hour, 30 minutes before Maria.

3. Listening to the radio helped one of the five get to sleep later than the one who took the sleeping tablets.

4. Reading helped one person drift off at 2:30; this wasn't the person who went to bed at 12:30, but who didn't listen to the radio.

5. The person who retired at 11:45 went to sleep later than the one who turned in at 11.

6. Roy sometimes resorts to sleeping tablets to help him sleep.

Name	Bedtime

	11:00	11:30	11:45	12:00	12:30	Herbal pillow	Hot drink	Radio	Reading	Sleeping tablets	2:00	2:30	3:00	3:30	4:00
Debbie															
Jeff															
Maria															
Peter															
Roy															
2:00															
2:30															
3:00															
3:30															
4:00															
Herbal pillow															
Hot drink															
Radio															
Reading															
Sleeping tablets															

Remedy	Fell asleep

SUDOKU

How to Play

Complete the grid so that every row, column, and 3 x 3 cube contains every digit from 1 to 9 inclusive with no repetition.

In Sudoku, you are given a 9 x 9 grid. Some of the grid squares already contain numbers—you cannot change these. To work the puzzle, fill in the empty squares of the grid with the numerals 1 through 9.

The puzzle is solved when each row, each column, and each 3 x 3 cube contains the numerals 1 through 9 with each numeral appearing only once. The 3 x 3 cubes are differentiated by shading.

8	3	7	1	4	6	9	5	2
9	1	2	3	7	5	6	4	8
6	5	4	2	9	8	1	7	3
2	8	6	9	5	3	7	1	4
4	9	5	7	2	1	8	3	6
3	7	1	8	6	4	2	9	5
7	4	9	5	8	2	3	6	1
1	6	8	4	3	9	5	2	7
5	2	3	6	1	7	4	8	9

7	5	2	3	1	8	9	4	6
1	8	6	2	9	4	3	5	7
3	4	9	6	5	7	1	8	2
2	1	3	4	6	9	8	7	5
9	7	4	1	8	5	6	2	3
5	6	8	7	3	2	4	1	9
6	3	5	8	2	1	7	9	4
4	9	1	5	7	3	2	6	8
8	2	7	9	4	6	5	3	1

8	4	1	5	6	3	2	7	9
2	9	7	4	1	8	3	5	6
6	5	3	2	7	9	8	4	1
3	7	8	1	9	5	4	6	2
5	2	9	8	4	6	1	3	7
1	6	4	3	2	7	5	9	8
4	8	6	7	5	1	9	2	3
7	3	5	9	8	2	6	1	4
9	1	2	6	3	4	7	8	5

3	6	1	7	2	5	4	9	8
7	9	4	1	6	8	2	3	5
8	5	2	4	3	9	6	7	1
1	2	6	8	5	3	9	4	7
5	4	3	2	9	7	1	8	6
9	8	7	6	4	1	5	2	3
4	1	8	5	7	2	3	6	9
6	7	9	3	1	4	8	5	2
2	3	5	9	8	6	7	1	4

★☆☆☆☆

4	6	2	1	8	3	7	9	5
5	7	9	4	6	2	8	1	3
8	3	1	7	5	9	4	6	2
2	8	3	5	1	7	6	4	9
6	5	4	9	2	8	1	3	7
9	1	7	6	3	4	2	5	8
3	2	6	8	4	5	9	7	1
7	4	5	2	9	1	3	8	6
1	9	8	3	7	6	5	2	4

978-505-
3192

4	2	3	6	7	1	8	5	9
7	5	1	9	2	8	3	6	4
6	9	8	4	3	5	2	1	7
2	7	6	1	8	4	9	3	5
1	3	5	2	6	9	7	4	8
8	4	9	3	5	7	1	2	6
3	6	7	5	9	2	4	8	1
9	1	2	8	4	6	5	7	3
5	8	4	7	1	3	6	9	2

2	4	9	5	3	6	1	7	8
3	6	5	1	8	7	4	2	9
7	1	8	4	2	9	3	6	5
4	8	7	3	1	5	6	9	2
5	9	2	6	7	4	8	3	1
1	3	6	8	9	2	5	4	7
6	7	3	2	5	8	9	1	4
9	5	4	7	6	1	2	8	3
8	2	1	9	4	3	7	5	6

8	4	2	3	9	1	6	7	5
7	1	9	5	2	6	8	4	3
3	5	6	7	8	4	1	2	9
1	2	7	8	5	3	4	9	6
9	8	4	6	1	7	5	3	2
6	3	5	9	4	2	7	8	1
4	9	1	2	6	8	3	5	7
5	7	8	1	3	9	2	6	4
2	6	3	4	7	5	9	1	8

7	8	3	4	1	6	9	2	5
1	6	5	3	2	9	4	8	7
4	2	9	7	5	8	6	1	3
2	7	4	8	6	5	1	3	9
3	5	8	1	9	4	2	7	6
6	9	1	2	3	7	8	5	4
5	4	2	9	8	3	7	6	1
9	1	6	5	7	2	3	4	8
8	3	7	6	4	1	5	9	2

	9			4			2	
7			9	6	5	4	3	8
4	5			8	2	1		
3	2							
1		9		2		7		4
							6	3
		7	2	3			1	5
2	3	1	6	5	7			9
	6			9			7	

8	4	2	6	5				
			4	2		5	7	
	6	7		1			4	
	8	3		4		7		
		5	8	7	3	2		
		4		6		3	5	
	5			9		1	8	
	7	1		8	6			
				3	5	6	2	7

		7			5	3		9
	9		3			8		1
		6	1	9			2	7
2	1				4			
8	7	4		5		2	3	6
			2				1	4
6	2			4	9	1		
7		1			2		8	
3		9	8			6		

		6	5	1				
	7			4	9		2	
8	5			3			1	
1	3	4			5			
9	8	7	3	6	4	2	5	1
			1			3	9	4
	4			2			3	7
	2		4	7			8	
			5	3	6			

7		4		8				1
		1		7	3	4		2
2	9			6			7	8
9			8	2		5	3	4
5								7
1	4	3		9	7			6
4	5			1			8	3
3		8	6	4		7		
6				5		2		9

			5	7		2		
		7		3	8	4	9	
4	8	2		9			3	
		3			7	6	1	
9			6	4	1			3
	1	6	3			9		
	3			1		8	6	9
	7	1	4	6		3		
		5		2	3			

4	9		1	7	2			
		3		6				
	5				4	1	6	2
	4	2		1	9	3		8
		1	4	5	8	6		
5		8	2	3		9	4	
3	1	4	6				8	
				8		4		
			5	4	3		1	6

			7	5		2		9
3		5	4	2				6
	7	9	8	6	1			
	6	7				8	9	2
				4				
1	3	8				4	6	
			5	8	2	6	4	
8				7	4	5		3
7		4		3	6			

		5			8			
	4			5	6	1	9	8
6	9		7	4		2		
	7	4	6	1				
8	2	6		3		9	7	1
				7	2	3	6	
		2		8	4		3	9
7	8	9	5	2			1	
			9			8		

6				5	9	1		
5			4		7	8	3	6
	7	3			6		4	
9	5		1			3		
	3	1		4		6	9	
		4			3		1	8
	8		9			2	5	
4	6	2	5		1			9
		5	7	8				3

	9	4		1		7	2	3
			7	4	2	5		9
	1				9			
3	2		5		7	9		
9		6		2		1		7
	5	8		1			3	2
			1				4	
6		8	2	7	5			
1	5	2		3		8	7	

1	8	9	5	4	7	2	6	3
2	3	6	8	1	9	5	7	4
7	5	4	2	6	3	8	1	9
4	2	5	3	9	1	7	8	6
9	6	7	4	2	8	3	5	1
3	1	8	7	5	6	9	4	2
5	9	2	1	8	4	6	3	7
8	7	1	6	3	2	4	9	5
6	4	3	9	7	5	1	2	8

9	6	8	4	1	3	7	2	5
3	7	1	8	5	2	6	9	4
5	2	4	6	7	9	3	1	8
2	8	3		4	5	9	7	6
1	4	5	9	6	7	8	3	2
7	9	6	3	2	8	4	5	1
6	3	7	5	8	1	2	4	9
4	1	9	2	3	6	5	8	7
8	5	2	7	9	4	1	6	3

183

7	4	5	6	3	9	1	8	2
6	8	1	5	2	4	3	7	9
9	3	2	1	7	8	4	5	6
1	9	8	2	5	6	7	3	4
3	7	4	9	8	1	6	2	5
5	2	6	3	4	7	9	1	8
4	6	3	8	1	2	5	9	7
2	5	7	4	9	3	8	6	1
8	1	9	7	6	5	2	4	3

184

3	6	5	8	4	7	2	9	1
2	7	4	9	6	1	5	3	8
9	1	8	2	5	3	6	4	7
4	5	2	7	9	8	3	1	6
1	3	9	4	2	6	7	8	5
7	8	6	3	1	5	4	2	9
6	4	7	1	3	9	8	5	2
8	2	1	5	7	4	9	6	3
5	9	3	6	8	2	1	7	4

★ ★ ☆ ☆ ☆

185

3	7	2	9	4	8	6	5	1
1	6	8	3	7	5	9	4	2
9	5	4	6	2	1	7	8	3
5	3	6	1	8	9	2	7	4
4	2	1	7	5	3	8	6	9
8	9	7	2	6	4	1	3	5
2	1	5	8	3	7	4	9	6
6	8	3	4	9	2	5	1	7
7	4	9	5	1	6	3	2	8

4	7	8	1	2	5	9	6	3
9	3	2	4	7	6	5	1	8
6	5	1	8	3	9	4	2	7
5	9	6	3	8	7	1	4	2
8	4	7	6	1	2	3	9	5
1	2	3	5	9	4	8	7	6
2	1	5	7	4	8	6	3	9
3	6	9	2	5	1	7	8	4
7	8	4	9	6	3	2	5	1

★ ★ ☆ ☆ ☆

5	7	3	6	8	4	2	9	1
1	6	9	2	5	7	8	4	3
8	2	4	9	1	3	6	5	7
9	4	2	3	7	5	1	8	6
7	8	1	4	2	6	5	3	9
6	3	5	1	9	8	4	7	2
2	9	7	5	4	1	3	6	8
3	5	8	7	6	2	9	1	4
4	1	6	8	3	9	7	2	5

7	6	3	4	9	8	2	5	1
4	8	1	7	2	5	6	9	3
9	5	2	6	1	3	7	8	4
5	2	4	5	8	7	3	6	9
6	1	9	3	5	4	8	7	2
8	3	7	9	6	2	1	4	5
2	9	6	8	4	1	5	3	7
1	7	8	5	3	9	4	2	6
3	4	5	2	7	6	9	1	8

★ ★ ★ ★ ★

8	4	7	1	9	5	2	6	3
5	2	3	7	8	6	9	4	1
6	1	9	3	2	4	8	7	5
9	7	2	8	6	1	3	5	4
1	5	6	4	3	9	7	8	2
3	8	4	2	5	7	6	1	9
7	3	5	6	1	2	4	9	8
2	6	1	9	4	8	5	3	7
4	9	8	5	7	3	1	2	6

4	2	1	6	9	8	5	7	3
7	3	8	5	1	2	4	6	9
9	6	5	3	4	7	8	2	1
2	7	9	4	3	5	6	1	8
6	5	4	1	8	9	3	7	2
1	8	3	7	2	6	9	4	5
8	9	7	2	5	4	1	3	6
3	4	2	9	6	1	8	5	7
5	1	6	8	7	3	2	9	4

★★☆☆☆

5	1	2	8	7	9	3	4	6
4	7	6	5	1	3	2	8	9
3	8	9	4	2	6	7	1	5
1	6	7	2	8	5	4	9	3
9	4	5	3	6	7	1	2	8
2	3	8	1	9	4	5	6	7
6	5	1	7	4	8	9	3	2
8	2	3	9	5	1	6	7	4
7	9	4	6	3	2	8	5	1

7		4		1	8		2	
		3	5		9	8		
					2			
5		2						7
	7	6		8		5	3	
3						6		2
			1					
		9	8		5	3		
	5		7	2		4		6

					1		7	2
				5	2	3		
6			3		8	5		1
	1			4	7		3	
	8			2		1		
	7		1	8			9	
7		1	8		4			9
	9	2	1					
4	6		5					

5	8	3	7	4	6	1	2	9
7		6	2	1			8	5
1		2	8	5				
3	1	8	9	6	7	5	4	2
9	6	7		2		8		
4	2	5	1	3	8	6	9	7
8				9	1	2		
2				8				
6	5			7	2	9		8

9	2	8	5	1	6	4	3	7
4	3	5	7	9	2	6	1	8
7	6	1	8	4	3	9	5	2
3	8	2	9	5	4	7	6	1
5	1	4	3	6	7	2	8	9
6	7	9	1	2	8	3	4	5
1	5	6	2	3	9	8	7	4
8	9	3	4	7	5	1	2	6
2	4	7	6	8	1	5	9	3

196

7	4	2	3	8	9	1	5	6
3	6	5	1	4	7	2	8	9
1	9	8	2	6	5	3	7	4
9	1	7	4	3	6	5	2	8
2	5	4	8	7	1	9	6	3
8	3	6	5	9	2	4	1	7
6	7	1	9	2	4	8	3	5
4	2	3	6	5	8	7	9	1
5	8	9	7	1	3	6	4	2

★★★☆☆

8	4	1	6	2	3	5	9	7
2	9	6	5	4	7	1	8	3
5	3	7	8	1	9	2	4	6
7	5	4	2	9	6	8	3	1
3	1	8	4	7	5	9	6	2
6	2	9	3	8	1	7	5	4
1	6	2	9	3	8	4	7	5
4	8	3	7	5	2	6	1	9
9	7	5	1	6	4	3	2	8

6	4	3	7	2	5	8	8	9
1	5	9	3	4	8	2	6	7
2	7	8	6	9	1	4	5	3
	6							8
				8				4
8							2	4
9	2	5	8	1	7	3	4	6
3 7	3 8	7	4	6	2			5
4	8	6	5	3	9	8	7	2

2	9							
3		1			7			4
7				9		2		
				7			8	2
9	7			3	8		5	1
5	8			4				
		3		1				8
4			8			7		5
							4	6

		4		6			7	
	7	8		5		2		
				7	2			5
	5	9	2	1		3		
	3			8			6	
		2		3	4	5	1	
3			8	9				
		6		2		1	9	
	9			4		6		

4		6			9	5		7
7	1			5			9	
8	9			3				
				6				
	2		9	8	5		3	
				7				
				9			5	6
	7			2			4	8
5		8	3			1		9

		1	9	4			6	
7	4		3	6		1		
	9			8	2		4	
		8	2					9
4								1
2					9	8		
	1		5	2			7	
	7			9	1		8	2
	2			7	8	5		

1	6			4	8	5		
2				9			3	
	5			7		2		6
		7		2	1			
3				8				5
			5	3		7		
8		9		5			6	
	3			6				4
		5	3	1			7	2

9	3	2			8			4
	5		9	7	4		6	
		6		3				
	4	7						
3				1				8
						2	7	
				2		4		
	8		3	9	7		2	
2			8			9	1	7

				5	2			7
		1		9	8	4		3
8				3			5	9
	2							
9				4				5
							1	
7	8			6				4
1		6	4	7		3		
3			8	2				

		1	7	2	6			8
		4	9				2	
7		2		5				6
8			2	6				7
		3		9		2		
2				1	7			9
4				7		5		3
	1				2	6		
3			1	4	5	9		

1		9	7	5				6
							7	
		5		8				9
	9					3	5	
5				7				8
	1	3					6	
6				9		8		
	8							
3				4	8	9		2

				6			9	
3		9	1	7				2
	4	1		9		5		
			9		7		2	3
				1				
1	7		4		2			
		6		2		7	4	
8				4	6	3		5
	1			5				

	9		3	2			5	
	3	7		4				
5								7
7	4				3			2
	5			7			4	
6			9				1	3
1								9
				6		3	8	
	6			1	9		7	

7	8				4	3		
		2		8				7
1			7	9	2	4		
		7	9	2				
6								1
				6	1	2		
		9	2	1	6			8
3				4		5		
		8	3				1	4

		7		9	3		5	
6				7	1			
	3			6				7
						9	6	
		2		3		8		
	4	5						
8				5			7	
			2	1				4
	1		9	8		5		

8				1	2	3	5	4
								9
			3	6			2	
	7	1		5		9		
				7				
		4		9		1	8	
	5			2	7			
2								
4	9	7	8	3				1

					3			
6	1		2	4	8			
	4	8		7				
5	6			2			3	
		7		9		2		
	2			3			9	1
				6		4	1	
			1	5	9		2	8
			3					

		6		4	7			
		8	9		6		4	
	4			5	3		8	6
6							2	
			2		4			
	5							4
7	2		5	3			6	
	1		6		2	3		
			4	1		7		

3				9	6		4	8
	6		7	3				
9				4		6		
					9		8	
	9			6			7	
	8		5					
		4		5				6
				7	1		5	
6	5		9	8				1

	6			3	9		5	4
	1	4	6	7	2			
				1		7		
3				8		5		9
				5				
6		9		4				2
		8		9				
			1	6	4	2	7	
1	7		3	2			4	

				8				4
				9		3		
	1			7	4	5	8	
2	6				8		9	5
	5			2			3	
8	4		9				2	7
	3	8	2	4			7	
		5		6				
4				3				

		5	8	3		7	4	2
		3		7				
	6	4		9				
	3				2	4		9
				5				
4		2	7				3	
				1		5	6	
				4		9		
6	5	1		2	7	3		

			4				1	
8	7	2	6		5			
5	4	7	8			6		
7		5						
8	2					5	6	
				4		9		
6			7	8	9	2		
	2		5	9	6	7		
7			3					

				2	7			1
2	8			1	9			
		1	5					
		2		5			8	
9				6				4
	7			4		1		
					1	6		
			6	3			1	5
6			8	7				

3		9				8		1
					9			
	1			5			9	
	3			1			7	4
2				4				5
4	9			3			1	
	5			8			4	
			3					
1		2				6		3

5	2			8			4	
				4	7		5	
	4	8	5					1
1		9		7				5
				6				
7				1		9		2
8					9	2	3	
	3		1	2				
	7			3			1	8

		1		4	6		5	3
	4							
		6	2		8			
7				2	4			
	1			6			7	
			5	7				1
			6		1	3		
							8	
5	6		4	3		2		

★ ★ ★ ★ ★

1				3	8			
8		3	2	5				
5	2			4				
		2		9	7		5	3
				2				
7	5		8	1		4		
				7			6	2
				6	2	3		8
			1	8				7

				2	5	9		6
	6				3	1	2	7
			6					
	2		5				8	
3				7				4
	5				8		6	
				9				
9	7	6	8				1	
1		2	6	3				

				3			8	2
3	8			4	2		6	
		2		5	8	3		
						8		7
				2				
7		1						
		5	2	6		7		
	9		1	8			4	3
8	3			7				

	6			5	2		1	
8				4		9		
5		2		7				
6				3				7
	4			6			8	
9				2				1
				8		3		4
		8		9				6
	9		7	1			5	

8				1		9		5
	9				5	8		
4				9	8		6	
	7	4		8				
				7				
				5		1	9	
	4		7	3				2
		9	8				4	
3		1		4				9

		5		4				
7				6				9
				9	2	7	1	
	1				8		6	
		6	2	7	4	1		
	2		6				7	
	5	9	4	8				
4				5				7
				2		6		

		4			8	9	2	1
6	1			7				
			1	3				
2		5						
	6			8			3	
						6		9
				4	9			
				2			1	4
5	4	8	6			2		

	1		2	8	3		7	
								1
				4		9	3	
		4			2		9	5
	7						1	
2	6		5			8		
	8	2		9				
3								
	4		8	2	1		5	

★ ★ ★ ★ ★

	2			9	7		5	
4		6		5				
5	8		2	1			3	
			7			5		1
8		2			3			
	1			6	2		7	4
				3		6		5
	6		9	7			1	

			5		3	2		
	4			8		9		
			6	4				3
	2		3	6		4		5
	1			9			3	
6		4		2	5		9	
8				3	6			
		9		1			8	
		2	4		8			

7	6	2		5		8		
				1		6		
			4	2			5	
3	7			8		5		
				3				
		5		7			2	9
	8			6	7			
		7		9				
		9		4		7	8	5

					5	6		
	5	8	1	3	6			
9				8				1
						3	2	
			9	6	8			
	4	9						
5				1				4
			5	2	4	1	3	
		1	8					

		2		9	4			
	5			2				
		3		6				9
	9			8		2	1	
	3		7	1	2		9	
	6	1		5			4	
9				4		3		
				3			7	
			5	7		8		

	7	2	4					6
3	9			2		4		
	4			7				
			5			7		
2	8			6			4	5
		4			8			
				5			6	
		6		9			3	4
5					1	8	7	

★ ★ ★ ★ ★

		6	3	8				
		9		5				6
	4			9	2	7		
		1	9	7				8
	8			6			1	
6				1	3	5		
		2	1	4			7	
4				2		9		
				3	8	6		

	7			3	2	6		
				4	1	2		
1	5			9			3	
6	3							
			1	7	4			
							2	9
	9			8			6	4
		7	9	1				
		1	4	5			7	

		6			2	4	7	
				4			3	6
9				8				
			3	1		5		
6								4
		3		2	4			
				3				8
3	8			7				
	4	9	8			2		

242

				5	4			7
7				6		5		
	9	5			7			6
	3	9		2	8		5	
		8				9		
	5		4	9			3	
8			5	4		6	1	
5		6		7				2
9			6	8				5

4	1	2	9	8	6	3	5	7
8	9	6	3	7	5	4	1	2
7	5	3	1	4	2	8	6	9
9	8	7	4	3	1	5	2	6
3	6	5	7	2	8	9	4	1
2	4	1	5	6	9	7	8	3
6	3	9	2	5	4	1	7	8
1	2	4	8	9	7	6	3	5
5	7	8	6	1	3	2	9	4

				2			3	6
	4			8	3			
	9					2	7	
			8	4		6	9	
9				6				7
	1	6		3	9			
	8	7					5	
			2	7			6	
2	6			5				

		3	4			9	1	
				7	1			2
		8		9		5	4	
9							5	
			9	2	4			
	3							8
	8	7		5		4		
3			6	4				
	2	6			9	7		

	3			6	9			
					8			4
	4			3				6
	7		3	9				5
		6		2		8		
5				8	4		9	
4				1			5	
3			8					
			2	7			8	

4				1	5	2	3	
9			8			4	6	
				4				1
		1				9	5	
				5				
	3	9				1		
1				7				
	9	2			4			7
	5	8	1	9				6

☆ ☆ ☆ ☆ ☆

			8	3	2			
				5	6		7	
5	6							3
	8			4				6
		1				8		
3				7			2	
4							6	9
	2		7	8				
			1	6	9			

		6			4			1
	3					8		
1				6	8			
6	2		4	5				
3				2				5
				9	7		2	4
			7	4				6
		5					3	
8			5			4		

3		7		5	6			9
6	9			8			4	3
1	4		3	9				
	7		9		3	2		
	1		5		2	9	7	
		9	7		8			
9				3	4		5	
7	3			2	5		9	6
5			6	7	9	3		

WORD ROUNDUP™

How to Play

Find the hidden words in the puzzle looking horizontally, vertically, and diagonally. Unlike traditional word searches, Word Roundup™ gives clues to the words hidden within the puzzles. The words themselves are for solvers to figure out.

```
J Z D G S L M U G M S C
X U J E I H R J H T A Z
S Z N R C E A S X R L Y
M V P E B E U R C O M B
E A X O P R M J K S O Y
L Z T U B Z V B J E N L
T C C S N A P P E R Z U
O A U G U S T Z J R X J
```

FIND AND CIRCLE . . .

Seven months   ☑☑☑☑☑☑☐

Four fish that start with S   ☑☑☑☐

Two things used on hair   ☑☑

Two drink containers   ☑☐

Vacation/recreation area   ☐

```
B G S X E Z P S S L H S
R O Z A E U T C P O Z A
E P O O N E R H O T C G
K E H T K D J O U S E K
A S Z S I X A O N I L Z
E O U L H Z Z L D P F Y
N M O D O L L A R X I E
S S Z X S L I P P E R N
```

FIND AND CIRCLE . . .

Six things worn on your foot

Five currencies

Three types of guns

Two forms of matter

Public or private _____

```
N D P E C R C T A N R L
C O U I A A Z X O E E S
D L O D N Z T O H V N C
B R A N U K R C E E I I
D R E H X A T L H U X V
E Z A D M I Z T A E Z I
E O Z Z P J A M Z J R C
D R A C E C A R O T O R
```

FIND AND CIRCLE . . .

Seven palindromes (four-letter minimum) ☑☐☐☐☐☐☐

Five colors ☐☐☐☐☐

Two baseball positions ☐☐

Two Hawaiian islands ☐☐

City named after a goddess ☐

```
C R K C J F U N D S H B
W A V X U S O L E G O R
O F S A M R Y V U K R E
C T N H O Z R O X P E A
L U O X O I D E Y A N D
T O J Y L P Y X N Z I G
Z R O C A N O E R C D I
D T D T H S M E L T Y P
```

FIND AND CIRCLE . . .

Eight words that mean "money" ☑ ☐ ☐ ☐ ☐ ☐ ☐ ☐

Four fish ☐ ☐ ☐ ☐

Four words that start with Z ☐ ☐ ☐ ☐

Two types of watercraft ☐ ☐

Two common farm animals ☐ ☐

```
M J D Z X N Z R M O L E
C U J I O L E B A N O N
Z T L I N Z S E E I Z S
J A L E W N L L H A N X
A O Z O L C E C E L R N
M G N A R X N R I E X Y
U S V I H U J A E Z T L
P O C Z L X H D S E A L
```

FIND AND CIRCLE . . .

Nine mammals with four-letter names ☑☐☐☐☐☐☐☐☐

Four forms of precipitation ☐☐☐☐

Two meals ☐☐

Two shapes ☐☐

Country on the Mediterranean Sea ☐

```
B C Z N J Y C R I M E R
A L L X Z B G J N M Z A
T T E A N L X O I J R D
L I X U M O Z L U S O D
A M E R I C A N S D J E
S E C A P T A I N I A H
P R I M E Z W C D M M C
S N A I L S J H G E Z J
```

FIND AND CIRCLE . . .

Six types of cheese	☑☐☐☐☐☐
Five words that rhyme with "rhyme"	☐☐☐☐☐
Two military ranks	☐☐
Two mollusks	☐☐
Bound collection of maps	☐

```
L D Z X L O C A L G W C
L U M B E R M I L L H D
Z C L J O T T E R Z I Z
X K Z L H A Z T O N T L
P U M P E R N I C K E L
L E T H A L H G Z B C R
Z S W A N L E G A L X Y
S E A L O Y A L Z C D E
```

FIND AND CIRCLE . . .

Seven words that begin and end in L ☑☐☐☐☐☐☐

Four types of bread ☐☐☐☐

Two aquatic mammals ☐☐

Two waterfowl ☐☐

2,000 pounds ☐

```
O J O H N R K U W A I T
A B S Z A P I C C O L O
Y D O T C L A R I N E T
Z X I E U L I I D G X O
H U Z O O A J B R R N D
G A X H S J R O Y A U C
Y T R U M P E T I A N M
X Z Y P V G J P P A U L
```

FIND AND CIRCLE . . .

Eight musical instruments	☑□□□□□□□
Three countries	□□□
Three Beatles	□□□
Spanish "good-bye" and "hello"	□□
Mary _____ Masterson	□

```
L R J S E O U L V D A C
N I Z L E T R T E Z F V
I A M M I E A B U K O I
L H O A S S B B S N S E
B R O S V O B E L Z A N
U X E U C Z D O X E D N
D R O W S Y M A N I L A
D T A I P E I O S L O Z
```

FIND AND CIRCLE...

Nine country capitals	☑☐☐☐☐☐☐☐☐
Five pieces of furniture	☐☐☐☐☐
_____ salad	☐☐☐
Tired	☐
_____ follicle	☐

```
R V C Z T X D G H O T Y
H A Z A S O N O F S D X
I L I U N I N L G A E O
L L N N K Y O I H T L F
L E Z N X W O Z C U T I
V Y I M A R S N N R T C
H R M O U N T A I N O E
D Z S P R I N G Z X B J
```

FIND AND CIRCLE . . .

_____ water   ☑ ☐ ☐ ☐ ☐ ☐ ☐

Four land formations   ☐ ☐ ☐ ☐

Three planets   ☐ ☐ ☐

Three canines   ☐ ☐ ☐

Small unit of distance   ☐

```
U P E R I O D U E X Y H
N N Z J C J H L M E Z N
R D I X A O C Z K P O X
U I H T Y N M N Z L R R
A M J F U J O M O X U E
P E I Z X M H C A Z M D
E N U G H G R E G P E N
U Z U N A W A R E K L U
```

FIND AND CIRCLE . . .

Nine words that begin with U	☑☐☐☐☐☐☐☐☐
Three punctuation marks	☐☐☐
Three primates	☐☐☐
Two "Brady Bunch" children	☐☐
U.S. 10-cent piece	☐

```
A Y D X H E G A M M A N
Z U H A C E D Z H X O N
A Z N E U L W E D S Z I
X L I T B G E T L A X S
J N P Z E A H A L T D U
M Z Y H T E P T Z I A O
X O J X A B E S E J M C
L E M O N J N E Z R J E
```

FIND AND CIRCLE . . .

Eight relatives	☑☐☐☐☐☐☐☐
First four Greek letters	☐☐☐☐
Two citrus fruits	☐☐
Type of hound	☐
Property with a large home	☐

263

```
F X T W E L V E X Z S E
J O E I G H T Y B T R X
Z C U X B Z R Y R O I S
A R R R Z E T E O S A K
R I J A N R B M S D Z U
B T Z N I O Z B N X O N
E I O H R G X A A B W K
Z C T T E N P Z N H T H
```

FIND AND CIRCLE . . .

Eight even numbers	☑☐☐☐☐☐☐☐
Four actors who've played James Bond	☐☐☐☐
Three black-and-white mammals	☐☐☐
"Notting Hill" star	☐
Word that begins and ends in C	☐

```
P D E M E R A L D Z K E
E A I G A Z X S J A A N
E U L A H F S Z O X I I
C X R M M E R S O B S P
U R Z O R O I I R P A G
R H U P P R N E C E A X
P Z Y B A E V D Z A L L
S C X P Y Z C E D A R M
```

FIND AND CIRCLE . . .

Seven types of trees   ☑ ☐ ☐ ☐ ☐ ☐ ☐

Four birthstones   ☐ ☐ ☐ ☐

Three continents   ☐ ☐ ☐

City on the Seine River   ☐

Type of word that denotes action ☐

```
N S H O E E N K I N G H
Z I J X N E S F E Z N D
E J N O V U T E I E Z N
L A Z E C K T A E V W E
E S S A C R F T N A E E
V L B O I Z F C P G H R
E A S H J I R O O K O H
N S T Z F W A L T Z G T
```

FIND AND CIRCLE . . .

Eight odd numbers	☑ ☐ ☐ ☐ ☐ ☐ ☐ ☐
Three styles of dance	☐ ☐ ☐
Three chess pieces	☐ ☐ ☐
Two things worn on the foot	☐ ☐
Early calculator	☐

```
C X T E R R I E R Y C B
F H H C Z O L Z R D E A
D Z O Z O G G U H Z L R
R S P W A L C E T M D L
E R S E J R L S R A O E
X A B Z E X E I A L O Y
O M J M X W J X E T P C
B H O U N D V E N U S D
```

FIND AND CIRCLE ...

Seven dogs	☑☐☐☐☐☐☐
Four planets	☐☐☐☐
Three common beer ingredients	☐☐☐
Moore or Maris	☐
Compass direction	☐

```
L J D C T R E S A J R D
B A L O H Z J I Z E C A
E P O Z S E R C L J H Y
L E J S B E C L A Z E B
U E X E B X I K O R S I
G J U I Z K N N E D S L
A L L V A N U X Z R H Z
B L I T H U A N I A S L
```

FIND AND CIRCLE . . .

Four countries that start with L   ☑ ☐ ☐ ☐

_____ whale   ☐ ☐ ☐

Three types of automobiles   ☐ ☐ ☐

One, two, three, in Spanish   ☐ ☐ ☐

Two games played on the same board   ☐ ☐

```
T D A Y F Z F Z Z Y D H
S E O U L I T I E Z E Y
T J A Z P E F S E V H T
A Y X M M L R T L L N N
D T E L E E A E Y O D E
I Z E A J R W Y R Z M W
U H X N R T I U E A X T
M Z C O A C H E G R G H
```

FIND AND CIRCLE . . .

Football _____   ☑☐☐☐☐☐☐☐

Four two-digit numbers   ☐☐☐☐

Two Great Lakes   ☐☐

Two units of time   ☐☐

South Korean capital   ☐

```
R D J Z C H L X P L Z O
X O B H I O N O E O J G
S Z C M Z O U P U Z P A
H P A K T M S N S S X C
J I O S X O E R T J E I
M A U U G U U O A R D H
D O Z X S S L C T X Y C
H C H Z H E B A E R A P
```

FIND AND CIRCLE . . .

Seven styles of music	☑☐☐☐☐☐☐
Three large U.S. cities	☐☐☐
Three words that end in OUSE	☐☐☐
Oak tree beginning	☐
Alaska or Hawaii, for example	☐

FIND AND CIRCLE...

Seven words that end in ULL ☑☐☐☐☐☐☐

Six signs of the zodiac ☐☐☐☐☐☐

Two coin-flip results ☐☐

Two forms of precipitation ☐☐

Jennifer Garner TV show ☐

```
E Z J X D G A M M A Z M
K U V Z K O P O U N D A
A O R X I C L A D J X L
T S Y O N S Z L H O Z C
L E J A G N A P A D W N
E P R Y Z A T H E R E N
D F Z X J I E A C Y C P
S J A C K L B D A Z U X
```

FIND AND CIRCLE . . .

Six currencies ☑ ☐ ☐ ☐ ☐ ☐

First four Greek letters ☐ ☐ ☐ ☐

Three playing cards ☐ ☐ ☐

Two mollusks ☐ ☐

Two opposing directions ☐ ☐

```
B D T C P B H T C U P R
X E D A M O R U X P T E
D Z A U B E T N Z I U D
B X H N T L T A M N R N
R T Z L P U E A Z K K I
E H I M O E L J X Y E R
A F A R U A R J R C Y G
K X T M S G Z U C A K E
```

FIND AND CIRCLE . . .

Coffee _____

Three deli meats

Two fingers

Two fish that start with T

Country on the Pacific Ocean

```
H B Y X T D J Y C L Z N
R A J Z R U A Z A U I X
A N R A J D E K D L B Y
T J Y P S I C S O O A A
I O F R W A N I D D G D
U H U O J O V C N A X N
G H Z H X Z L O H Z Y U
T C E L L O M F O O T S
```

FIND AND CIRCLE . . .

Five string instruments	☑☐☐☐☐
Four days of the week	☐☐☐☐
Four canines	☐☐☐☐
Three units of length	☐☐☐
Largest island in the West Indies	☐

```
R Z X S T R A I G H T Y
X A Z F Y C N F K Z T A
P L F V L I A A E I E C
C A X T U U Y N L R A H
L J I G X A S P O Z R T
E Z N R K Z S H X E T Y
E E G O N D O L A Z H G
P H Z X F D I N G H Y H
```

FIND AND CIRCLE . . .

Seven types of watercraft	☑ ☐ ☐ ☐ ☐ ☐ ☐
Three poker hands	☐ ☐ ☐
Banana _____	☐ ☐
Flightless bird	☐
Your home	☐

```
C Z C H O C O L A T E Z
C U L A O S S E T L X U
I Z B L H E V K G E R G
R F L A E L L N I E N E
C O B I E M A E P M Z L
L R V W M I O H V J H O
E T T A R E Z N Z E X H
B Y Z T L Z I R A N N W
```

FIND AND CIRCLE . . .

Four countries with four-letter names	☑☐☐☐
Four two-digit numbers	☐☐☐☐
____ milk	☐☐☐
Three shapes	☐☐☐
Two citrus fruits	☐☐

```
F J Z H C L O U D Y Y J
V A J A C K Y H X N R O
H D I Z A N S W Y N U B
H L V R I R E E T U J R
U O J A V H M S Z S A B
M C R U L Z A T H E Z J
I B H Z N E G Z L O X A
D J A B Z K G C H Z T Y
```

FIND AND CIRCLE . . .

Eight weather conditions	☑☐☐☐☐☐☐☐
Six words that begin with J	☐☐☐☐☐☐
Two opposing directions	☐☐
Two human appendages	☐☐
Uno, Scrabble and Monopoly	☐

```
G Z A W A N G R Y S Z G
G R E G Y C W J S W G X
A F E B I E L I X E N Z
X C L W I L W U Z R E Z
Z O T V X S E J B H W W
C X D I A M O N D S E Z
N A S H V I L L E R Z H
C L U E L E W H B L E W
```

FIND AND CIRCLE . . .

Nine words that rhyme with "stew"	☑ ☐ ☐ ☐ ☐ ☐ ☐ ☐ ☐
Three adjectives that begin with A	☐ ☐ ☐
Two types of cheese	☐ ☐
Two playing card suits	☐ ☐
Country Music Hall of Fame home	☐

```
B H C A Z R D S C E N E
Z I M O E X H J Z A Z X
B I L B M T J A C K L Z
L A M L O P X D S C E L
H U N O J Z A J O A M R
N B B D Z H Z N N I I O
E N S E M B L E Y R R M
O R C H E S T R A O C E
```

FIND AND CIRCLE . . .

Phone _____	☑ ☐ ☐ ☐ ☐ ☐
Three words for musical groups	☐ ☐ ☐
Three country capitals	☐ ☐ ☐
Gil Grissom's C and S	☐ ☐
Large Japanese conglomerate	☐

```
C C L A N K Z B A N D M
J R Z H E B E C H Z A X
P X E E R U S T R E A M
O C R W E T E B T O O H
O C R B B T E R M T W G
R H I E M E H O T I N D
T R Z X A R C O Z A L X
T C L U B M B K G X Z K
```

FIND AND CIRCLE . . .

Nine words for groups of people	☑☐☐☐☐☐☐☐☐
Four dairy products	☐☐☐☐
Three moving bodies of water	☐☐☐
Top's antonym	☐
Yellowish-brown color of resin	☐

```
A T H R K X A Z A R S Y
X S E R U T E C Z E O T
X S I N S G I U T C U T
S K U A N R B S R C T O
P Z N L F I E Y X O H C
O A J A U W S Z H S P S
C A N T A R C T I C A E
K E A S T H B O X I N G
```

FIND AND CIRCLE . . .

Four continents ☑☐☐☐

Four classic "Star Trek" characters ☐☐☐☐

Four sports ☐☐☐☐

Three directions ☐☐☐

Card game related to rummy ☐

```
J C O U G A R P I R K K
L E Z J K S E Z U C Z R
Y V R R T T V U M E E
N Z E K E I E P E H A P
X L H K G C H A T N Z K
C J N H I K C N M Z R D
D I Z J T Z A L I O N D
R L U R K P M Z W X C O
```

FIND AND CIRCLE . . .

Six words that rhyme with "quirk"   ☑ ☐ ☐ ☐ ☐ ☐

Six felines   ☐ ☐ ☐ ☐ ☐ ☐

Hockey _____   ☐ ☐ ☐ ☐

Two types of numbers   ☐ ☐

Large, heavy knife   ☐

```
S O L D S M O B I L E N
X I H W G F N B S Z R G
G Z N N I I R E U U B N
H O I G T N L E T I X I
G D L A J G G A N D C R
N X L D A Z S J X C B K
I C H E V R O L E T H J
K R U S S I A N Z I N G
```

FIND AND CIRCLE...

Six words that end in ING	☑☐☐☐☐☐
Four GM divisions	☐☐☐☐
Three languages	☐☐☐
Large, soaring birds of prey	☐
Element with the symbol Au	☐

```
W H P O W E R P O I N T
K O H Z E J S S Z S R A
O T R P V M W I R O U L
O H A D S O O E X N M L
L R H J D A I N J E E G
T E Z N O L W V K C L N
U E I W P T W O X E H O
O W K C H I S E L J Y L
```

FIND AND CIRCLE . . .

Five Microsoft products	☑☐☐☐☐
Four one-digit numbers	☐☐☐☐
Three primates	☐☐☐
Three tools	☐☐☐
Two opposites of short	☐☐

```
L S E A X F P T Y M H C
I A X A L S G U B E U J
N D K U C T Z O D A A G
L N G E N E X R B D Y R
E O Z R A I P T Z L L H
T P Y C E N T U R Y E E
H A Z U C M O N T H X T
D C J P O Z H A R B O R
```

FIND AND CIRCLE . . .

Nine bodies of water   ☑☐☐☐☐☐☐☐☐

Four units of time   ☐☐☐☐

Four drinking vessels   ☐☐☐☐

Rainbow or lake _____   ☐

High or low playing card   ☐

285

```
G X S H P T C Y Z H C M
D A H T S E E A K Z N A
Z F M E A S R C S M E E
A I W E R D I I L H H T
M E X E Z L I I O X P T
M L J H F X F U Y D Y O
O D C O L O N Z M Z H O
C E A S T P L A Y E R L
```

FIND AND CIRCLE . . .

Football _____ ☑☐☐☐☐☐

Four punctuation marks ☐☐☐☐

Two words that mean "movie" ☐☐

Two words that mean "money" ☐☐

Two opposing directions ☐☐

```
B E H J Z C H U R C H M
H A Z X U L I M E Z A A
J R R J Z N T H G V L Y
S T X N I S E L N E A E
T H J B U S I O A N S Y
O Z A G R R M X R U K L
R C U A P E Z J O S A U
E A M A L S C H O O L J
```

FIND AND CIRCLE . . .

Six types of buildings   ☑☐☐☐☐☐

Five months   ☐☐☐☐☐

Three citrus fruits   ☐☐☐

Planetary second, third and fourth   ☐☐☐

The largest of 50   ☐

D D B K I T T E N N T D
R E R E G X Z R Z I A E
I J S E V L T E H L B B
A Z X K S E A I Z E L H
H C H C L S R S J S E A
C H A G O J E A G Z F C
X Z I L X L X R G O Z U
J P C Z F J T F S E W B

FIND AND CIRCLE . . .

Six pieces of furniture	☑ ☑ ☑ ☐ ☐ ☐
Five young animals	☑ ☐ ☐ ☐ ☐
Two Cranes	☐ ☐
Drink	☐
Scottish city	☐

```
B R O N I O N N B R L X
N E Z P X P M Z E Y E Z
U T E Z I U A L R B T G
B N J F T C D R L A T N
X I Z U Z D K X I B U I
Z W A R O M E L N S C R
M A S T E R P I E C E P
T O M A T O A T H E N S
```

FIND AND CIRCLE...

Six things associated with a Whopper

Four European capitals

Three seasons

Two words for a young child

An 11-letter word

```
S P N T S D S T Z X J N
Z O X S L L O A T B I Z
R M C O N O I E N T E C
E O G K B E K P Y D N E
V T A Z X C A N P I A D
L H L J I H N K Z E A L
I H O R N E T Z E E R H
S X C J B Z X J L R Z X
```

FIND AND CIRCLE . . .

Five things worn on your foot	☑ ☐ ☐ ☐ ☐
Five metals	☐ ☐ ☐ ☐ ☐
Five insects	☐ ☐ ☐ ☐ ☐
Hill or Goodman	☐
Coke or Pepsi	☐

```
F G X H Z C X Z S S A L
G A R Z J F R S X N P L
N N C E E P E E I O O A
I A A E E N O H D W U B
L P B C I T C R X I L E
L A Z S R Z I Z K X T S
A J U V I E T N A M R A
C B L A O S S Z G X Y B
```

FIND AND CIRCLE . . .

____ card ☑ ☐ ☐ ☐ ☐ ☐

Four East Asia countries ☐ ☐ ☐ ☐

Three protein sources ☐ ☐ ☐

Land units ☐

A form of precipitation ☐

```
A R I F L E H A L S J A
M R X B R X E O U L D X
A H E O I L T N J A T Z
R Z J A A S E Z M R E A
S A H Z I V H R J E K U
M J A P J Z A O Z N S R
A M N E S I A J P E U A
A L P H A K I N G G M H
```

FIND AND CIRCLE . . .

Six words that begin and end with A	☑☐☐☐☐☐
Three types of guns	☐☐☐
Two military ranks	☐☐
Two chess pieces	☐☐
Two planets	☐☐

```
N G Z H O C E A N N S H
O O U L A K E E Z I U N
T S O L J M M A R X O N
I E Z N F O L A L I Z O
O A U X R Z P E T L J E
N O T I F I C A T I O N
N L O N D O N J Z B A Y
H N Y L O N N E U R O N
```

FIND AND CIRCLE . . .

Nine words that begin and end with N ☑☐☐☐☐☐☐☐☐

Five bodies of water ☐☐☐☐☐

Three large European cities ☐☐☐

Shakespearean tragedy ☐

Brass, for example ☐

```
P D E A L E R H P Z H A
X A U B C H I L E E D F
H J R J O C E L X O E H
A X E T Z L I A S Z W L
E L P H X Z I D L H A N
E Z A Z A H Z V E T S A
R A P R I C O T I N H O
T H B X M S H O W A T L
```

FIND AND CIRCLE . . .

Car _____   ☑ ☐ ☐ ☐ ☐ ☐ ☐

Four South American countries   ☐ ☐ ☐ ☐

Orange _____   ☐ ☐ ☐

Yellow-orange fruit   ☐

Word that begins and ends with H   ☐

```
Y Y M J C R A H X Y S T
X E Z I I L T R E Z E H
D Z A A N N I L M T C G
F E P R O U L F O Y O I
H L C M X A T P F X N A
L I U A V Z A E Z J D R
B H L S D C H A S M A T
D B C L H E N A V Y S
```

FIND AND CIRCLE . . .

Six units of time ☑☐☐☐☐☐

Four land formations ☐☐☐☐

Three poker hands ☐☐☐

Two branches of the U.S. military ☐☐

2005 Philip Seymour Hoffman movie ☐

```
P T O R N A D O N D Y Y
Y I H J X Z N E R T T D
E X T Z J I V A N R N A
N J H T C E Z E O U X M
O Z E A L Z W F C C N O
O T P E I T H N Z K A N
L J E L P Z A M A C G R
C Z B N X C H E A D L E
```

FIND AND CIRCLE . . .

Six "Ocean's Thirteen" stars	☑ ☐ ☐ ☐ ☐ ☐
Four double-digit numbers	☐ ☐ ☐ ☐
Four types of vehicles	☐ ☐ ☐ ☐
Two storms	☐ ☐
Mexican resort city	☐

```
A F D Z J S E N I O R H
Z U R E N U N C L E Z S
F K N E N I E J R W R I
A C B T S S E O X E X B
T U J U O H I C H H N L
H D O O N N M T E P A I
E C G X U N O A Y E W N
R J Z J H M Y Z N N S G
```

FIND AND CIRCLE...

Nine relatives	☑☐☐☐☐☐☐☐☐
Three student classifications	☐☐☐
Three waterfowl	☐☐☐
Amount per unit size	☐
Rabbit	☐

```
G X G T H N S C Z W L G
Z R A U W E N H A R P I
P B I O I I L C Z X G P
E E R N L T H L E H Z E
P F C O Z J A O O L L C
A J I A H D X R W I L W
Z V X J N Z G H M D O O
G R I M A C E S Z C Y B
```

FIND AND CIRCLE...

Four facial expressions ☑☐☐☐

Four string instruments ☐☐☐☐

Four mammals with three-letter names ☐☐☐☐

Two words that mean "hi" ☐☐

Species of hickory ☐

```
L J L T G Z P B R A N D
Z A A E J E R O L I M E
E R S H M E R H S Z O Z
L J Y T P O J B H T U T
D H Z O H X N G I J S S
D A R E D E V I L L E R
I P O R A N G E Z J D I
M X S T A G E X F C B F
```

FIND AND CIRCLE . . .

____ name ☑☐☐☐☐☐

Three citrus fruits ☐☐☐

Three rodents ☐☐☐

2003 Ben Affleck movie ☐

Large Washington, D.C. newspaper ☐

```
K B K B L I S B O N E P
L I X N Z B E X Y B S A
A S N Y I V U D Z N R W
R H B G I G I L I R E N
E O R R B R H L B O V X
D P D O D I R T Z M E Z
E Z X A O E B X Y E R B
F B M Z B K A T H E N S
```

FIND AND CIRCLE . . .

Five chess pieces	☑☐☐☐☐
Five European capitals	☐☐☐☐☐
Two automatic transmission gears	☐☐
Two words that begin and end with B	☐☐
The FBI's F	☐

```
B H T J Z E J W F C D B
X I H O N V K G H R A Z
N J K A A C S O Y A O R
I Z L E U D U O A J L G
A P S D V X R S V L Z E
R X H W Z J L E H X A S
T S A L A M A N D E R U
F E E T X N W N E W T B
```

FIND AND CIRCLE . . .

Six ways to get from place to place	☑ ☐ ☐ ☐ ☐ ☐
Four amphibians	☐ ☐ ☐ ☐
Three waterfowl	☐ ☐ ☐
Two marine mammals	☐ ☐
Animal native to Australia	☐

D A D R I A T I C P Z C
I E E C Z W H X Y U F A
R K A Z O T E Z H F G S
I C S D R R H S U F N P
S A T O B G A H T X I I
H L N A U A T L A S R A
G B R O U G H Z X H E N
D C T A R A B I A N B Z

FIND AND CIRCLE . . .

_____ Sea ☑☐☐☐☐☐☐☐☐☐

Four words that rhyme with "bluff" ☐☐☐☐

Two opposing directions ☐☐

Son of Iapetus and Clymene ☐

Animal with five pairs of legs ☐

```
P X J Z Y L S L E E P L
Y I K J L V S N W X L L
V N L I S J E Z I I J I
S E F L L A R M S L L H
L E N V Z L T Z A Z E L
L H P U J Z T U X R L L
I S Z J S P A Z R I S I
G S H E E T M J B N L T
```

FIND AND CIRCLE . . .

Nine four-letter words that end in "ill" ☑☐☐☐☐☐☐☐☐

Three words associated with a bed ☐☐☐

Three planets ☐☐☐

Charlie or his father Martin ☐

River that flows south-to-north ☐

```
F H O R R O R G J H G Y
H A C H I N E S E U D Z
J E S W E B Y H D E N X
W X L T G E Z L M P S K
C I Z M S H R O V U E C
D J D R E O C X B O D T
Z O E E W T V Z H C A Z
D J G L X M Z G Y C N B
```

FIND AND CIRCLE . . .

_____ food   ☑ ☐ ☐ ☐ ☐

The W's in www.usatoday.com   ☐ ☐ ☐

Two movie genres   ☐ ☐

Two things worn by a football player   ☐ ☐

Two styles of cars   ☐ ☐

```
P J A M F E J A S O L E
R I J Z I L N X O P N D
E S K R J U O I J A O T
P H E E T H R U I G R R
P A J Z C A J D N O U O
A R X R T X N Z X D H U
N K E N L I G H T A E T
S P O Z H A D D O C K R
```

FIND AND CIRCLE . . .

Nine fish   ☑☐☐☐☐☐☐☐☐

Three Great Lakes   ☐☐☐

Traffic _____   ☐☐

Eastern structure   ☐

Home to more than 1 billion   ☐

FIND AND CIRCLE . . .

Six words that begin and end with K ☑☐☐☐☐☐

Four mammals that start with M ☐☐☐☐

BMW's B, M and W ☐☐☐

Two crossword directions ☐☐

Pertaining to sound ☐

```
C T E M P E R A T U R E
S O L I B Y A J T L N E
K T S I D A Z P X E I M
I H Y T Z N Y E E K A I
P G R A H G Z N M C P T
P I I L E U J N I I S E
E E A Y X S Z Y D N G C
R W B G I L L I G A N B
```

FIND AND CIRCLE . . .

Five things often represented as numbers	☑ ☐ ☐ ☐ ☐
Five countries that border the Mediterranean	☐ ☐ ☐ ☐ ☐
Three U.S. coins	☐ ☐ ☐
Big and little sitcom buddies	☐ ☐
Breed of cattle	☐

```
L Z I L L E A G U E A P
Y A L N R Z P Y L Z D I
X A N A D M T I H X V N
B L E E U I H A I T I N
C L Z D L C A C X N S A
D E V A S T A T E D O P
Z Y E S P A I N Z X R A
D R M A N D A T O R Y J
```

FIND AND CIRCLE . . .

Bowling _____ ✓☐☐☐☐

Five countries with five-letter names ☐☐☐☐☐

Four four-syllable words ☐☐☐☐

Garbage _____ ☐☐

Hearing organ ☐

```
H Z E M U R Y X K C N Y
H A T Y G P O R Z O A R
C D W E M E O B R M C R
I U Z K N T O U I B I E
R C J R S S O R Z N L J
T K Z U J F I Z G G E O
S J H T N Z V X A E P W
O K R A M E R E Z X H T
```

FIND AND CIRCLE . . .

Nine birds	☑☐☐☐☐☐☐☐☐
Four even numbers	☐☐☐☐
Three "Seinfeld" characters	☐☐☐
Two months	☐☐
It has teeth but it's not an animal	☐

```
P N O V E L Z R H R C K
R A J R Z G O X E K H I
E X G H I H J L R O A N
V T K E T G D X M O P G
O F Z U B D H J I H T E
C E A J I Z N T T Z E U
D L Z F A N G L E R R L
I N D E X Z D U N K Z B
```

FIND AND CIRCLE...

Six words related to books   ☑☐☐☐☐☐

_____ crab   ☐☐☐☐

Two turn options   ☐☐

Two basketball shots   ☐☐

Fisher   ☐

```
S D R B T S H Z B S D N
C T Z O B A Z X D P O X
K J A U O H L N B I S H
C T L G B S O O L N T Z
U C U M X M T L N K R B
B J U L A Z A E H Y A U
Z H X I I T G X R Z E L
T Z D H S P A D E S H L
```

FIND AND CIRCLE . . .

Five male animals	☑ ☐ ☐ ☐ ☐
Four playing card suits	☐ ☐ ☐ ☐
Two fingers	☐ ☐
Bird of prey's claw	☐
Flower with many varieties	☐

```
C J A X J E Z A A X F C
X U Z N O X I I Z E L A
A S B B G S L N C E U Y
Y E O A S O A I D N T B
N V Z U G J L S O I E I
E E R N X S Z A I N A L
K N O E U R O P E A E Z
Z M F I V E Z A M B I A
```

FIND AND CIRCLE . . .

Eight countries with names ending in A ☑☐☐☐☐☐☐☐

Four odd numbers ☐☐☐☐

Two continents ☐☐

Two woodwinds ☐☐

Piece of pizza ☐

```
H Z F Z M N Z E J D X E
C E N I O A K J E I O Z
C A A S X O T R S Z F A
T I R T M C A C T U S L
O A R S G R A Y H K J B
M V Z C T R I A N G L E
I J A J L Z J I Z H E X
X Z B L U E P B D D C G
```

FIND AND CIRCLE . . .

Five words related to fire	☑☐☐☐☐
Five colors	☐☐☐☐☐
Five three-letter words ending in X	☐☐☐☐☐
Three shapes	☐☐☐
Succulent desert plant	☐

```
M B J H B A R K O X K C
X E Z X I Z R O J H N H
G J O P N S M U T Z I I
H Z A W G H T A S H O R
G C G X O J M O X S A P
I X H E L M E T R Z I T
E R O A R X Z B J Y X A
N S C I E N C E H I S S
```

FIND AND CIRCLE . . .

Eight animal sounds	☑☐☐☐☐☐☐☐
Three school subjects	☐☐☐
Three things worn on the head	☐☐☐
The largest country in the world	☐
A game of chance	☐

```
T P Z D D X N G S Z T H
Z I X E I W O L F L S W
D N M R P Z J X U I O H
O B L E L R Z P L N S T
G A A N O X A G S A Z V
E L T R M T N I C Z G X
C L I O A E Z J N J A H
I Z N C T F O X J F Z G
```

FIND AND CIRCLE . . .

_____ machine	☑ ☐ ☐ ☐ ☐ ☐
Three canines	☐ ☐ ☐
Three eight-letter words	☐ ☐ ☐
Two languages	☐ ☐
Two forms of precipitation	☐ ☐

```
L L X J P N V Z J E E P
J I Z L O U R A X G P Z
X O M M I E L Z N N O A
P N E E T Z W P P A L M
U L J S B Z A E X R P A
M X B R H U E R S O X L
P O A Z J P S Z D T Z L
L C T A N G E R I N E X
```

FIND AND CIRCLE . . .

Four citrus fruits ☑☐☐☐

Four animals with names that begin with L ☐☐☐☐

Four words that begin and end with P ☐☐☐☐

Four types of automobiles ☐☐☐☐

The _____ Indies ☐

```
P A C H J E H R C A T C
B U X O F Z E I I C U T
X D C A L Y M N R R O E
J I S K A O Z G A O Z A
K E X L N H N S B N E M
N N P O H Z J I R Y M X
I C C Z J C X D A M A G
R E S O C K Z E B L G C
```

FIND AND CIRCLE . . .

Hockey _____   ☑☐☐☐☐

Five eight-letter words   ☐☐☐☐☐

Two baseball calls   ☐☐

Two things worn on the foot   ☐☐

OPEC, for example   ☐

```
G S E A I Y P J X M G Y
E I J Z B N R E Z J A Z
K T R A X E F Z R B L N
A A B L L D P A V U I T
L L X D L Y E I N Z T L
B Y D I J P X J N T E U
Z O H G U L F Z X T R D
T C Y O U N G S T E R A
```

FIND AND CIRCLE . . .

Nine types of people	☑☐☐☐☐☐☐☐☐
Four bodies of water	☐☐☐☐
Two units of volume	☐☐
Two countries	☐☐
Bartlett ____	☐

```
C N H J M Z B R O W N H
S A Z U P A S J X B S G
P J A O S D D M Z A R A
A H T N O H O I H R O R
D D I O J T Z X S K O N
E N W G T L E A F O T E
R O Z O H A G G I S N R
X B B C A M E R O N Z D
```

FIND AND CIRCLE...

James _____	☑ ☐ ☐ ☐ ☐ ☐ ☐ ☐
Three words that begin and end with H	☐ ☐ ☐
Three parts of a tree	☐ ☐ ☐
Two opposing ends	☐ ☐
Scottish meat pudding	☐

319

```
H J F L U S H Z T H L J
E A E X A J N H X A Z T
L R N L Z N G O E J E A
K A Z D B I K R W B R N
C I Z J A O T L X M I T
U S X R Z N W J E Z A E
N E T T O R O N T O P N
K S Z M S O L O F O L D
```

FIND AND CIRCLE . . .

Eight words related to poker ☑☐☐☐☐☐☐☐

Three human joints ☐☐☐

Two Canadian cities ☐☐

Frosty the _____ ☐

"Star Wars" character played by Ford ☐

```
G J Z E B U M Z E S T P
M A K E Y B O A R D A R
O L M J Z E D E N K C O
N A Z E S I N E C I E G
I E X U X O N A U R L R
T Z O Z Z J J C D C Z A
O M S O F T W A R E E M
R X Z E R O P V I R U S
```

FIND AND CIRCLE . . .

Computer _____   ☑ ☐ ☐ ☐ ☐ ☐ ☐

Six four-letter words that begin with Z   ☐ ☐ ☐ ☐ ☐ ☐

Three playing cards   ☐ ☐ ☐

The capital of the Philippines   ☐

Spanish father   ☐

```
L H I G H W A Y R B X Z
X A B C E L L C Z O E H
T D N O J Z S E D V A D
N O V E U C U T Z E J D
U N Z J I N H X R J S A
O O X V E X T A Z E F K
C R I V J Z V Y I O E Z
Z C A H B A N K S R X T
```

FIND AND CIRCLE . . .

Five thoroughfares	☑ ☐ ☐ ☐ ☐
Four pieces of furniture	☐ ☐ ☐ ☐
Blood _____	☐ ☐ ☐ ☐
Type of reward	☐
Popular Honda model	☐

```
H V M H C K J S O L I D
Z A Z O C H S P A I N K
Y C C A N F I U X Z V C
Z A R K H D R L N Z J A
K Z K J O E A I E D K L
C G M Z N D X Y D C A X
A X A U S T R I A A V Y
S J Z S H X P J Z H Y C
```

FIND AND CIRCLE . . .

Six words that rhyme with "back"	☑☐☐☐☐☐
Three of seven	☐☐☐
Three countries	☐☐☐
Two forms of matter	☐☐
Frank Hardy's sleuthing brother	☐

```
S C A N D I N A V I A N
J O S C F N H D B E Z T
D X D I Z L L F G E J A
O J C A L O O A I X E C
G Z B A G V B O Z S H R
T D W J X R E J R X H C
D I C T A T O R S H I P
C Z N G X H Z S P R A Y
```

FIND AND CIRCLE . . .

_____ can   ☑ ☐ ☐ ☐ ☐

Three animals commonly kept as pets   ☐ ☐ ☐

Two 12-letter words   ☐ ☐

Two room surfaces   ☐ ☐

Second- and first-place medals   ☐ ☐

```
B C D B F O R E M A N N
B U C K L E W Y J Z V O
L Z S L Z X R H T X A S
U N V H O O B I I N R I
C E I E V O A E W T I R
A E R I N R N O I Z E R
S R G C T U R E E G S A
D G O S Z B S L Y Z E H
```

FIND AND CIRCLE . . .

George _____ ☑☐☐☐☐☐

Five five-letter colors ☐☐☐☐☐

Three zodiac signs ☐☐☐

Belt _____ (cowboy accessory) ☐

Goddess or planet ☐

```
N V C Z J P L A C E Y O
Y A X O S T O P Z T X G
T R M Z U E X T I T Z G
D O Z E S S H C N Z N X
O O W A B G I O D I Z A
W L B N I A R N N A Y I
N F J N J F C N J A T D
D E G R E E I K D Z J E
```

FIND AND CIRCLE . . .

First _____	☑☐☐☐☐☐☐☐☐☐
Two types of communities	☐☐
_____ row	☐☐
"A Hard _____'s _____" (Beatles song)	☐☐
What red and green mean	☐☐

HIDATO™

How to Play

Each Hidato™ puzzle starts with a grid partially filled with numbers.

6		⑨
	2	8
①		

The goal is to fill the grid with consecutive numbers that connect horizontally, vertically, or diagonally.

6	7	⑨
5	2	8
①	4	3

Hidato™ Tips

Tip #1: Each puzzle has only one solution.

Tip #2: Hidato™ puzzles can be solved using 100 percent logic. No guesswork is needed.

Tip #3: The first and last numbers of a puzzle are circled.

Tip #4: It is not necessary to start from the first number. Sometimes it is better to start elsewhere.

Tip #5: Working backward (counting down in numbers) can reveal key clues to solving the puzzle.

A Sample Hidato™

The following example demonstrates how to solve a Hidato™ puzzle.

	8		4
			3
	10		①
12		⑯	15

The circles indicate that the lowest number in the grid is 1 and the highest is 16. Start by trying to complete chain 1 to 3. There are two possible places to put the 2.

It is not clear which position is correct. Therefore, look for other connections that will provide the clues needed to place the 2.

	8		4
		2	3
	10	2←	①
12		⑯	15

As you scan through the puzzle, you'll see there is also not enough information to solve chains 4 to 8, 8 to 10, and 10 to 12. However, there is only one way to connect 12 to 15. By working backward, you'll see only one position for the 14 because the 15 has only one open box connected to it. With the 14 placed on the grid, the locations for the 2 and the 13 are revealed.

	8		4
			3
	10	14	(1)
12		(16)	15

	8		4
		2	3
	10	14	(1)
12	13	(16)	15

Now, numbers 5, 6, and 11 also have exact positions. The final numbers can now be placed to complete the puzzle. These strategies can be used to solve all levels of Hidato™ puzzles.

	8	5←4	
	6	2	3
11	10	14	(1)
12	13	(16)	15

7	8	5	4
9	6	2	3
11	10	14	(1)
12	13	(16)	15

⑯			
	11	14	
	10	3	①
7			4

PRACTICE

(16)			
(1)	2	14	5
8	10	6	
	7		

PRACTICE

		28	25		
31	27			21	23
	34		(36)		
33		3	(1)		
	4		12	14	

	25		2	①	
23	27	4	3		
	29				11
19			32	10	
	18				
			14	34	㊱

30			(36)	11	13
	29			16	
					(1)
	19	21	23	5	
		24			3

★ ☆ ☆ ☆ ☆

8	10		4	2	①
			5		
13		25	24		
				18	
㊱					
34	33	31			

23	21	19	28	29	31
					33
	4			16	
①			15	12	
6				13	㊱

333

①1	21				
	3	20	25	24	
5			18	15	
	8			30	
35			10		
㉝36					

(36)	20				
	17	23	22		28
16			4		29
	15	(1)	2	9	
13				8	

36	34			29	28
		33	1		30
	6	14			
		7			24
			17		21
9					

(36)		33	32	25	
		5			26
7	6	3			27
	9				21
12			(1)		
13	14			18	

	23			4	3
22		25		①1	
19	26				11
	27			10	13
					35
			32		㊱36

	20	18	17		10	
	19				11	8
26				14		6
27					4	
						42
	29	34	36	39	41	
	31			37		1

★ ☆ ☆ ☆ ☆

	37				5	
㊵		33	35		4	
		31			8	2
						①
29					15	
	22				14	12
	25	23	19			

	33			9	
35			3	8	6	
						12
37		①|		14	
					㊷	
	24	23				17
	26		21	19		

	34		44	43			
	31	33		38		42	50
	18	19		39			
28			21			52	2	(1)
			56		54		4	(68)
		15		60			
25			59		8	6	
	13			9			

	52		50	49		62	
54				48	63		
	57				44		66
	32		35		39		41	
	30	36			14			68
	22		19	17	15	12	
					5		9
		24		2	1	8	

	10	13	16		21		
9		14		18		22	
7	6	4					26
	56				①		30
	54				29	31	
59		49		44		38	
	63			47			39
			66	42			

	7					
3		8	11	15	17	(60)
	5		10		20	
(1)	42	46			50	
37		43	47			52
38				54		
	34			24	28	
	33	31			27	

	49	51		55		64		
		52	54		3	①		
	45	▓	▓					⑥⑥
43		▓		6	8	10	59	
	41		28			▓		
	35		29	27	▓	▓		14
	36	34		25			18	15
38							17	

							65
9					(72)	63	
		5		57	54		
	3		21	52			70
13		(1)				45	
	17	19			49		46
16			26				43
32	29					42	
31					38		40

①1		7	9				
	2					13	15
		69			63		16
⑦72	71				61		
27				23			
28	26			66			59
			38			55	54
	35				44	43	
			46	49			

348

51		54			69		
	52			70			
	48	43	(72)			61	
	44		4	2		62	
		40		10	(1)	18	
	38						
	37	8		15			
	32	30	28			23	
						24	

		①1	4	6		11	
	32			7	9		
		30		19	17	15	
	36			66			
	28		68				
39					59		
42	40	70	25				61
		㉒72	47				54
			51	52			

350

		53					
55	57				40	42	43
	64		67	48	41		37
		63	68				36
			3		6	34	
	(1)	14	(72)	70			
	15						32
		11			23		25
	19		10		28	27	

	20	19	18	9		①	
	16				7		
24			13			39	
	29		12			40	
		28				42	
63	64	65	32		47		
	61			33	70	46	
	60		68		53		
58							㉒

				(72)				
	19	20			12		69	
	25			10	8	65		
27			17					
	28	59					5	6
33			56	(1)				
	34	41			2	53	52	
35		40		44		49		
36	38				48			

353

		5		26		19	
2	1		27	24		20	
31	29			9	23	14	
32					11	13	
		36			50		
39		37	47	46	51		
	72	42		65			
		43				63	
					59		61

★★☆☆☆

354

42				13			
	41		12		16	17	
		35	33	9			5
45	46	34		8			
50		48				3	
						24	1
			29	27			68
61	62	63			72		
			64				

				6		4	①(1)
	54				5		2
51		55	9	13		18	
	62					19	16
49				69			
48	46		67			⑦(72)	
44			33	34		24	
	40					28	23
42		39			31		29

	(100)		30		36				45
	96		32	31		39		43	
	95	27	85		82		41		
			87			81	80		48
	93	88				75		49	
24		90	5	4		73			51
	8			(1)	70	71			52
22						67		60	
			18		68		66	59	
		20		17				58	

★ ★ ★ ☆ ☆

18			10			4			57
					6	(1)	3	58	
		21	22			86	53		59
	13		92			87	50		
	14							62	
98		25			83				64
		34	35			47		80	
(100)			36		69				79
	30							75	
	31			38			73	77	

		92	90	88			55	57	
96	94			86	85		56		
(1)				48	49		84	60	
2		46	(100)						61
	3	44			40	38			
	8	10		41		37			
		11		19	30			77	
					33			76	
		21	24		32	68	70	75	
							71		73

			31						
				33	34				
	79	72		25	27		46	41	
87			69			45		48	
		81				23		49	
			90		64	22		18	
	84			60	63		54		
97		2	(1)				55	11	
				4		57	10		15
			(100)		6		9	13	

	94			7					
		4	3		9		23	15	
96					①1			21	
					85	26			18
99			88		37	28	29		19
	⑩⑩100		79	83			39		
			76						
67			77		81		50	41	43
66				57			51	47	
63	62	60	59	58					45

39					53	55		77	
	41		50	71				58	
	42			68			75	80	
						73			
		32			84				61
34			89			64		4	
29							99	100	
22	21		91	92	93		1	7	
			17		15			8	
	25	18				14			

100					86	85	84		80
	99	93		28				79	
	98			30					1
	25	12				32	4	2	
	14		35	9					
	23						68	75	
16				7				65	
17	19			39	41	72			
47		50	52	43		56	58	60	
									62

	83	46	48	39					33
	81		45			37	30	31	
85		43						28	
						53		27	
	99					65		24	
100		97		69	67			57	
		71	70			63			
95				6		59			19
91		1		5	8		13		18
92			3			11		17	

		87				65	63	61	60
(96)			89						56
		83	81		77				55
	92		82				74		53
	93					71	73		
		15					50	49	
	(1)		19		33				
		18	20		28			46	
	6		23	27			44	37	38
		4				42	41		

365

	77				92		45	
86			76		49		46		
							43	42	41
			53				58		39
	4				55		34		38
1	3		13	7				33	37
			12					62	
16			20	10			30		
	18								
	23	24		26		68	67		

		C3							
		2							
	4		(1)	16			21	22	23
6	7	12			30				
	8		10	33		27	69		66
			(96)	35	36	71		68	
	94					72	61		
	93		39		75	77	58		
92			80				59		
	89		44		47	49		53	
	42			46		50	52		

			29	27	25	24		
	36	34	30		28			20	
	40							16	
42					82		15	
43					68			14
	45			70			12	
	46		75	73				10
	51						8	
	52	57	58			64	1	7
			60	61	63			

76	75	74		69	71			34
						29	32	
	44		▓	▓		37		
			▓	▓			27	
		▓	▓			▓	▓	23
		▓	▓		41	▓	21	
	52		62	▓				
		60		▓		16	15	
		54		5		8	9	13
57	56		3		1			

(76 and 1 are circled)

	72	75	
	73		
	68		
		67	
47		66	
		(84)	44
	51		
	52	56	
			61
54			

36	35	34	
		27	
24		26	
		(1)		4
	20	6	7
19		9	
18	16		
15		12	

			36	35		39	40	47	
	26				44				49
	25							54	53
	21								
	20	22						61	
									58
	13	10							69
12		9		79		65		68	71
		8		78	82				
2	①		㉟84						

371

	53	51							
54						7			11
	58	61	48					13	2
59			63	46		16	14		①
		41		43	18				
			83	㉘					
		81			37				
			68	38	21	34		31	
76		71			23			30	

		64		66	70	69		
52	63							
56	58			48	(78)		76	74
59						77		75
			25	27				
			▓	▓				
	19				30			
	18	17			31		35	
	(1)		9	10		34	36	
					13			

57				78	79	81		87	
	53						82	89	
	54	60		49	75		90		
70				48					
	67	63							
					25			40	39
						27	29		38
							30		37
	8		14		18	19			36
	7	5		1			21	34	

						50	48	47
58	60	53				44		
59	64	63					40	
68	66			29	17		42	
69		22		27	32			
	23		26					
85				91	(92)	14		
86		76				6	11	
	88				4		9	
82			78	(1)	8			

	13					⑨2		85	
	14	11					91		86
17		10			80			89	87
18				78	7				
		21					33	34	
	22	76			①		36		
66	67		75	62		52	37		49
				60				50	
			57		54	39	41	43	
									45

(121)			104	103	102					
	120					92	100			
	108	112			90		12		95	
		83	111		15	14	13	6		8
	114		84						4	(1)
	115		79			68			3	
55				78	77	76		20		
	53	57	58			75	71	21	23	
51					38	74			28	
	46	45	43	41	39			32		27
						36	34			

					(121)					
		22	14		16			110		
	23				18		106			112
	24		4	20	103		107	74		113
	28	94	3					75		72
	29			(1)	99	100			76	
			92			84	82		68	
	35			97			65		67	
	36		44			87	64	62	59	58
	39	42	45							56
		41	46	48		51				

378

10		(1)			53	54	55	57		
	12		7	4						60
13	19			5		45		49	62	63
	16						47	67		
	17		23					68	69	
					34	39				
28	27					38		111		
		26					107	112	74	114
	87	100					106		76	
91		86			80	(121)				116
	89			102	103				117	

				26			23			
	35	37	29	27		24		21		19
		38		11			16	4	(121)	
		57	60		9	7	6			3
52		59								2
	53	44					112	111		(1)
	50						110			106
	46	72	70	68			91			
	75			67	65				93	
	78	80	83	85	89		103			
		81				87			97	

				52	54	55	57	67		
	38	47		51					66	
33			43					65		
	32		42		72	73				
31			41							
29	27						95		76	78
			10							80
21		8		(112)		102		91		82
20		12				109				
19	17	13			(1)	104		85		89
				2		105	106			

381

		52			57			
	①1						59	
45				79	81			
		48	10		80	66		
	42	47			76		67	
41		15	12	85			68	
40		13	33		30		88	73	71
17			29			89		⑤105
		26	25		93			
	20		27		98		102	
		95						

382

	56	58	66						
		59					83		
	49		60		68	85	88	81	
	48			63	69	71		87	
	43	42	62			7		96	91
	44	-	39	15		9	6		97
117				16					98
	116			113	17	18	20		4
	35	28	114					105	
		30			110		1		
				24	108		103		

	3		117				104	103	101		
	①1			113						97	98
5		16			111						96
7				21		110	91	89	93		136
13	8		20		123		125				134
12						126				138	
11		24	26				86				139
47			32	30	84		79		74		
		39	33		83	81				72	
		50				61			77	71	
	41	51		55	56		63	65			143
43							59	66	68		⑭144

30	32			47	49	50		69	70		
29		35	44	46			67			100	
		41	43				66				103
	37		42			64			86	98	
		39			62			84		97	
	24	58		60		79		83			106
	23		59			78	80	89	94		
	21			1		129		92		109	
	19		9	126				122			
						131		120	111		
	15	6						135			117
13		144		141		133	138				

113	112	110			126			(144)			
115				125		106	(1)		130		
116				101		3			141		134
	120		122	102				37			137
	92				8	7	5	39			136
	91		97		10						34
	89		95							41	43
87			13	14		22			31		44
86	84				16	18	20		30		
80	81		71	69					48		
	77		64		68			56	55	53	
	76			66			60			52	

386

	65						26		17		15
63		61				28	25			19	
55	57	58	59		71	75					11
54			47	72		77					10
		50	46	80				31		8	
							33		5	3	
	90	88	86	85	42	83		134			
			40				136			1	
	93			38	144		137		122		
	97	103		109			139				
	98		106	108		141	115	117			124
		101			113			118	125		

6	7		10	11	12						99
5		2				15	24			100	
	3	(1)	41			25			22	101	
		49		39	37	35	28		104		96
	53	48		43	36	34					
(144)		47	45			33	31	106		94	
143						67	69		108	93	
142		139		64		70		110			90
141		138	63	62	73	72		111		88	
129			136	135		74			114	84	
			123		120	118	116	77			85
	127	124		122		119			79		82

388

	13	11	9	7			29	28	33		
	14			6	4					37	36
								25		38	
63	61	59	57		53			①		39	
64			56	54				47	⑭⁴		
65		70	110			50					
66	68	72		109	112	117		45	140		
	75		73	107						139	
		78			104		115		122		
	88	80		105				129	131		136
				91		97	128				
			93			96		127		134	133

	64	69	70			3	5	7		11	
				49		2			8	10	
67		61		50	(1)	75					14
			47						16		(144)
	59		55			80	136	138			
.	41		57	54	53	82				18	
38			86		84			26			
39		36	87			119	27				
			32		106		117			23	
	102				108	116		121			
101		93			109				123		
		97	95	111		113	125	127			

390

70	69						59	116	115	121	
	72	67		105		61				117	119
74				107	106			57		123	
	78	77		103					(128)		
		100	101								126
80			98					54		49	
82	83		97							45	
85								51		41	
86			26			30	33		40		
87	89			24	23	31		9	5		
		18				12	10		6		
	19		21		14						(1)

		7		(1)							(132)
			5			124	128		115		
9	14		4		122						113
	20		▓		76		▓		118		110
19			▓			77	79	▓		108	
	18					80			87		
	72	70			60	63		84	88		
			▓			61		▓		93	
			▓		58		▓		92		103
	37	38	29				54			97	
		30		41		46			96		101
	33	32			43	44	49	50			100

		65	67						76		
						70	72	74	77		
63		59	23		16		13	9		79	
			24		17	14	12			83	
57		53		18					6		82
56		48						3	5	85	
51		47								86	
		42						1		100	
		41						104			
	40									98	97
	37	35									95
			32						108		

			(108)		94				
82		87	89		107		99	97	(1)		7
	83			105						6	
											9
	71			102						10
	70					17		19	
68		73					14		23
65	66			42			15	22	
	64		43						25
	63		52				27	
	56	51			38			32	
	58	55		48		46	34	35	31	

			64		60						■
				63	53	55			41	■	
		69			56	47		■			
	95			51	77		■				
				76		■			27		
			74		79	■	30		26		
91		89		81	■	130	(132)	(1)	32		25
		88	83	■					3		
	86		■			117		122	4		21
		■		126		118			8		
	■	109			115	12	11	10	9		
■		108	112	113					16		

★ ★ ★ ★ ☆

						26	23	21	19		
	34	35	36	37	28		24			17	
			39				(1)				
	44	42	40						12		
	48		54					5			10
		49	50				102	7	8		
				52			103		99		
67		65									95
	66	63									
	69	73					109			91	
71			77	79	82	83					92
				80			(112)	111		89	

396

102			107	117			114		129		
	104	105						126		130	
	98		91		110					135	
99		93	(1)		(144)		122			134	
		2				142			15		
	87							13			21
		84		61		9		17			
66	65		63	62		10			19		26
68			82				44		40	25	
69		78	80					38			28
70			79		55			37			29
73					54			47	34		

★ ★ ★ ★ ☆

					24						135
	16	14	12	10	8	6					134
							①1	⑴140			
						45			50		128
	36	38		42			52			129	
		39	41		▓	▓		54			
					▓	▓			55		
	100	102	104	106			61	64	66		
	95	93	91				62			68	
					87						121
81				85					70		118
	79	78	77	76	74		72	115			

398

		90	85						30		
	93		86	83			79		31	28	
95		88			74	78		18	19		
	98	69									25
	99		71	102		105	15				24
					104			13	39		
	117	116				112			38		42
	64		115	120		111		11			43
62					135	51		10		45	
	125										
	124	128		57		54		(1)			
				131	55			(140)	4		

94						42					
	96	92	99					46	47		50
			102		104			38	52	53	
	88	█	█				36	█	█	55	56
86	85	█	█		108		34	█	█		
83						32			59		
	80	113						68		61	63
81				28	27					21	
			116	█		█		9			
124		77			█		3				18
		120	129		(132)			4			
	127					(1)	6			13	

20						86	88			
	18	23	30		84			91	94	
16			28						93	
		39			80	102				
				37						
	41	10		136	76		107	105		
		43		134	65					
						68				
	47		4		7	63				113
49	50	1		6			129		72	
53							126			118
	55		58	60					125	120

Crossword Solutions

1

```
S W E A T   L A O S   C A L M
P A R K A   O G R E   O R E O
I H E A R D T H A T   R E N T
T I C   N A T A L   G N A S H
E N T W I N E S   M A C
D E S I S T     B E G O N I A
    T H E P I L L S B U R Y
A P O   E V E     T E E
D O U G H B O Y W A S A
S I R L O I N   S I M P E R
    E G G   R E T R I E V E
A L I A S   F O L I O   R O D
T O R N   F L O U R C H I L D
O B O E   L A D D   C A L V E
M E N D   A P S E   O L S E N
```

2

```
C A L F   S A R D I S   M A S
A L I A   A T E A M S   A X E
N I C K E L O D E O N   V E X
D E K E D   M O W N   R E L Y
O N S I D E   O T T E R
    D I M E N O V E L I S T
S A S   E U R O   X A C T O
H T T P   S A R G E   X K E S
A T R A S   T O R O   S T S
Q U A R T E R H O R S E
    P S Y C H   S T R I P S
B A L E   Z I G S   E R N I E
A G E   P E N N Y L O A F E R
B U S   A M O U N T   N O T A
Y E S   M A S S E D   T R A C
```

3

```
L E A S E   A B L E   F L A P
P O B O X   G O A L   L O B E
S N A F U   I O T A   A V O N
    A D E N T I S T W E D A
A L E   E D G Y   T A S S E L
T E R E S A     G I G
B A N D   M A N I C U R I S T
A S I D E   L U G   P U S H Y
T H E Y R E A T I T   S L A P
    I A N   A D H E R E
I M P A C T   A S T O   S K A
T O O T H A N D N A I L
S O S O   W A D E   N O T C H
O R E M   A S E A   G O A P E
K E D S   Y A R D   S T R A W
```

4

```
S C A R   D R A W   C S P O T
T A D A   R A R A   O H A R A
A L A N   A P E T   V A P O R
F L Y I N G S A U C E R
F I T   A S H   S A N D B A R
S T O A T   E V I L   A W E
    F U S E S   I D O N O T
T H E A R C T I C C I R C L E
H E A R E R   G H O S T
I R S   O M N I   M S D O S
N O T A B L E   G O A   E L O
    G O L D E N G L O B E S
C L E A R   I D O L   A B O O
D A N Z A   A N N E   K I L O
C O D E X   N A S D   S E E N
```

5

```
CALF   HAREM   BOSH
LUAU   AROMA   OLIO
ATCROSSPURPOSES
DOE  SHOE    LIEGE
    GLEN   PLANNED
PERIOD   SLANG
ALAS     PHONE   DDT
CANTSEEEYETOEYE
TNT   CAKES    GENE
    ERROR   FORDED
HEMLINE   BODE
BROOM    LUGE   ICE
ONOPPOSITESIDES
MIRE   HEFTY   KEEP
BEES   MATES   EASY
```

6

```
HAWN   MILD   UPEND
ALOU   ANEW   MAYOR
HARDDRIVE   PLEBE
ASKIN   TILT   EWES
    SARI   LENTILS
ALOT   AAA   LOTT
DOC   ZITI   EVENTS
DUE   ONELOVE   ERA
STARRY   EVIL   SUN
   NERD   YES   USED
OFFLOAD   REST
POLE   YIPS   AUNTS
ALONE   JETSTREAM
RIOTS   OREO   NATO
TORSO   NIPS   STAG
```

7

```
MANE   ALEUT   NERF
AMYS   BALSA   ODIE
JAMSESSION   SETS
ONE   NOTE   TBONES
RATEDR    RIA
    CUBSCOUTPACK
USURP   WARMS   URN
SULU   HERBS   IRAE
MEN   COATI   INAWE
CRAMFORATEST
    YOS    ALLPRO
ODENSE   DARE   OAF
POLA   GREENSTUFF
ANKH   OHARE   ARTE
LESS   WEDID   USSR
```

8

```
CEIL   PESTO   ACME
OSSA   REARS   CHIC
HANDFELLOWBEACH
OUTER    ETAL   TAO
    NONE   SLUM
CAT   GOAT   DIADEM
AREA   GRAD   SCARE
BENBROTHERHORNS
ANELE   HOLE   NESS
LATEST   EVEN   STY
    REAM   EKES
USA   APER   AEGIS
SIGHTEDSTOPWAVE
ETUI   RIVAL   ELAN
SEEP   SAPID   DENT
```

9

```
CORK   CHANT   DDAY
OMEN   AERIE   RAGE
LINE   CRONE   AURA
ATTACHEDATOWBAR
    DIE    OWL
LAM   STRAITS   OAF
ISAAC   ULNA   GALA
KINGOFSOULMUSIC
EDGE   LESS   UNITE
NEY   BASSETS   SOT
    SAM    EEC
LETTHEWOUNDHEAL
ACRE   NORSE   AXLE
BRIM   CREST   FIDO
SUPS   ODORS   ETON
```

10

```
BOLA   CALM   AMBLE
IRIS   ALOE   GREER
GENE   NOUS   ABHOR
SLICEOFTHEPIE
USN   NOT   LEGMAN
REGARD   STY   ORA
    SILICA   HETUP
   PIECESOFEIGHT
SARAH   NUTMEG
APO   SOT   BISTRO
MANIAC   BAN   HOP
   SPLINTERGROUP
SHOAL   YORK   ORSO
PAUSE   ERLE   APES
ANTSY   TEED   MERE
```

11

```
SPED  PROP  CEDAR
ALTO  RODE  ARENA
CANOPENER   MALTS
SNARES  SUM  STEP
      MATS  UNEASY
POTATOPEELER
IRONS  HULAS   SOP
GEL   RERAN   WOE
SOD  PEROT  AMAZE
   CHEESEGRATER
LIQUID   DOGS
ABUT  SHE  BUSSED
DEALT  EGGBEATER
LAKER  RAIL  GALA
EMERY  EDGE  ERST
```

12

```
DEBT  ESTAB  ACTS
INRI  AORTA  CHAI
SDAK  SLATS  DENT
HAWKEYEPIERCE
ELNINO   CPA   RCA
SLY  GNAT  ASKFOR
   GREGORYHOUSE
ABRA   ERA   BLTS
FRASIERCRANE
TEMPTS  HERE  TSA
SAP  OTS  SACRED
  DEREKSHEPHERD
SHOD  LETON  OVAL
KIWI  LIANA  ROPE
ISNT  ANGEL  DRED
```

13

```
CLEF  EMMAS  BASS
HERR  COALS  ALMA
ANNEMORROW   NLER
TOSEE  TIN  OSOLE
    DTS  NEOPHYTE
LABORED   RAE
ONEMOMENTPLEASE
OON  ISIAH   RES
MNEMONICDEVICES
   IRA  SUITSME
TRIALRUN   SRS
RICHE  RAT  GOATS
ALIA  NINEMONTHS
CLEM  CANTO  MOAN
TERM  OHYES  EMTS
```

14

```
GRO  AWACS  COLAS
EEL  MALLE  EDITH
IHAVENEVERLETMY
SEVERE     TELL
HAITI  SCHOOLING
ARI  CHIDE    SOL
    TAUPE  AMANDA
REFINES  ENACTED
ARENAS  ODORS
VIE  BRINK   LOP
INTERFERE  TRINE
    TERR  AWAKEN
WITHMYEDUCATION
ADIEU  FERMI  NNE
DOERS  TWEEN  GED
```

15

```
SHOP  INKS  APART
TUNA  REEL  TACOS
YEAR  KARATECHOP
   DOC  RIO   KIM
DAILYGRIND  MEIR
SWEEPEA   DOUSED
TET  RAVED  ULTRA
    FIREGRATE
ASTRO  LOUIS  EVE
STRATA  IDIAMIN
SPEC  LOADEDDICE
   AMT  ESC   EON
RUBIKSCUBE  NEAR
ALLOF  ATIT  INCA
NSYNC  REBA  STEW
```

16

```
CHILI  CARES  ADD
EOSIN  ORONO  XII
LOUISBMAYER  LAN
STP  IAMBS  BEENE
    AGRO  SEEGER
STEPHENFOSTER
COVET  URNS   EAT
ALEX  APSES  LAMA
MER  GLUE  AESOP
  GERALDORIVERA
WARSAW   RORY
ATEAM  PAPAL  IKE
TOE  MITCHMILLER
EON  ADAMA  FAKER
RTS  RISEN  TBSPS
```

17

```
HIHO  MARA  EJECT
ETON  ITON  MORAY
ROPE  SITZ  PERPS
ROSANNECASH  ORO
 CLIO  CHAPLIN
AMO  AMPS  ETA
BETS  ELMO  ISLES
BACKGROUNDCHECK
ETHEL  DREI  ACHE
 EAR  FLED  TOW
PASTDUE  TOFU
LIL  DEPTHCHARGE
ADAZE  CIAO  SEAR
ZEVON  OMSK  TRIO
ASSES  TETE  SSNS
```

18

```
ITSME  TOWER  OCT
BREED  RAISE  NOW
MINTTRUFFLE  ELI
SODA  OISE  LEMON
 PASS  OSCARS
EIGHTYMILLION
CDROM  DEAN  BOP
HEIR  AMITY  MALL
OSE  CLIO  RINGO
 VALENTINESDAY
FRACAS  TUFT
LANES  DECK  ATIT
UPC  HERSHEYKISS
TIE  ERASE  DELLA
EDS  DATES  SNEER
```

19

```
CZAR  BRAT  ABFAB
COVE  EWER  PRIME
ROADFLARE  PURSE
 REIN  SPONSOR
MAJORED  BRITT
AZUSA  ASIAN  ASA
CAMELS  TENT  ILL
ALPS  TRUNK  CDEF
WEE  TREF  SMOKER
SAR  WOLFE  ALIVE
 COOKE  STILTED
ARALSEA  TUNA
DEBIT  SPARETIRE
DELVE  ESTO  EROS
SLEEP  STEW  DAZE
```

20

```
GATES  RAKE  ABED
ABASH  UNIX  DIVA
MARCO  NONO  IGET
 WHANGDOODLE
GYM  MAT  MUMS
ROOFER  LISA  USC
OOZE  SHAD  HENNA
WHATCHAMACALLIT
TORAH  CASH  BETH
HOT  ASKS  ITASCA
 INCA  ALI  SHY
THINGAMAJIG
ROLE  ROMA  HOGAN
IPSE  ERIC  TWICE
MEAD  DESK  SETTO
```

21

```
HAGS  TRESS  ASAP
AREA  SANTA  GIRL
HANDMAIDEN  EGGO
ABODE  NERD  SNOW
 SALAD  DNALAB
 ENUF  LAGOON
TESS  PLAY  SOAMI
ACH  DEALOUT  ROB
CRONE  PEWS  ADOS
OUTEAT  LAHR
 GENIES  FETES
TOLD  NULL  RIATA
ERAS  GROUNDCREW
NEST  LOTTO  LEER
SOSO  ESSEN  EDDY
```

22

```
RUST  CUPID  EFOR
INCH  ETUDE  SARA
FLOE  CAPON  ANEW
FORTHEHALIBUT
LANAI  SAO  ALI
EDS  DECK  LOGSON
 LEMANS  RIOT
CANYOUTUNAPIANO
USER  STORED
THWACK  EWAN  BAT
SEW  AAH  CRESS
 OHWHATTHEHAKE
AGRA  LIVIA  ONIT
FOLD  IFALL  DENS
TADA  LADLE  EDGE
```

23

```
SOLD   SARGE   EMIL
OLEO   ONEUP   BETA
HIGHPROTEIN BRAS
ONO ETD  SCI  CLE
   GROANS  THEIR
CAULIFLOWER ERAS
ERROL   SHOOS
EMI   SITON   AHS
   EDINA  MAGOO
THETERRIBLE TOWS
EELER   ENROLL
NAM EAP  IND  IRA
STICKTOONES GNUS
EERO   OSLER  ERNE
DDAY   NEEDS  LISA
```

24

```
LOVER   AMES   ASA
CHASES  TALISMAN
DIRECTMARKETING
SOY  LIEN   RENDS
  WANT  PER  OPT
STRAIGHTAWAY
WHELM   RIO  ABBA
ARAL  FRANK  CLAW
TODO  LEI  WHALE
  PLAINCLOTHES
SSA  OWN  OARS
CONIC   ASPS  HUT
OPENANDSHUTCASE
ROASTERS  PEAHEN
ERR  EAST  DYADS
```

25

```
LODI   RAPS   AVES
ICON   ERROR  NEXT
STEAKDIANE  NAPA
PESKIEST  SAILOR
STANLEE  MIMEO
   OOM  RUDE  SLY
CAST   BEGUN  COO
OIL  ICEAGES  ASK
IDO  DALLY   ERSE
REP  ATOM  LID
  PSHAW  NIAGARA
ANYHOW  SEAMILES
DOJO  BROWNBETTY
ODOR  AISLE  SERE
SEEN   BOYS   TROT
```

26

```
HALTS   SWAMP  ILE
ONION   OILER  NOW
ONCLOUDNINE  LOO
TAKEON  SELF  ASK
   DDAY  NOODLES
ALSO  WOES  REA
LET  ARM  EMPLOY
DIAL  RECAP  TAPE
AFRAME  EDS  NIA
  GOO  BEAT  ODER
MAANDPA  MEMO
ERZ  ERSE  IAMSAM
ALI  LOSTINSPACE
DEN  EVENT  KARAT
ENG  DETAT  SHADE
```

27

```
BOP   CRANE  SHEBA
ETA   APNEA  TOMEI
GONEWITHTHEWIND
GOADS   RIOTER
ALMA  FAUNS  AMA
REAMERS  GENETIC
   RAID   AMEND
THESOUNDOFMUSIC
OILED   ELEE
TRITEST  DESERTS
ETC  HOLES  VERA
  IODATE  PENAL
ONTHEWATERFRONT
KEENE  LILAC  ICE
SODOM  SNIPS  RED
```

28

```
ASSAM   GIGI   GLAD
SENNA   OMAN   ROBE
HAITI   TINA   EDEN
 SPINNINGWHEEL
   SOT   HAT
REPEAT  PRIM   BAA
ATARI   KAEL   ERIC
WHIRLINGDERVISH
LOGS  NEED  EAGLE
SSE  AVER  RINSES
   EGO   IAN
 REVOLVINGDOOR
DARE  VISA  EGRET
ERIN  ETON  ELENA
MEET  SANE  RESET
```

29

```
R A J A S   E S P Y   I T C H
A F I R E   N O L O   M A R E
S A V E T H E D A Y   P L E A
P R E S T O     Y O D E L E D
      L L A M A   I D Y L S
S O L V E T H E C A S E
I L I E   A N T I C   A L A
T I P T O E     D O L L A R
S O S   C R E D O   E M I T
    L E A V E I N T E A R S
S E P I A   I N L A W
A R S E N A L   S E A N C E
C R A G   G E T T H E G I R L
R O L E   E Y R E   D E C A L
A R M S   D E A N   S E E M S
```

30

```
W O O L F   T O D D   A M A S
I N D I A   S T E I N B E C K
S T O P T H E I N S A N I T Y
P O R   C U T S   A V E R S E
      S A S S   T B A R
D R O P T H E B A L L   M A S
R O B E S   A R E   W E N T
E P I C   C Y S T S   A R G O
S E E K   H O I   D I C E R
S S S   R O L L T H E F I L M
      K I R K   O A T S
A P P E N D   D A Z E   T A I
F I R E S A F E T Y C L A S S
A T O N E T I M E   T O X I N
R A M S   A R I E   S W I F T
```

31

```
E A S E   M I T E R   D I P S
P L U S   A D I E U   A D I T
I S N T   R E E L S   H O L E
C O N   S T A R S H O L L O W
    Y O K E L   H O I S T S
O R D A I N   H O O H A
L E A R N   B O N U S   C O G
G A L S   B O R E R   C A V E
A L E   T O A D S   B A B E L
    S H O R E   W A G O N S
A B L O O M   C A R E T
W A L N U T G R O V E   C B S
I R A N   O L I V E   S O L O
N O M E   W E B E R   O V E R
G N A T   N E S T S   N E W T
```

32

```
C A S E S   E D G E   A B E D
A C H O O   R E A D   R A T E
P H O N O G R A P H   C R A M
P E P   N E E D S   P A B L O
      N E R D S   M A R E
L A H O R E   E P I S O D E S
O G E E   H A R E S   W I T
V I L L A G E   O N E S I D E
E L I   C O R P S   P R E P
R E C O R D E R   S H E E R S
      O R E S   A N T E D
H O P I S   K N O L L   H A M
A L T O   M I C R O P H O N E
R E E L   O L E S   E A R N S
M O R E   P O R E   D Y N E S
```

33

```
A S C O T   A H A B   W A G S
B U B B A   S E G A   I S L E
I C E S K A T E R S   L I E N
T H R E E M I L E I S L A N D
    S R I   E L H I
A N T S   T A M S   A W A C S
P O E   F I N I   A R A B L E
H U N D R E D A C R E W O O D
I S S U E S   M A T S   D A G
D E E R E   S I M I   P E K E
    A L I T   S P A
F I F T Y C U B I T S W I D E
A L A I   A P P L E A N N I E
R E M O   N O O K   L E G A L
O X E N   T R E S   M E A L S
```

34

```
H U R   A M F M   S O C C E R
E V A   D E L I   A P O L L O
R U N   M R I S   F E M A L E
O L D W I V E S T A L E S
N A D I R   S T I R   S E A
    N E W B E G I N N I N G
S S S   H Y P E   P E C A N
T A T T O O   C R E A T E
U B O A T   B A S H   L E S
B O R R O W E D T I M E
S T Y   R A M A   A I L E D
    B L U E R I B B O N D A Y
S C O U R S   T B A R   O R E
L O O K A T   T E R I   P E R
Y O K E L S   O D D S   A D S
```

35

```
DUPES · BARE · STOW
ATALL · ONEA · TORE
MAPLELEAFS · AXLE
PHASEII · SESSION
· · PEND · TINNY
OAKRIDGEBOYS · ·
GLEAN · LADE · OLD
RELY · THINE · ERIE
ESP · TWIG · ABATE
· PEACHCOBBLER
SHEER · TODD · ·
YARDMAN · BOURNES
NINA · CEDARCHEST
OLIN · MAIL · TEASE
DEET · ERST · SALEM
```

36

```
CLOD · STOAT · JAM
ROPE · PLANE · SERE
AGEBRACKET · TRIM
TOLTEC · MAKESDO
ESS · NEB · INANE
· WORLDCUP · YDS
EMMA · SUE · SPECIE
BOONE · EVA · ALONE
ATODDS · IRS · AWED
YEN · DEALMEIN
· RAINS · SEA · FHA
FAIREST · SMORES
LIVE · ORDERBLANK
IDEA · RAISE · DICE
PAR · SYNOD · SLEW
```

37

```
SATUP · PILAF · AVS
AMIGO · ITALO · LOW
REDHOTPOKER · AWE
ANY · CRI · TIRED
· WHITEKNUCKLE
BABIES · MAINE
MULES · TENNESSEE
OTO · SARGE · AVA
COWABUNGA · ANGER
· CRETE · CSHARP
BLUEEYEDSOUL
AANDW · OPS · HEA
NUB · STARSTUDDED
FRO · KOREA · ANTED
FAX · IMMAD · LAVES
```

38

```
DELIS · AREA · BLAB
ORLON · FORM · LIMO
GRANOLABAR · AVOW
MOM · WORE · ASSESS
ARABIA · DOTS
· ONTHEAIR · TMC
ADDN · HORROR · OIL
DROOP · IAM · YUCCA
ANY · LUSTER · SKEW
MOO · UPTODATE
· USMC · DEDUCT
HOMEEC · SWAN · SYR
ELIE · OUTERSPACE
RIND · DRUB · EAGLE
ENDS · EBBS · STEED
```

39

```
ARID · STOMP · OKAY
RIDE · TIDAL · VICE
APES · ANERA · EDEN
LEAPINGLIZARDS
· OLD · LEAHS
MALTESE · SEEPIN
AMA · IRMA · ALENE
JUMPINGOFFPLACE
OSIER · OPAL · CUD
REATAS · RIOTERS
· EQUAL · NAH
· SPRINGINGFORTH
TORO · NONCE · MORE
ALAS · EGGAR · AVER
ROME · DOORS · SEED
```

40

```
HAAS · RAPS · CRAZE
ISNT · ABET · HAVEN
GREATDANE · AMEND
HERMAN · NACL
· DAMIEN · MALTESE
· EGRET · RAILED
SUTRA · GREYHOUND
TSU · BEERS · TAI
RETRIEVER · CRETE
ANTONS · DOGIE
POINTER · RUDDER
· OTIS · MERLOT
SALON · DOGBREEDS
ADORE · OHIO · SNIP
GATED · FOGS · SANS
```

41

```
BODY SECTS ALAS
OHIO AWARE MOLE
SONG NEPAL BAKE
SHOULD SPIDERMAN
    ROC  LOBO
CULTURED MOSES
ABU  ARIA  LITHE
POST ABLOG VIA HIS
OATHS EDIE  ENS
 TYROS ENROLLEE
  OLES  SDI
OWN WORLDWIDEWEB
LEAS VIREO LIVE
DEMI OCEAN OPEN
EDEN SEARS WENT
```

42

```
GALA SIAM ALDER
AMIS OPIE POILU
MUSHROOMS RAVES
EST END SPINACH
RESUME  ILE
   PARTIAL DIRT
ABBOT ANNAS DUE
FRENCHMENUITEMS
AIL HIPPO LISPS
ROTE KATYDID
   ACE  ICEAGE
OYSTERS OBI GAS
RATED LAMBCHOPS
SNORE ABEL AREA
OKAYS GENE LADY
```

43

```
MAMAS LOP STUNT
ARENA IVE HIFIS
LITTLEMEN ENOLA
EDS VAIN GEYSER
  PERT HERB
LAKERS MEASURED
OGEES LIAR BELA
VIEW FOLDS BRAT
ELLE APES PLATE
DESERTER KEENED
  REED TARS
ASCEND LULU GAS
BERET MINISKIRT
ERASE AVE EERIE
TAMED PER DYLAN
```

44

```
POET BLAB TALKS
ALSO YOHO ELIOT
LIAR PREY ALONE
LOUISARMSTRONG
   USE OUT
HAREMS LAMP CAL
ARENA FACE ARNO
LOGICALTHINKING
AMID RATE EIEIO
SAS CITE CAMDEN
   BEE CAT
LOYALFOLLOWING
GANGS ABEL EVEN
ONCUE TEAM LAMA
DEEMS EYRE KNOT
```

45

```
ACTOR LAMP ALES
LLANO OLEO TIME
FAMOUSDAREDEVIL
AWE LIGNITE ELM
  DETEST LENYA
GROUTS  GIN
REACT LORE GOBI
INTHEMIDDLEAGES
NOSE ADDS GREEN
  SRO  RODENT
BALSA DILUTE
AHA CORSAIR OFF
MEDIEVALKNIEVAL
BALD EPEE PRATE
IDEA NESS SALSA
```

46

```
MEALS AGOG DART
ATRIA RAVI UTAH
LABEL CRABAPPLE
ELI ACHY STEALS
  TAME POT RYE
HERRINGBONE
URAL TALE NORSE
NITER MAT DREAD
SCENE BRIG ACID
   SOLECUSTODY
REA EYE LEER
EXISTS SOLD DAM
FISHSTICK AMINO
ELLA ETUI TONTO
REED ROTE EDGED
```

47

```
SOLD  IDES  PLUMB
OVER  MEAT  EASEL
MISSAPPROPRIATE
EDS  WATTLE  RBIS
   SOS  HERS  LET
ASPERSE   ORDER
MISSDEMEANOR
ARIA  UPI  YARD
   MISSINFORMED
 FRESH  TIPOFFS
TOO  MERE  NET
AGUA  BOXCAR  TRA
MISSCALCULATION
PETER  LORE  AMMO
ASSAY  ONES  PEEN
```

48

```
EMIR  PACK  IDEAL
BARA  ALOE  CARGO
BURNONESBRIDGES
 LESS  STAIN  ODE
  SOME   BOGS
BOOMORBUST  AMPS
ELL  NIBS  ADORE
EDU  DECIMAL  VIE
CITES   NORA  IMP
HEEL  BAGOFBONES
   FROG  SANG
ADO  INERT  MEAL
BABESONBROADWAY
CLINK  DION  GAZE
SEEDY  ASTO  EYES
```

49

```
ASHES  MAPLE  PEA
SPEAK  ORION  ACT
FURRYFRIEND  PRO
ORBS  LED  GIVEUP
RNS  SIS  AVER
  STROKEGENTLY
 ASCOT  EGO  THEE
INTOW  PEG  SUITS
STEN  PAL  BARNS
TEACHERSFAVE
 LEER  ERE  OAT
MEASLY  ELK  ABLE
AWW  PEEVISHMOOD
LEA  MAVEN  AMEND
TRY  ERASE  MOSEY
```

50

```
BELOW  AMPS  OHNO
ADANA  BORE  RAID
JEWELRYBOX  ARNO
ANN  NOSY  TINEAR
   DUBS  PANG
POLITE  KENNEDYS
AMASS  COLT  CREW
TEMP  SORES  ROME
EGAL  CREE  RANEE
SARATOGA  LATENT
  YETI  DANE
FORCES  PAID  INK
ARIA  MILKCARTON
NAPS  AREA  LEAVE
GLEE  NEAR  LALAW
```

51

```
STEM  BLIMP  MAAM
PISA  LANAI  ONTO
ANTI  ERODE  IAMB
CHAMPAGNETASTE
EAT  ORE  NTH
STEEL  AMOK  EAR
 DOUBLEWHAMMY
ATRA  KEANE  RAYE
CHAMBERMUSIC
TET  ASTO  CHAFE
 HOB  FRO  MEN
 ABRAHAMLINCOLN
CLOD  ALOUD  ERIE
AONE  STAKE  LANA
PEER  HONES  SLED
```

52

```
DNAS  SILT  CRASH
ACOP  KNOW  LISLE
MAKEMINCEMEATOF
PASEOS  OREO  ROT
  DOLT  POPTOPS
LAWS  OHS  WAH
ALE  SPEAR  TAROT
MOPTHEFLOORWITH
PETRI  TAMPA  VIA
  OPT  DEE  JEST
ROADMAP  ONEA
EBB  ACES  ANGSTS
BEATTHETAROUTOF
ESTEE  PERM  ALFA
LEEDS  SPAS  ROUX
```

53

```
WALE  GRASS  WASP
ONYX  RESET  ALOE
ETNA  ENTRY  SOUR
 INCREDIBLEHULK
    TET   SERA
NEPALESE  SAWERS
ONA   RIVA  TAROT
FANTASTICVOYAGE
ATEAM SARI   SEW
TELLER NESTLERS
   ENOS   IRA
GRANDTHEFTAUTO
LIST  GALLO  NONO
ACHE  UNBAR  CREW
DEED  TEENS  HOSE
```

54

```
PAPAL  SLOBS  WEB
ECOLE  TEPEE  OAR
CHEFGUEVARA  RTE
SEMI  SPILL  SKEW
    ECHO  SITTERS
ASP  HENS   THOR
CUR  ERIE  ZOMBIE
ERODE  TIC  UPEND
DEFERS  SHAG  EGG
   AGUE  MOTH  FEE
CANAPES  ROTC
ODDS  PAEAN  YMCA
PAC  BATTLESCARF
EGO  AGATE  ALTAR
DEN  GENUS  GETGO
```

55

```
SUSHI  MATER  VAT
ANTON  ALAMO  ALI
GUESS  KARMA  CAN
EMPTYNESTER  ANT
   SNEAKS   ENDS
APB  COLA   DART
BALL  INDONESIA
CLAUSES  EGGCELL
DONKNOTTS   TAIL
  KALE  OMEN  TEA
VACS   ANORAK
ISH  MISSINGLINK
TOE  INFUN  GIVEN
ARC  NOIRE  ENATE
LEK  ANTES  DENSE
```

56

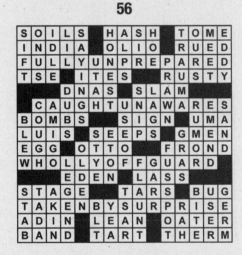

```
SOILS  HASH  TOME
INDIA  OLIO  RUED
FULLYUNPREPARED
TSE  ITES   RUSTY
   DNAS  SLAM
 CAUGHTUNAWARES
BOMBS  SIGN  UMA
LUIS  SEEPS  GMEN
EGG  OTTO   FROND
WHOLLYOFFGUARD
   EDEN  LASS
STAGE  TARS  BUG
TAKENBYSURPRISE
ADIN  LEAN  OATER
BAND  TART  THERM
```

57

```
USPS  LOGE  GAMIN
SPEE  ADOG  ROONE
MARAUDING  ENJOY
CRUMPLEZONE  ONO
   ALE  ONICE
BRANIFF  NEVADA
IAM  NUEVO  EXES
CRINKLECUTFRIES
EENY  TRIAL  ORA
PRONGS  STEMMED
  YAHOO  TWO
ADJ  BUCKLEUNDER
QUELL  HAIRPIECE
UNTIE  EPEE  ELHI
ASTER  RIND  DION
```

58

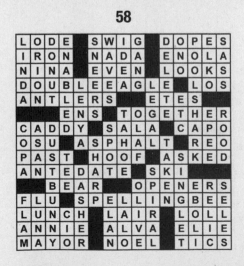

```
LODE  SWIG  DOPES
IRON  NADA  ENOLA
NINA  EVEN  LOOKS
DOUBLEEAGLE  LOS
ANTLERS   ETES
   ENS  TOGETHER
CADDY  SALA  CAPO
OSU  ASPHALT  REO
PAST  HOOF  ASKED
ANTEDATE   SKI
  BEAR  OPENERS
FLU  SPELLINGBEE
LUNCH  LAIR  LOLL
ANNIE  ALVA  ELIE
MAYOR  NOEL  TICS
```

59

A	G	R	A		A	V	O	N		D	O	G	I	E
R	E	E	L		L	I	M	A		A	L	U	M	S
M	I	S	T		A	X	I	S		P	E	E	P	S
A	G	O	O	D	M	E	T	A	P	H	O	R		
D	E	L		E	O	N		O	N	S	I	T	E	
A	R	D	E	N		S	L	A	T	E		L	E	T
		D	I	R		I	K	E		A	L	E	C	
C	A	N	M	A	K	E	A	N	Y	B	A	D		
D	A	T	A		F	I	G		T	I	E			
I	V	Y		A	F	T	E	R		E	L	B	O	W
N	E	P	A	L	I		O	I	L		O	B	I	
	I	D	E	A	S	O	U	N	D	G	O	O	D	
D	I	C	E	R		E	R	S	T		O	B	I	T
A	D	A	P	T		N	E	E	R		B	O	S	H
B	O	L	T	S		D	O	D	O		S	O	T	S

60

M	B	A	S		A	L	G	A		A	B	C	S	
A	A	R	E		S	C	O	R	N		S	L	U	E
C	R	I	C	K	E	T	B	A	T		P	A	R	T
H	E	A	T	U	P		E	D	I	F	I	C	E	S
O	D	S		D	A	B	S		O	R	K			
			S	U	L	U		R	E	N	E	G	E	D
S	E	P	T		T	W	E	E	D		O	V	O	
P	L	A	Y	W	I	T	H	D	O	U	B	L	E	S
A	I	R		A	D	I	O	S		I	D	L	E	
R	A	K	E	D	I	N		E	U	R	O			
		P	R	E		T	A	M	E		A	H	A	
P	O	L	A	R	I	Z	E		P	A	S	S	U	P
A	L	A	S		P	E	P	P	E	R	C	O	R	N
N	I	C	E		O	R	E	A	D		A	N	T	E
G	O	E	S		D	O	E	R		M	E	S	A	

61

M	I	S	C		J	I	F	F	S		A	G	I	N
A	L	M	A		A	P	L	E	A		L	O	C	I
G	O	O	D	Y	G	O	O	D	Y		K	O	O	K
E	S	T	E	E		D	E	U	S		A	N	N	E
S	E	E	N	A	S		S	P	O	O	L	S		
			C	R	I	B			P	I	Q	U	E	
R	A	G	E		R	E	C	I	P	E		U	R	N
E	G	O		D	E	E	P	R	E	D		A	G	O
N	E	O		D	E	B	R	I	S		I	D	E	S
D	E	L	T	A			S	T	E	M				
	A	N	Y	O	N	E		O	S	P	R	E	Y	
N	O	G	O		R	O	M	A		P	R	O	N	E
A	L	O	T		G	O	O	G	O	O	E	Y	E	S
R	E	N	E		A	S	T	E	R		S	A	M	E
C	O	G	S		N	E	E	D	S		S	L	Y	S

62

A	C	M	E		I	W	O		C	H	E	E	S	E
T	H	O	R		S	O	W		H	U	R	R	A	H
T	A	X	I		S	U	E		A	M	I	G	O	S
I	F	I	C	O	U	L	D	L	I	V	E			
C	E	E		R	E	D		O	N	E		A	D	A
			S	O	D		E	S	S	E	N	C	E	S
B	R	A	I	N		R	A	T	A		A	U	N	T
L	I	F	E	O	V	E	R	I	W	A	N	T	T	O
A	V	I	V		I	C	E	T		S	N	E	E	R
B	E	R	E	A	V	E	D		A	N	Y			
S	T	E		L	A	D		E	V	E		U	S	A
			L	I	V	E	O	V	E	R	A	B	A	R
G	A	Z	E	B	O		D	E	N		G	O	L	D
I	R	O	N	I	C		O	R	G		E	A	S	E
G	R	O	S	S	E		R	Y	E		S	T	A	N

63

L	A	U	G	H		H	U	T	S		P	A	R	T
E	N	S	U	E		E	C	R	U		A	L	E	E
A	T	S	E	A		E	L	A	N		P	I	N	E
F	I	R	S	T	C	L	A	S	S		E	V	E	N
			S	H	U			H	E	B	R	E	W	S
H	A	W		S	P	A	T		T	A	C			
O	L	A	F		I	C	E	S		A	L	L	O	T
S	E	C	O	N	D	H	A	N	D	L	I	O	N	S
E	C	O	L	E		E	M	I	R		P	I	T	A
			L	A	P		S	P	I	T		N	O	R
O	C	T	O	P	U	S			E	O	N			
P	L	O	W		T	H	I	R	D	W	A	T	C	H
T	A	X	I		T	O	D	O		A	D	O	R	E
E	R	I	N		E	R	O	S		R	I	G	O	R
D	A	N	G		R	E	L	Y		D	R	A	W	S

64

C	O	L	T		S	C	A	N		B	A	M	B	I
A	S	I	A		O	H	I	O		I	L	I	A	D
G	L	E	N		L	E	N	S		R	A	D	I	O
Y	O	U	K	N	O	W	T	H	E	D	R	I	L	L
				Y	E	S			A	I	M			
B	E	H	O	L	D		W	A	V	E		E	S	P
E	R	A	T	O		T	A	L	E		A	Q	U	A
B	U	S	I	N	E	S	S	A	S	U	S	U	A	L
O	P	T	S		R	A	T	S		N	A	I	V	E
P	T	A		D	I	R	E		Z	I	P	P	E	D
			T	I	C			L	O	T				
H	O	W	I	T	A	L	W	A	Y	S	G	O	E	S
E	D	I	T	H		O	A	T	S		R	O	I	L
R	I	F	L	E		V	I	I	I		E	Z	R	A
S	N	E	E	R		E	T	N	A		W	E	E	P

65

```
CAPON   VET   OTTER
ANODE   IVY   CARLA
SONYOUVEPUTYOUR
ENDS  PINON  LYLE
      SETA  LAO
SHOESONTHEWRONG
HORUS   WISE   COL
EYAS  PRESS  CANE
ALT  FLOE  ROLES
FEETBUTDADTHATS
      AIR  ROSE
ITLL  ATALL  SAGS
THEONLYFEETIGOT
CRANE  PAN  UVULA
HURST  ERE  BEEFY
```

66

```
SHAG  MAGUS  BETH
PALO  ADOPT  ATEE
ELOI  SALSA  RULE
COUNTERFEITBILL
      TAR  TREE
SABOTAGE  SECEDE
HEE  TURN  TUNAS
ARTIFICIALHEART
DIANA  KEPI  TEE
YESSIR  SANENESS
      IRES  SLO
FALSECONFESSION
EXIT  AFIRE  HOME
DEKE  LIPID  EWER
SLED  LASTS  SAND
```

67

```
ROCS  NPR  POSSE
HAHA  ELI  EATIN
ORATORIO  ANTEGG
   REEVE  CNN  ANI
BOLERO  BOGEYMAN
AVON  USAGE  ABLE
BET  ASHY  LIMO
ENTWINE  RIPSAWS
   EIRE  VINO  TOE
SLAM  LLAMA  GWEN
PAMPHLET  JURIST
AMA  AID  TOTAL
RELATE  COLESLAW
KNIFE  OUI  PIPE
STETS  ORE  SEED
```

68

```
ITS  SINCE  APSES
TAP  TREAT  REPRO
CHINESECHECKERS
HIRAM  HANSEL
ETAT  SPEND  LIU
SILESIA  SWAINS
      AMISS  HINGE
CARRYINGCHARGES
OGEES  STAIR
DISCOS  REFUSAL
ANT  TALES  ROVE
   OPIATE  AGUES
CARLSBADCAVERNS
ONEAL  ROUTE  EGO
MARNE  INTER  DEN
```

69

```
SABRA  AJAR  SALE
CLEAR  GUSH  PLED
AFACEINTHECROWD
MATE  VEE  URANIA
   PEW  IMAGES
SHADES  ASIN
LOVES  APSE  ARGO
EYESOFLAURAMARS
DARK  RICE  GIROS
   FATE  BODEGA
MEDICO  BAG
SILENT  ARK  FLOP
PRICKUPYOUREARS
ETTA  REEK  ORCAS
WHEY  EASE  KNELT
```

70

```
ARCH  ALUM  ALERT
CAFE  SEMI  METAL
INCA  SAPS  IONIC
DISTRESSSIGNAL
   HERE  OBOE
JAM  STRAUSS  CAM
UNITE  PRE  CLUE
DISHWASHINGPADS
ASSE  LEI  OASIS
HEY  COLDWAR  STY
   BEEF  ASKS
ABBASHITSINGLE
BLOGS  ELSE  AMEX
ISSUE  LION  PANE
BOSNS  PANT  ENDS
```

71

```
P R A M . S A B E R . A H A B
L A N E . A G A V E . L O R E
O V E R L O O K E D . L U I S
D E W L A P . E N I D . S E E
. . I S A . S T A R K E S T .
S I G N S U P . S L A N G . .
O S U . O L A F . . M O U T H
F L E E . O X I D E . W E R E
T E S L A . T O U T . S E I .
. T U L S A . G R I F T E R .
A T H L E T I C . O R E . . .
B O O . F A R R . P E D A N T
O P U S . L O O K E D O V E R
M E S A . L U C I A . R O S E
B R E W . S T E R N . A N T S
```

72

```
T U B A S . A D A P T . A M T
O P E R A . L U R C H . X I I
E T E R N A L C I T Y . I L L
S O F A . B I T . . A O N E .
. . E N D L E S S S U M M E R
L E A G U E S . L O S E . . .
A C T E D . C O L A N D E R .
I R E . . S H O E D . E R A .
D U R A T I O N . G A M I N .
. . P O L O . S M I T I N G .
N O N S T O P F L I G H T . .
A L O E . R A N . L A B S . .
V I M . I N F I N I T E S E T
E V A . F E A S T . A T S E A
L E D . S O A K S . T E E N Y
```

73

```
W A L S H . L A P S . A H A B
O N I C E . O K R A . G A G A
O N E A L . K I E V . E R R S
F O U N T A I N P E N . D E E
. . T E L . P R I C K E D . .
M A I . R A L L Y . T A N . .
U L N A . R E A . M R M O T O
C A T C H M E I F Y O U C A N
H I A T U S . R E O . S K I T
. . N I N . A D E P T . S L O
D I G I T A L . I R K . . . .
A L I . S W A M P C O O L E R
N I B S . A S E A . O R A T E
T A L E . S K I N . P E D A L
E D E N . H A R E . S A D L Y
```

74

```
R I S K . T A L C . F A M E D
A S H E . I D E A . L L A N O
B L O G . S L A T . A G G I E
B E T S T H E F A R M A I D .
I T S . O R R . C U B E . . .
. . T A I . H O M E . D E N .
O V E R S . T O M B . E U R O
M I L I T A R Y B A N D A I D
S N A P . M I L S . O G L E S
K E N . K N E E . A V E . . .
. . . C O I N . M B A . G S A
. W H O S O N F I R S T A I D
R E I C H . I O T A . I T E M
C A N O E . A X E D . L E V I
A L T A R . L Y R E . E D E N
```

75

```
S A L S A . B U M S . H A L F
A L I E N . E S A U . A R E A
C O A S T . N A N N Y G O A T
S T R A W S . F I D O . L S T
. . . M E T E . L O Y A L T Y
C O V E R E D W A G O N . . .
A P E . P E E R . . S T R A P
T E E M . P R I N T . I A G O
S C R A G . T E R M . G A L .
. . G R O C E R Y C L E R K .
I N D I A N A . D I C E . . .
L A O . P E P S . T O S S E S
I R I S H M O N K . U S A G E
A C N E . A T O M . R O M A N
D O G E . N E W S . T R E N T
```

76

```
F L A Y . O P E D . C L O T S
I O W A . T A P E . R A T I O
G R O W . I R I S . U T T E R
S E L L S T O C K S S H O R T
. . . S L I D . A T E . . . .
O V A . A S Y L U M S . U P S
B A S I N . I T O . A R E A .
A L I T T L E L E A R N I N G
M O D S . E R A . I N A N E .
A R E . E G G C U P S . H E S
. . S U I . S E E M . . . . .
S M A L L T I M E C R O O K S
C A M E O . D O N A . T H E E
U N P E G . O V E N . T I L E
T E S T Y . L E T S . O O P S
```

77

```
U T A H   W H I P   I D E S T
A H O Y   R I S E   G I R T H
W A K E   O G L E   E R N I E
  W I N S T H E L O T T E R Y
      A T E     S K I P
A N I S E O I L   S T O C K S
C O N   A F L A T   O R A L
C L A I M F I R S T P R I Z E
R A N A     A V A I L   M A P
A N E M I A   A R M A M E N T
    I N C H     E N O
H I T S T H E J A C K P O T
A N E A R   N O N O   S H O E
A T R I A   C L A D   U N I X
G O R D Y   E T T E   P O L E
```

78

```
W A G S   O F A G E   I S N T
A B L E   N O M A D   B A I O
T O O T H F A I R Y   E N N A
T O P S O I L S   S O R T E D
        A R E S   R I A
M A T U R E D   P A L A C E S
A M I T Y   V E R Y   L A C
C O N E   D R E A M   S A G A
A R K   B E E T   Y O U L L
W E E K E N D   P R E S S E D
    R E A   P R O A
S A B E R S   R E T R E A T S
O M E N   T H E S A N D M A N
P I L E   E M E E R   D A D A
H E L D   M O N T Y   A S A P
```

79

```
S O C K S   H O S T   A P E S
A K E L A   I D E A   D O M E
F A D E D   G I T S   S P A R
E Y E I N T H E S K Y   C I G
      N E A T   A S A R U L E
S P F   S T I L T   L O L
M A L   S A M E   K E T T L E
E R I S   M E T A L   H U E S
W A P I T I   B N A I   R A T
    W T S   B E T A S   E N D
W H I S K E R   I T L L
A O L   S T A R Q U A L I T Y
L A S E   T H O U   M A D R E
E G O S   E M M E   I M E A N
S Y N C   S A P S   C A M P S
```

80

```
B A S E   C A R O M   E T N A
E R A S   A G A N A   T H O U
E M I T   L O U T S   C O A T
P A N E O F G L A S S   R H O
E N T E R     P I E   A S P
D I S   L A L O   F R A C A S
      L O L I T A   W I R Y
  P A I N I N T H E N E C K
C A L M   T E M P U S
A L P A C A   R E A R   R E M
T O A   A L P   S I E V E
S A C   P A I N E W E B B E R
P L I E   S P A R E   S A N G
A T N O   K E V I N   E T T E
W O O S   A R E N T   N E S S
```

Logic Solutions

81. San Guinari Border Post

The priest was found hiding in a shipping crate (clue 2), and Carlos Ortiz is a teacher (clue 1), so Juan Rivera, who was hiding under a railway car and who isn't a physician (clue 3), must be a journalist. Carlos Ortiz, the teacher, wasn't disguised as a tourist (clue 1), so, by elimination, he must have been in the back of a truck, and it must have been the physician who was disguised as a tourist. The priest isn't Diego Valdez (clue 2), so he must be Ramon Gomez, leaving Diego Valdez as the physician. Since Dr. Diego Valdez and Carlos Ortiz are in even-numbered cells (clue 1) and Father Ramon Gomez isn't in the highest- or lowest-numbered cell (clue 2), the man in cell 1 must be Juan Rivera the journalist. We know that the man in cell 3 can't be Dr. Valdez or Carlos Ortiz, so he must be Ramon Gomez, the priest found in a shipping crate. Dr. Valdez can't be in cell 2 (clue 3), so he must be in cell 4, leaving cell 2 occupied by Carlos Ortiz, the teacher who was found in a shipping crate.

1, Juan Rivera, journalist, under railway car.
2, Carlos Ortiz, teacher, in back of truck.
3, Ramon Gomez, priest, in shipping crate.
4, Diego Valdez, physician, disguised as tourist.

82. Add Up: 75

83. Add Up: 68

84. Wordwheel: Warehouse

85. Codewords

86. Grandmother's Pride

Girl 1 does not play tennis (clue 1), nor is she the one who plays the guitar and enjoys running (clue 2). Clue 3 rules out squash, so number 1 must be the basketball player, Katherine (clue 4). So, from clue 4, girl 3 plays the piano. Number 4 cannot be Judith (clue 1), and, since the cello player is not number 2 (clue 3), that clue also rules out Sonya as number 4. Therefore girl 4 must be Michelle. She is not the runner who plays the guitar (clue 2), and we know the latter is not in positions 1 or 3, so she must be number 2. Michelle cannot be the squash player (clue 3), so her game must be tennis, leaving the pianist in position 3 as the squash player. So, from clue 3, Sonya must be girl 2, and girl 4, Michelle, must be the cellist. This leaves Katherine's instrument as the clarinet, and, by elimination, the squash-playing pianist must be Judith.

1, Katherine, clarinet, basketball.
2, Sonya, guitar, athletics.
3, Judith, piano, squash.
4, Michelle, cello, tennis.

87. On the Leash

Francesca lives at number 15 (clue 5). The owner of Butch at number 8 is not Joel (clue 6), nor can he be Susie's collie (clue 2), and Julie's pet is Danny (clue 3). So, by elimination, Butch must belong to Aaron. Therefore, from clue 1, Rex must live at number 20. Clue 7 rules out numbers 3 and 27 for Arthur, and we know he does not live at 8 or 20, so he must belong to Francesca at number 15. We have now matched three pets' names with house numbers. Titan cannot live at number 3 (clue 4), so his home must be number 27, and number 3 must be where Danny lives with his owner Julie. From clue 6, Joel cannot live at number 20, and own Rex, so Susie must, leaving Joel at number 27 with Titan. Now, from clue 4, the Labrador must be Butch, whose owner is Aaron at number 8, so, from clue 7, Julie's pet, Danny, at number 3, must be the Alsatian, and the retriever must be Joel's Titan at number 27. By elimination, this leaves Francesca's pet, Arthur, as the Dalmatian.

Number 3, Julie, Alsatian, Danny.
Number 8, Aaron, Labrador, Butch.
Number 15, Francesca, Dalmatian, Arthur.
Number 20, Susie, collie, Rex.
Number 27, Joel, retriever, Titan.

88. Cell Blocks

89. Battleships

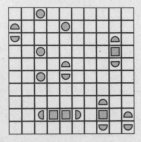

90. Replacement Polvonis

The dancer who quit in March played Momo (clue 4), so Gary Hurst, who left after Sue Ridley took over as Sese (clue 1), can't be the one who quit in April and was replaced by Kate Johns (clue 5); nor is Cathy Day (clue 5), while Nick Oaks quit in July (clue 3) and Annie Bird was replaced by Mike Lamb (clue 2), so it must have been Todd Usher who was replaced by Kate Johns. As Nick Oaks was replaced by a male dancer (clue 3), the dancer replaced by Sue Ridley, who can't have been Gary Hurst (clue 1), must have been Cathy Day. From clue 1, she can't have quit in October, and we know she didn't quit in April, or July; since she was playing Sese she can't have quit in March, so must have done so in September. Therefore, from clue 1, Gary Hurst quit in October, and, by elimination, it was Annie Bird who quit in March, and Mike Lamb who took over as Momo. The dancer replaced by Pete Olsen can't have been Gary Hurst, who quit in October (clue 6), so must have been Nick Oaks, leaving Gary Hurst's replacement as Danny Crane. From clue 6, Todd Usher, who quit in April, can't have played Baba, and neither can Nick Oaks, so it must have been Gary Hurst who played Baba. Finally, from clue 3, Nick Oaks, who didn't play Dudu, must have played Vivi, leaving Dudu as Todd Usher's role, in which he was replaced by Kate Johns.

Annie Bird, Momo, March, Mike Lamb.
Cathy Day, Sese, September, Sue Ridley.
Gary Hurst, Baba, October, Danny Crane.
Nick Oaks, Vivi, July, Pete Olsen.
Todd Usher, Dudu, April, Kate Johns.

91. Wordwheel: Solitaire

92. Cell Blocks

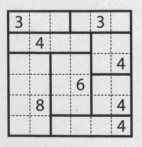

93. *Classic Mystery*

Wayne's story will be in the June issue (clue 2), so, from clue 4, Joseph's must be going to be in the September issue, Wayne's story must be "Point of Honor," and Knapp's story must be in the December issue. The March story, "Memento Mori," isn't by Sheldon (clue 3), so must be by Gordon, and Sheldon must be Knapp, who wrote the December story. We now know the title or writer's surname for the stories for three months, so Darby, who wrote "Eye Witness" (clue 1), must be Joseph and, by elimination, Sheldon Knapp's December story must be "Night Work." Finally, Wayne, author of the June story "Point of Honor," isn't McMillan (clue 2), so must be Saxon, leaving McMillan as Gordon, who wrote the March story.

March, "Memento Mori," Gordon McMillan.
June, "Point of Honor," Wayne Saxon.
September, "Eye Witness," Joseph Darby.
December, "Night Work," Sheldon Knapp.

94. Codewords

95. Spring Color

We did not plant 35 daffodils (clue 1), tulips (clue 2), hyacinths, of which there were 20 (clue 6), or narcissi, of which there were more than 50 (also clue 1), so we must have planted 35 "Midas" crocuses (clue 5). These were not planted along the hedge (clue 1), in the lawn (clue 5), in the terraced bed, where 60 bulbs went in (clue 4), or in the island bed, where the "Golden Beauty" variety were planted (clue 3), so they must be under the apple tree. The 45 bulbs were not the "Golden Beauty" or "Sky Queen" variety (clue 3), nor were they the 35 "Midas" bulbs or the 55 "Misty Morn" variety (clue 2), so they must have been "Fanfare." As the 60 bulbs were planted in the terraced bed, the "Golden Beauty" variety in the island bed must have been the 20 hyacinths. By elimination, the 60 bulbs must have been "Sky Queens." These were not narcissi (clue 1), so we must have planted 55 of those, and they must have been the "Misty Morn" variety. The daffodils were not "Sky Queens" (clue 1), so must have been the 45 "Fanfare" bulbs, and, as they were not planted along the hedge, they must be in the lawn. By elimination, "Sky Queen" must be a variety of tulip, and the narcissi must have been the 55 bulbs planted along the hedge.

Crocus, "Midas," 35, under apple tree.
Daffodil, "Fanfare," 45, in lawn.
Hyacinth, "Golden Beauty," 20, island bed.
Narcissus, "Misty Morn," 55, along hedge.
Tulip, "Sky Queen," 60, terraced bed.

96. Battleships

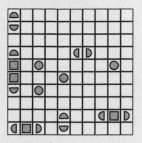

97. Cell Blocks

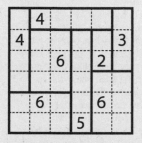

98. Colonies

The Melisari settlement is Orspi (clue 2) and the Zastrians are beetle farming (clue 4), so the race that has built the settlement of Avwasil for its lizard farming colonists, which isn't Saltlik, the planet colonized by the Quirrigi (clue 5), must be the Corians. Effraj isn't the settlement of the Zastrian beetle farmers (clue 4), which must therefore be Ul-Boc, leaving Effraj on the Quirrigi-colonized planet Saltlik. Ul-Boc isn't on the planet Frolik (clue 3), and, as they're beetle farming there, it can't be Darlik, where coal is being mined (clue 1), so it must be Garlik. As Avwasil is the lizard farmers' settlement, it can't be on Darlik either, so it must be on Frolik, and Darlik, the coal-mining planet, must be where the Melisari have built their settlement of Orspi (clue 2). By elimination, on Saltlik, where the Quirrigi have built Effraj, they must be nut farming.

Darlik, Melisari, Orspi, coal mining.
Frolik, Corians, Avwasil, lizard farming.
Garlik, Zastrians, Ul-Boc, beetle farming.
Saltlik, Quirrigi, Effraj, nut farming.

99. Add Up: 100

100. Add Up: 93

101. Wordwheel: Promotion

102. Codewords

103. Healthy Occupations

House 8 is the radiographer's (clue 8). Even if this was Martin, clue 2 rules out house 6 for the health-food store owner, and the ambulance driver (clue 1) and Neil, the physiotherapist (clue 7) have odd-numbered houses. Clue 4 rules out house 6 for both the chemist and the osteopath, and clue 9 rules out the nurse, so, by elimination, house 6 must be the dentist's. Since a man lives in house 4 (clue 5), clue 3 places Hester in house 1. Even if Martin was the dentist in house 6, clue 2 rules out house 4 for the health-food store owner, and we know it does not belong to the dentist, the radiographer, the ambulance driver (clue 1), the osteopath (clue 4), the physiotherapist (clue 7), or the nurse (clue 9), so, by elimination, it must be the chemist's. Clue 4 now tells us Lily's house is number 8, so she is the radiographer, and, from clue 4, the osteopath must live in house 5, and is therefore Iris (clue 6). The fact that Lily lives in house 8 rules out Jim as the chemist in house 4, and we know he (clue 7) is not Neil, nor can he be Graham (clue 9), so he must be Martin. Therefore, from clue 2, house 2 belongs to the health-food store owner. From the names and occupations inserted and clue 1, the straight line referred to is houses 6, 7, and 8, so the ambulance driver must live in house 7, and Jim must be the dentist in house 6. So, from clue 9, Graham must be the ambulance driver in house 7. Now, Neil, the physiotherapist, must be in house 3 (clue 7). By elimination, Kath must be the owner of the health-food store who lives in house 2, and Hester, in house 1, must be the nurse.

1, Hester, nurse.
2, Kath, health-food store owner.
3, Neil, physiotherapist.
4, Martin, chemist.
5, Iris, osteopath.
6, Jim, dentist.
7, Graham, ambulance driver.
8, Lily, radiographer.

104. A Gentleman in America

Sir Emmett was in Montana in 1893 (clue 6). In that year, he wasn't known as Jack Steel (clue 5), Matt Flint (clue 4), or Sam Nails (clue 1); he was Joe Stone in 1865 (clue 1), so in 1893 he must have been Dan Leathers. His crime in 1865 wasn't smuggling (clue 5), train robbery (clue 4), bank robbery (clue 3), or stagecoach robbery, his 1872 crime (clue 2), so must have been rustling, and he was thus in Arizona (clue 2). He was Jack Steel in New Mexico (clue 5), and we know that he was Dan Leathers in Montana and Joe Stone in Arizona; his assumed name in Texas wasn't Matt Flint (clue 3), so must have been Sam Nails, and he must have called himself Matt Flint in California. In 1879, he wasn't known as Sam Nails or Matt Flint (clue 3), so he must have been Jack

Steel in New Mexico that year, and was therefore smuggling in 1886 (clue 5). In 1893, as Dan Leathers, he wasn't a bank robber (clue 3), so must have been a train robber. By elimination, he must have been a bank robber in 1879. From clue 4, he was Matt Flint in California in 1886, leaving his 1872 career as a stagecoach robber as the one he pursued as Sam Nails in Texas.

1865, Joe Stone, Arizona, rustling.
1872, Sam Nails, Texas, stagecoach robbery.
1879, Jack Steel, New Mexico, bank robbery.
1886, Matt Flint, California, smuggling.
1893, Dan Leathers, Montana, train robbery.

105. Cell Blocks

106. Battleships

107. Scent Packing

Giveninch make Infatuation (clue 3) and La Roma's scent is sold in spherical bottles (clue 2), so La Luna, which is sold in a crescent-shaped bottle, but isn't the Hicoste scent in its black packaging (clues 1 and 4), or the De Klein offering (clue 1), must be a Christophe Eor perfume. The ice-blue packaging does not contain a teardrop-shaped bottle (clue 3), a spherical one, or a square one (clue 5), nor is it the crescent bottle (clue 5), so it must be tall and thin. It does not contain Giveninch's Infatuation (clue 3), so it must be made by De Klein. Infatuation is not sold in teardrop-shaped bottles (clue 3), so it must be in square bottles. By elimination, Hicoste must use the teardrop-shaped bottles, and the black packaging. The silver packaging does not contain the spherical bottle (clue 6) or the crescent-shaped one (clue 1), so it must be the square one. By elimination, the spherical bottle must be in the red and gold packaging. Sirène is not made by La Roma (clue 2) or, as it is not sold in a teardrop-shaped bottle (also clue 2), Hicoste, so it must be a De Klein scent. Coquette is not manufactured by Hicoste (clue 4), so it must be La Roma. By elimination, Craving must be the Hicoste fragrance.

De Klein, Sirène, tall and thin, ice-blue.
Christophe Eor, La Luna, crescent, yellow.
Giveninch, Infatuation, square, silver.
Hicoste, Craving, teardrop, black.
La Roma, Coquette, sphere, red and gold.

108. Wordwheel: Diversion

109. Battleships

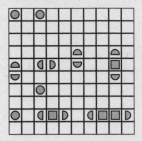

110. Outside the Silver Dollar

Horse 3 was gray (clue 5). Since Windy was horse 4 (clue 3), clue 1 rules out horses 2, 3, and 5 as the sorrel, which must therefore have been horse 1. Thus, from clue 1, horse 2 must have belonged to Lute Judson, and horse 3, the gray, must have been Trooper. Since Bucky belonged to Hondo Pike (clue 4), we know it can't have been horse 2, 3, or 4, and clue 4 tells us it wasn't horse 5, so it must have been horse 1, the sorrel. So, from clue 5, the pinto that belonged to the cowhand must have been horse 2, and the cowhand was therefore Lute Judson. Crowbait can't have been horse 5 (clue 2), so, by elimination, it must have been horse 2, Lute Judson's pinto, leaving horse 5 as Hero. Trooper, the gray horse 3, didn't belong to Key Moffit (clue 5), and we know it didn't belong to Hondo Pike or Lute Judson; nor was it Ollie Lane's horse (clue 2), so it must have been Sam Riley's. From clue 6, the horse breaker's mount wasn't horse 1, 2, 3, or 5, so must have been horse 4, Windy, and horse 5, Hero, was therefore the palomino (clue 6), and, by elimination, Windy was a bay. So Sam Riley, owner of Trooper, wasn't the trail-boss (clue 6), nor was he the sheriff (clue 1), so he must have been a rancher. Hondo Pike, owner of Bucky, horse 1, wasn't the sheriff (clue 1), so must have been the trail-boss, leaving the sheriff as the owner of Hero, the palomino horse 5. He was not Key Moffit (clue 5), so he must have been Ollie Lane, leaving Key Moffit as the horse breaker who owned horse 4, Windy.

1, Bucky, sorrel, Hondo Pike, trail-boss.
2, Crowbait, pinto, Lute Judson, cowhand.
3, Trooper, gray, Sam Riley, rancher.
4, Windy, bay, Key Moffit, horse breaker.
5, Hero, palomino, Ollie Lane, sheriff.

111. Codewords

112. Not-So-Merry Men

The mason lasted 7 days in the forest (clue 6) and the thatcher complained that his feet were constantly wet (clue 5), so the man who was an outlaw for just 4 days complaining that he was cold at night, but was not the cowherd (clue 1) or the potter (clue 4), must have been the blacksmith, Jethro Growse (clue 3). Dickon Grype lasted only 5 days (clue 2), so Cedric Grumbell, who hated the monotonous food (clue 1), must have lasted at least 6. Therefore the cowherd must have lasted longer than that. It was not 7 days (clue 6), so must have been 8. He was not complaining about the lack of privacy (clue 2), so it must have been the hard ground that they had to sleep on. Dickon Grype lasted 5 days as an outlaw, but didn't object to the hard ground or the lack of privacy (clue 2), so it must have been the wet feet, and he must have been the thatcher. By elimination, the outlaw of just 6 days' standing must have been the potter. Barney Crabb didn't complain about the lack of privacy (clue 2), so he must have left after 8 days because of the hard ground to sleep on. Finally, Billy Akins wasn't the outlaw who gave up after 6 days (clue 3), so he must have been the mason who lasted 7 days, and, by elimination, the lack of privacy must have been his main complaint. This leaves Cedric Grumbell as the potter who stayed in the forest for 6 days before returning to his trade of potter.

Billy Akins, mason, 7 days, no privacy.
Barney Crabb, cowherd, 8 days, hard ground.
Jethro Growse, blacksmith, 4 days, cold at night.
Cedric Grumbell, potter, 6 days, monotonous food.
Dickon Grype, thatcher, 5 days, constantly wet feet.

113. Battleships

114. Cell Blocks

115. Mugs Game

The Tuesday winner was the student (clue 7). The Friday caller cannot have been John Sage, the builder (clue 1), the unemployed listener, or the secretary (clue 2), so, by elimination, it must have been the sales manager with the answer "Saturn" (clue 3). So, from that clue, Joyce Brainey won on Wednesday with the answer "Plutonium" (clue 4). John Sage cannot have won on Thursday (clue 5), so he must have been the Monday winner, and, from clue 1, "the magpie" was the student's answer on Tuesday. We have now matched four days with a name or an answer, so Mary Wise, whose answer was "Venezuela" (clue 6), must be the woman who won a mug on Thursday. Now, by elimination, John Sage's Monday answer must have been "Charles Dickens." Clue 2 rules out Tuesday for Graham Nozett, so he must have been the Friday winner, leaving Sandra Smart as the student who won on Tuesday. Clue 2 reveals the secretary as Joyce Brainey, who won on Wednesday, and the unemployed winner as Mary Wise, the winner of the Thursday mug.

Monday, John Sage, builder, "Charles Dickens."
Tuesday, Sandra Smart, student, "The magpie."
Wednesday, Joyce Brainey, secretary, "Plutonium."
Thursday, Mary Wise, unemployed, "Venezuela."
Friday, Graham Nozett, sales manager, "Saturn."

116. Add Up: 99

117. Add Up: 56

118. Wordwheel: Adventure

119. Massaging the Figures

Mr. Aiken is not being treated in Room 4 (clue 1), so osteopath Gunther Hertzum is not treating Mr. Aiken, Mrs. Smart (clue 2), Mr. Twist, who is Rick Yorbach's patient (clue 4), or Mr. Crick, who is in Room 3 (clue 5), so it must be Ms. Sharp, and he must be treating her neck (clue 6). The patient with the bad leg is not in Room 1 or 2 (clue 1). We know that Ms. Sharp's neck is being treated in Room 4, and since the osteopath is Gunther Hertzum, the bad leg is not in Room 5 (clue 1), so it must be Mr. Crick's ailment in Room 3. Therefore Anne Culpayne must be in Room 2 and patient Mr. Aiken in Room 1 (clue 1). Rick Yorbach is treating a painful hand, so Anne Culpayne in Room 2 must be treating Mrs. Smart, and, by elimination, Rick Yorbach must be in Room 5. We know that Mr. Aiken in Room 1 is not being treated by Amy Leggerts (clue 3), so it must be French osteopath Paul de Muselle, and Mr. Aiken must be having trouble with his arm (also clue 3). This leaves Amy Leggerts as the osteopath treating Mr. Crick. Finally, the patient with the painful hand is not being treated by Anne Culpayne (clue 2), so it must be Rick Yorbach, leaving Ms. Culpayne as the osteopath treating Mrs. Smart's back.

1, Paul de Muselle, Mr. Aiken, arm.
2, Anne Culpayne, Mrs. Smart, back.
3, Amy Leggerts, Mr. Crick, leg.
4, Gunther Hertzum, Ms. Sharp, neck.
5, Rick Yorbach, Mr. Twist, hand.

120. Codewords

```
E X E M P T   B R E E Z E
X   X   O     I   V     I
P U P I L   M U S T A N G
O   O   A   E   O   D   H
S Q U A R E D   T W E E T
E   N   I   T       I   H
    D E L I C I O U S
R   Y   I       E     A
E N T E R   N E G A T E D
F   I   I   A   L   T   J
O P T I C A L   I G L O O
R   L   A       D   E   I
M E E K L Y   T E N D O N
```

```
K A S O X Z C G V Q Y P R
T E J U W B N F M L D I H
```

121. *Heading West*

Picture D shows Ross Benmore (clue 4). Matt Rideau isn't shown in picture C (clue 2), so must be in picture A or B, and, by the same clue, Joe Whitney must also be in A or B. Gus Hayden being on the top half of the poster (clue 3), he must be Matt Rideau's character. Duke Logan's picture, which we now know is either C or D, is horizontally opposite that of Kenny Van Ern (clue 1), which we know isn't D, so Kenny Van Ern must be in picture C and Duke Logan in picture D. By elimination, picture C must show Seth Barry. From clue 1 we now see that Grant Leopold must be in picture A and must have played Joe Whitney. This leaves Matt Rideau, who played Gus Hayden, as the man in picture B.

A, Grant Leopold—Joe Whitney.
B, Matt Rideau—Gus Hayden.
C, Kenny Van Ern—Seth Barry.
D, Ross Benmore—Duke Logan.

122. Poster Parade

Poster 5 advertises the fridges (clue 4). The Wogan's product on poster 1 (clue 3) cannot be the cigarettes (clue 1), the soap powder, made by Hogan's (clue 2), or the canned soup (clue 7), and, since Anna Peel designed poster 3 (clue 7), clue 5 also rules out the beer for poster 1, which therefore must feature the cereal, and be designed by Tim Flogham (clue 6). So, from that clue, the Logan's product must be on poster 4. Since we know the cigarettes are not on poster 5, clue 1 now tells us they must be advertised on number 3, designed by Anna Peel, and it must be Dick Sellett who designed poster 2. We now know Walter Cokes's poster for Regan's (clue 5) is either 5 or 6, so, from that clue, the beer, which we know does not feature on poster 3, must be on number 4, and be made by Logan's, and the Regan's poster must be number 6. By elimination, poster 2, by Dick Sellett, must advertise Hogan's soap powder. Also by elimination, Regan's product on poster 6 must be the canned soup. Therefore, from clue 7, Jack Kidham's poster must be number 5, leaving Phil Craven as the designer of the poster for Logan's beer. So, from clue 3, Deacon's must be the makers of the cigarettes advertised on poster 3, leaving the fridges as the Fagan's product.

1, Wogan's cereal, Tim Flogham.
2, Hogan's soap powder, Dick Sellett.
3, Deacon's cigarettes, Anna Peel.
4, Logan's beer, Phil Craven.
5, Fagan's fridges, Jack Kidham.
6, Regan's canned soup, Walter Cokes.

123. Cell Blocks

124. Battleships

125. Independence Day

Steuben comes from Utica (clue 6), and the actor comes from El Paso (clue 4), so De Kalb, the cartoonist, who isn't from Anchorage or Orlando (clue 2), must come from Indianapolis. His first name isn't Wayne (clue 3), Earl, the first name of the man from Anchorage (clue 1), Lewis, the first name of the diplomat (clue 4) or Ches, which is Revere's first name (clue 5), so must be Ross. Earl from Anchorage isn't Jefferson (clue 1), so he must be Hancock. He's not the historian (clue 3), so must be an aero engineer. Wayne's not the historian either (clue 3), so he must be the actor from El Paso. By elimination, the historian must be Ches Revere, who, also by elimination, must be from Orlando. Therefore Steuben from Utica must be Lewis, the diplomat, and Wayne from El Paso must be Jefferson.

Ches Revere, Orlando, historian.
Earl Hancock, Anchorage, aero engineer.
Lewis Steuben, Utica, diplomat.
Ross De Kalb, Indianapolis, cartoonist.
Wayne Jefferson, El Paso, actor.

126. Wordwheel: Transport

127. Battleships

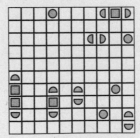

128. Unlucky for Some

Ralph's shot ended up in the trees (clue 1), and the third player finished in the sand (clue 3). Don, who drove off second, did not land on the fairway, so he must have landed in the rough. The player who found the fairway was not George (clue 4), so he must have been Eddie, who is number 1 in the line (clue 5). By elimination, the third player, whose shot landed in a bunker, must be George. Ralph did not play fourth (clue 1), so he must have been first off the tee, leaving Eddie as the fourth to play. We now know number 1 did not go first and number 4 did not go fourth. Clue 5 rules out Don, who went second, and landed in the rough, as number 2 in the line, so, from clue 2, George, who teed off third, must be number 3 in the line. From clue 1, Ralph must be number 2, leaving Don as number 4.

1, Eddie, fourth, on fairway.
2, Ralph, first, in trees.
3, George, third, in sand.
4, Don, second, in rough.

129. Codewords

130. Around the Course

Jane rested by the 8th green (clue 6), so the first name of March, who rested by the 16th tee, which must have four or five letters (clue 2), must be Terry, who rested after 2 miles (clue 1). Stride, who rested at 1 mile, isn't Jane or Nicholas (clue 1), nor Amanda, whose surname is Foote (clue 5), so must be Donald. Nicholas isn't Toddell (clue 4), so must be Pace, leaving Jane as Toddell. Nicholas Pace didn't rest by the driving range (clue 4) or the lake (clue 3), so he must have stopped at the half-mile mark by the green keeper's hut (clue 2). The golfer who stopped at 1.5 miles must have a six-letter first name (clue 2), so must be Amanda Foote, leaving Jane Toddell as the one who rested at 3 miles. Finally, as Donald Stride didn't stop by the lake (clue 3), he must have stopped by the driving range, leaving Amanda Foote as the one who stopped by the lake.

Amanda Foote, 1.5 miles, lake.
Donald Stride, 1 mile, driving range.
Jane Toddell, 3 miles, 8th green.
Nicholas Pace, .5 mile, green keeper's hut.
Terry March, 2 miles, 16th tee.

131. Battleships

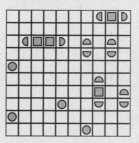

132. Cell Blocks

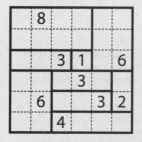

133. Let's Squirm Again

The 1963 dance craze produced the No. 1 hit (clue 6), so the "Jetplane" record that reached No. 3 in the charts and was released before Lola Powers's 1964 hit (clue 1) but that wasn't a 1961 hit (clue 3) must have been in the 1962 charts. The artist associated with it was neither Lola Powers nor Eddie Lewis, who reached No. 8 (clue 5), nor was it Scott Dillon, who popularized the "Squirm" (clue 6), and Gary Eden's hit didn't begin with the letter "J" (clue 3), so the "Jetplane" must have been the dance craze associated with Jessie Fisher. Eddie Lewis didn't have his No. 8 hit in 1961 (clue 3), 1962, 1963, or 1964, so it must have been 1965. Therefore, from clue 6, the "Corkscrew" must have been 1963's chart-topper. The singer was not Scott Dillon, so it must have been Gary Eden. By elimination, the "Squirm" must have been a hit for Scott Dillon in 1961. We now know that the "Jack-in-the-Box" must have been the 1964 hit (clue 3), and the "Whirligig" must have been the 1965 dance craze. Since Scott Dillon's "Let's Squirm Again" got higher in the charts than the "Jack-in-the-Box" record (clue 3), it must have got to No. 5, and Lola Powers's "Jack-in-the-Box" record must have got to No. 6.

1961, "Squirm," Scott Dillon, No. 5.
1962, "Jetplane," Jessie Fisher, No. 3.
1963, "Corkscrew," Gary Eden, No. 1.
1964, "Jack-in-the-Box," Lola Powers, No. 6.
1965, "Whirligig," Eddie Lewis, No. 8.

134. Add Up: 91

135. Add Up: 79

136. Wordwheel: Landscape

137. Codewords

```
L A R G E L Y   D R A G
E   R   R A     E     A
S U M M A R Y   D E P O T
Q   E   N   O   I   L   E
U N D I D   U N S A I D
I   P   T   O   C   P
R A S C A L   A B L A Z E
E   U   R   W   E     N
  G R I E V E   D I C E D
J   F   N   I   I     A
E X A C T   G R E M L I N
R   C   H   N   L   T
K N E E   S T A T I O N
```

```
Y O T F D R A L C S E H I
Z U J X G K N W P Q V M B
```

138. American Sportsmen

Since figure B is the ice hockey player (clue 2), Nick Flint from Connecticut, who is playing ball with the football player (clue 1), can't be figure A, who isn't the man from Illinois either (clue 5); it's figure D who's from Ohio (clue 4), so figure A must be from Nebraska. So, from clue 1, he's not the football player, and thus Nick Flint can't be figure B. Since he's from Connecticut, Nick Flint can't be figure A or D, so he must be figure C. So, from clue 1, the football player must be figure D, who comes from Ohio, and, by elimination, the ice hockey player must be from Illinois. We have now identified the name or sport for three figures, so Roy Lowell, the basketball player (clue 3), must be figure A, from Nebraska. So Carey Troy isn't figure B, the ice hockey player (clue 3), and must be the football player from Ohio, figure D. leaving the ice hockey player as Val Denver. Finally, by elimination, Nick Flint, figure C, must play baseball.

A, Roy Lowell, Nebraska, basketball.
B, Val Denver, Illinois, ice hockey.
C, Nick Flint, Connecticut, baseball.
D, Carey Troy, Ohio, football.

139. Lunch Hour

Paul lunched on chocolate (clue 8), and the receptionist had a cheese and pasta salad (clue 5), so, from clue 1, Claire, the secretary, who didn't have a corned beef sandwich or a ham salad, must have had tomato soup, and therefore went to the dentist (clue 4). We know that the person who did the puzzle book wasn't the secretary, and clue 3 rules out the contracts manager and the receptionist; the managing director visited a shoe shop (clue 6), so, by elimination, it must have been the accounts clerk who did the puzzle book. So, from clue 3, the contracts manager must have had a corned beef sandwich for lunch. We have now matched three job titles with activities; the contracts manager, who had the corned beef sandwich, can't have visited the garden center (clue 1), so she must have gone for a walk and is therefore Ellen (clue 2), and, by elimination, it must have been the receptionist who went to the garden center. The person who had the ham salad wasn't Jason (clue 7), so he must be the receptionist who had the cheese and pasta salad, leaving Val as the one who had the ham salad. She's not the accounts clerk (clue 9), so she must be the managing director who visited the shoe shop, leaving the accounts clerk as Paul, who ate chocolate.

Claire, secretary, went to dentist, tomato soup.
Ellen, contracts manager, walk, corned beef sandwich.
Jason, receptionist, garden center, cheese and pasta.
Paul, accounts clerk, puzzle book, chocolate.
Val, managing director, shoe shop, ham salad.

140. Cell Blocks

```
1 | 5
  | 4 |   | 2 | 2
  |   |   |   | 2 | 2
6 |   |   | 4 |
  |   |   | 4 |   | 4
```

141. Battleships

142. Setting the Scenes

The statue appears in the garden scene (clue 3) and the cupboard is in the scene where the prop is an umbrella (clue 6), so the knitting, which is the prop required for the sitting room scene but not with the armchair or the wicker chair (clue 5), must be accompanied by the standard lamp. The armchair is on set for Act 1, Scene 3 (clue 2), so the drawing room scene is not Act 1, Scene 1, which features the tea tray (clues 1 and 4), and that first scene is also not set in the restaurant (clue 1) so the play must open in a bedroom and, by elimination, the piece of furniture on stage for the opening scene must be the wicker chair. The prop for the garden scene is not the newspaper (clue 3), so it must be the suitcase, leaving the newspaper as the prop accompanying the armchair in Act 1, Scene 3. Now, from clue 4, the suitcase must be the prop for Act 2, Scene 1, the drawing room scene must be Act 1, Scene 3, and the knitting must be required for Act 2, Scene 2. Therefore the newspaper must be the prop for the drawing room scene and, by elimination, the cupboard and umbrella must be used in the restaurant scene, which must be Act 1, Scene 2.

Act 1, Scene 1, bedroom, wicker chair, tea tray.
Act 1, Scene 2, restaurant, cupboard, umbrella.
Act 1, Scene 3, drawing room, armchair, newspaper.
Act 2, Scene 1, garden, statue, suitcase.
Act 2, Scene 2, sitting room, standard lamp, knitting.

143. Wordwheel: Nightmare

144. Cell Blocks

145. Looking for Gold

Clues 1 and 6 rule out a corner box for both FISH and LEAF, and clue 3 rules out RUSH. Therefore, from clue 1, the word in question must be RING. Clue 8 rules it out for boxes A1, A4, and C4, so it must be in C1, and FINGER therefore in B2 (clue 8). FISH cannot be in A4 (clue 6), so, from clue 5, the word there must be FINCH. Clue 2 now places MEDAL in C4. So, from clue 5, the word in A3 must be MINER. We have now placed five words. We know A1 cannot contain FISH, LEAF, or RUSH (clue 1). Clue 4 rules out SMITH, and clue 3 CREST, and clue 7 also rules out DIGGER, so, by elimination, A1 must contain the word WATCH. Therefore, from clue 7, DIGGER must be in C3. Now, from clue 3, RUSH must be in row 2, and CREST in row 3. The only box left is B3, so CREST must be there. SMITH cannot be in A2 (clue 4), nor can FISH or LEAF (clue 6), so RUSH must be in that box. Clue 6 now places FISH in B1, and LEAF in B4, therefore leaving SMITH in C2.

	A	B	C
1	WATCH	FISH	RING
2	RUSH	FINGER	SMITH
3	MINER	CREST	DIGGER
4	FINCH	LEAF	MEDAL

146. Codewords

```
E Q U I T Y U P K E E P
X N R S A X O
P R I V A C Y S U E D E
I O W L T R T
R E N A L P L A T T E R
E E H E Y
Z E B R A B L A D E
O P A O L
B O I L I N G T A S T E
J S D R T H N
E B O N Y E L E M E N T
C D L E R A I
T R E B L E E Y E F U L
```

```
L D A W K G V Q U P B I N
S R F M T E Y Z J C H O X
```

147. Hall Earmarked

Mr. Hughes is the contact for the Tuesday booking (clue 1) and the contact for the upholstery class is Mrs. Muir (clue 6), so Monday's drama group booking, which was not made by Ms. Owen (clue 1), or Mr. Dobson's group, which is later in the week than the keep-fit class (clue 3), must have been made by Ms. Douglas and the time must be 7:30 (clue 2). Therefore the painting class, which takes place the day after the 10:30 booking (clue 4), is not the booking for either Tuesday or Thursday. As the 11 o'clock booking is on Thursday (clue 2), painting does not take place on Friday either, so it must be Saturday's booking and the 10:30 booking must be for Fridays. Line dancing begins at 4:30 (clue 5), it cannot take place on either Thursday or Friday, so it must be Mr. Hughes's booking for Tuesdays. Mr. Dobson's group is not the keep-fit class (clue 3), so it must be Saturday's painting class, and, by elimination, keep-fit must be Ms. Owen's group, which, from clue 3, must be Thursday's 11 o'clock booking. Finally, Friday's 10:30 booking must be Mrs. Muir's upholstery class, leaving the 2:30 booking as the painting class on Saturday afternoons.

Monday, drama group, 7:30, Ms. Douglas.
Tuesday, line dancing, 4:30, Mr. Hughes.
Thursday, keep-fit, 11:00, Ms. Owen.
Friday, upholstery, 10:30, Mrs. Muir.
Saturday, painting, 2:30, Mr. Dobson.

148. Battleships

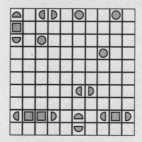

149. Cell Blocks

150. Sofie's Choice

Crispus, who suffered ill health, was neither athletic nor good-looking (clue 5); Lorenz was charming (clue 1), and the war hero was ugly (clue 3), so Crispus must have been the poet, and therefore came from Lohringia (clue 3). Patrizius came from Hochenberg (clue 4), and Archimbald from either Schwabenz or Westerfelsen (clue 2), so the prince from Drakenraupe, who wasn't Lorenz (clue 1), must have been Gotthart. The lecher wasn't Lorenz or Gotthart (clue 1), nor Crispus (clue 5) or Archimbald (clue 2), so must have been Patrizius. Archimbald wasn't the war hero (clue 3), and neither was Patrizius, who was a lecher, not ugly, so the ugly hero must have been Gotthart of Drakenraupe. Patrizius wasn't good-looking (clue 4), so he must have been athletic, and, by elimination, Archimbald must have been good-looking. He wasn't the one with no interest in women (clue 4), so he must have been the poor prince from Schwabenz (clue 6), and, by elimination, Prince Lorenz of Westerfelsen must have been charming but not interested in women.

Archimbald, Schwabenz, good-looking, poor.
Crispus, Lohringia, poet, ill health.
Gotthart, Drakenraupe, war hero, ugly.
Lorenz, Westerfelsen, charming, no interest in women.
Patrizius, Hochenberg, athletic, lecher.

151. Add Up: 99

152. Add Up: 62

153. Wordwheel: Tolerance

154. Intellectual Pursuits

Aubrey is Dr. Jekyll (clue 4), and, from the same clue, his hobby isn't collecting cola memorabilia or cryptology; nor can it be juggling, which is Dr. Dolittle's hobby (clue 5), or Elvish, which can't be the hobby of the lecturer with the shortest surname (clue 6), so it must be building model rockets. Aubrey Jekyll's subject can't be German literature (clue 4) or law (clue 6), while it's Dr. Strangelove who lectures in physics (clue 2) and Oliver who lectures in media studies (clue 1), so Aubrey Jekyll must lecture on economics. Ursula can't lecture on law (clue 6) or physics (clue 2), so her subject must be German literature. Her hobby thus can't be collecting cola memorabilia or cryptology (clue 4), nor can it be Elvish (clue 6), and we know it isn't building model rockets, so it must be juggling, and Ursula is therefore Dr. Dolittle (clue 5). Therefore the law lecturer whose hobby is Elvish must have a surname of more than eight letters (clue 6); he or she can't be Strangelove (clue 2), so must be Frankenstein. Thus Oliver, who lectures in media studies, must be Dr. Kildare. Dr. Strangelove, the physics lecturer, who has no interest in cryptology (clue 2), must, by elimination, collect cola memorabilia. Finally, Dr. Strangelove can't be Irving (clue 3), so must be Evangeline, leaving Irving as Dr. Frankenstein, the law lecturer whose hobby is Elvish.
Aubrey Jekyll, economics, building model rockets.
Evangeline Strangelove, physics, cola memorabilia.
Irving Frankenstein, law, Elvish.
Oliver Kildare, media studies, cryptology.
Ursula Dolittle, German literature, juggling.

155. Codewords

156. In Training

Nimbus has stall 3 (clue 1). The horse in stall 1 is not Milton (clue 2), nor can it be Sally Lunn (clue 3), or Scotch Mist (clue 5), and Jetstream's stall must have an even number (clue 7). Clue 6 rules out stall 1 for Yeoman Warder, so it must be occupied by Jerry's horse, Al Capone (clue 6). The lad grooming the horse in stall 7 cannot be Alan (clue 3), or Steffie (clue 5). Charlotte looks after the horse in stall 6 (clue 4), and, since this has a two-word name (clue 4), clue 7 rules out 7 as Maria's odd-numbered stall. On the same lines, since stall 5 also houses a horse with a two-word name (clue 4), clue 2 rules out stall 7 for Kevin's mount. Therefore it must be Ray who is exercising the horse in that stall. So clue 6 tells us Yeoman Warder must be Charlotte's horse in stall 6. Sally Lunn is not in stall 7 (clue 3), and we have placed three other horses. We know Jetstream's stall has an even number (clue 7), and clue 5 rules out stall 7 for Scotch Mist, so the horse there, exercised by Ray, must be Milton. Therefore, from clue 2, Kevin must exercise the horse in stall 5. Neither Maria (clue 7), nor Steffie (clue 5), can look after the horse in stall 2, so, by elimination, Alan must do so. Clue 7 also rules out stall 4 for Maria, so she must exercise Nimbus, in stall 3, leaving Steffie in charge of stall 4. From clue 5, Scotch Mist is Kevin's charge in stall 5, and clue 3 places Sally Lunn in stall 4, leaving the horse exercised by Alan as Jetstream.
1, Al Capone, Jerry.
2, Jetstream, Alan.
3, Nimbus, Maria.
4, Sally Lunn, Steffie.
5, Scotch Mist, Kevin.
6, Yeoman Warder, Charlotte.
7, Milton, Ray.

157. Hyperman

Clue 4 rules out the defeat of global warming as the first or fifth of Hyperman's feats, and, since Jupiter was the planet involved in the first (clue 5), and Al Smith supplied the report on the fourth (clue 6), clue 4 also rules out the defeat of global warming as the second or third achievement, so it must have been the fourth, reported by Al Smith. So, from clue 4, Saturn was involved in the third exploit, and Chuck Lomas wrote about the fifth. Clue 2 tells us this was sent in advance as Hyperman took all the world's diseases upon himself with fatal effect. We have now described or connected a planet with four feats, so the repair of the San Andreas Fault, requiring adjustment to Earth itself (clue 1), must have been the second task undertaken. Clues 6 and 7 rule out the carbon footprint transfer feat as the third performed, so it must have been the first, and Jim Robinson must have reported on the second, the repair of the San Andreas Fault (clue 7). This leaves the third feat as the decommissioning of all the world's weapons, reported by Tom Matthews (clue 3). By elimination, Hyperman must have used the pseudonym Sam Miller to report on the transfer of the carbon footprint to Jupiter. Finally, from clue 6, the global warming cure did not involve Pluto's gravity pull, so it must have depended on Mars, leaving Pluto as Hyperman's final destination, and the scene of the destruction of the world's diseases.
First, carbon footprint, Jupiter, Sam Miller.
Second, San Andreas Fault, Earth, Jim Robinson.
Third, lethal weapons, Saturn, Tom Matthews.
Fourth, global warming, Mars, Al Smith.
Fifth, diseases, Pluto, Chuck Lomas.

158. Wordwheel: President

159. Codewords

M	U		H	A	M		O		A			
C	O	R	N	E	A		E	M	B	A	R	K
T		Q		Z		T		J		I		
F	I	G	U	R	I	N	E		E	A	S	E
V		E		L		O		C		E		
J	E	R	S	E	Y		R	O	T	U	N	D
A		T				I		I				O
B	E	H	I	N	D		P	R	O	M	P	T
L		O		E		L		N		R		
L	I	O	N		R	E	A	W	A	K	E	N
X		I		N		B		F				
T	I	N	N	E	D		E	C	L	A	I	R
R		G		E	A	T		E		X		

L	D	A	W	M	R	Y	G	F	E	X	Z	T
S	U	K	C	J	P	I	B	Q	H	N	V	O

160. Wide-Awake Club

The person who went to bed at midnight and used the herbal pillow must have finally got to sleep at 2:30 or 3:30 (clue 1), but the person who drifted off at 2:30 had been reading (clue 4), so it must have been 3:30. Therefore Maria, who must have drifted off at half past the hour (clue 2), must have been the person who read before falling asleep at 2:30 (clue 1), and Debbie must have gone to bed at 11:30 and fallen asleep at 2:00. She didn't resort to listening to the radio, as that person fell asleep later than the one who took the sleeping tablets (clue 3), or take sleeping tablets, which was Roy (clue 6), so Debbie must have relied on a hot drink. The person who listened to the radio fell asleep later than the one who takes tablets (clue 3), he or she must have done so at 4:00, and the sleeping tablets must have taken effect at 3:00. The person who retired at midnight was not Jeff (clue 1), so it must have been Peter, and, by elimination, the radio must have had the desired effect at 4:00 for Jeff. The person who turned in at 12:30 didn't read or listen to the radio (clue 4), so it must have been Roy, who took the sleeping tablets. As the person who went to bed at 11:45 took longer to get to sleep than the one who went at 11:00, the former must have listened to the radio until 4:00, and the latter must have gone to sleep at 3:30, having resorted to the herbal pillow.

Debbie, 11:30, hot drink, 2:00.
Jeff, 11:45, radio, 4:00.
Maria, 11:00, reading, 2:30.
Peter, 12:00, herbal pillow, 3:30.
Roy, 12:30, sleeping tablets, 3:00.

Sudoku Solutions

161

8	3	7	1	4	6	9	5	2
9	1	2	3	7	5	6	4	8
6	5	4	2	9	8	1	7	3
2	8	6	9	5	3	7	1	4
4	9	5	7	2	1	8	3	6
3	7	1	8	6	4	2	9	5
7	4	9	5	8	2	3	6	1
1	6	8	4	3	9	5	2	7
5	2	3	6	1	7	4	8	9

162

7	5	2	3	1	8	9	4	6
1	8	6	2	9	4	3	5	7
3	4	9	6	5	7	1	8	2
2	1	3	4	6	9	8	7	5
9	7	4	1	8	5	6	2	3
5	6	8	7	3	2	4	1	9
6	3	5	8	2	1	7	9	4
4	9	1	5	7	3	2	6	8
8	2	7	9	4	6	5	3	1

163

8	4	1	5	6	3	2	7	9
2	9	7	4	1	8	3	5	6
6	5	3	2	7	9	8	4	1
3	7	8	1	9	5	4	6	2
5	2	9	8	4	6	1	3	7
1	6	4	3	2	7	5	9	8
4	8	6	7	5	1	9	2	3
7	3	5	9	8	2	6	1	4
9	1	2	6	3	4	7	8	5

164

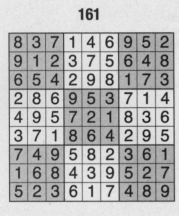

3	6	1	7	2	5	4	9	8
7	9	4	1	6	8	2	3	5
8	5	2	4	3	9	6	7	1
1	2	6	8	5	3	9	4	7
5	4	3	2	9	7	1	8	6
9	8	7	6	4	1	5	2	3
4	1	8	5	7	2	3	6	9
6	7	9	3	1	4	8	5	2
2	3	5	9	8	6	7	1	4

165

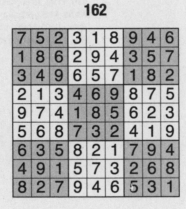

4	6	2	1	8	3	7	9	5
5	7	9	4	6	2	8	1	3
8	3	1	7	5	9	4	6	2
2	8	3	5	1	7	6	4	9
6	5	4	9	2	8	1	3	7
9	1	7	6	3	4	2	5	8
3	2	6	8	4	5	9	7	1
7	4	5	2	9	1	3	8	6
1	9	8	3	7	6	5	2	4

166

4	2	3	6	7	1	8	5	9
7	5	1	9	2	8	3	6	4
6	9	8	4	3	5	2	1	7
2	7	6	1	8	4	9	3	5
1	3	5	2	6	9	7	4	8
8	4	9	3	5	7	1	2	6
3	6	7	5	9	2	4	8	1
9	1	2	8	4	6	5	7	3
5	8	4	7	1	3	6	9	2

167

2	4	9	5	3	6	1	7	8
3	6	5	1	8	7	4	2	9
7	1	8	4	2	9	3	6	5
4	8	7	3	1	5	6	9	2
5	9	2	6	7	4	8	3	1
1	3	6	8	9	2	5	4	7
6	7	3	2	5	8	9	1	4
9	5	4	7	6	1	2	8	3
8	2	1	9	4	3	7	5	6

168

8	4	2	3	9	1	6	7	5
7	1	9	5	2	6	8	4	3
3	5	6	7	8	4	1	2	9
1	2	7	8	5	3	4	9	6
9	8	4	6	1	7	5	3	2
6	3	5	9	4	2	7	8	1
4	9	1	2	6	8	3	5	7
5	7	8	1	3	9	2	6	4
2	6	3	4	7	5	9	1	8

169

7	8	3	4	1	6	9	2	5
1	6	5	3	2	9	4	8	7
4	2	9	7	5	8	6	1	3
2	7	4	8	6	5	1	3	9
3	5	8	1	9	4	2	7	6
6	9	1	2	3	7	8	5	4
5	4	2	9	8	3	7	6	1
9	1	6	5	7	2	3	4	8
8	3	7	6	4	1	5	9	2

170

6	9	8	1	4	3	5	2	7
7	1	2	9	6	5	4	3	8
4	5	3	7	8	2	1	9	6
3	2	6	5	7	4	9	8	1
1	8	9	3	2	6	7	5	4
5	7	4	8	1	9	2	6	3
9	4	7	2	3	8	6	1	5
2	3	1	6	5	7	8	4	9
8	6	5	4	9	1	3	7	2

171

8	4	2	6	5	7	9	3	1
1	3	9	4	2	8	5	7	6
5	6	7	3	1	9	8	4	2
6	8	3	5	4	2	7	1	9
9	1	5	8	7	3	2	6	4
7	2	4	9	6	1	3	5	8
2	5	6	7	9	4	1	8	3
3	7	1	2	8	6	4	9	5
4	9	8	1	3	5	6	2	7

172

1	8	7	4	2	5	3	6	9
4	9	2	3	7	6	8	5	1
5	3	6	1	9	8	4	2	7
2	1	3	7	6	4	5	9	8
8	7	4	9	5	1	2	3	6
9	6	5	2	8	3	7	1	4
6	2	8	5	4	9	1	7	3
7	4	1	6	3	2	9	8	5
3	5	9	8	1	7	6	4	2

173

4	9	6	5	1	2	8	7	3
3	7	1	8	4	9	5	2	6
8	5	2	7	3	6	4	1	9
1	3	4	2	9	5	7	6	8
9	8	7	3	6	4	2	5	1
2	6	5	1	8	7	3	9	4
5	4	9	6	2	8	1	3	7
6	2	3	4	7	1	9	8	5
7	1	8	9	5	3	6	4	2

174

7	3	4	2	8	5	9	6	1
8	6	1	9	7	3	4	5	2
2	9	5	1	6	4	3	7	8
9	7	6	8	2	1	5	3	4
5	8	2	4	3	6	1	9	7
1	4	3	5	9	7	8	2	6
4	5	9	7	1	2	6	8	3
3	2	8	6	4	9	7	1	5
6	1	7	3	5	8	2	4	9

175

3	6	9	5	7	4	2	8	1
1	5	7	2	3	8	4	9	6
4	8	2	1	9	6	5	3	7
5	4	3	9	8	7	6	1	2
9	2	8	6	4	1	7	5	3
7	1	6	3	5	2	9	4	8
2	3	4	7	1	5	8	6	9
8	7	1	4	6	9	3	2	5
6	9	5	8	2	3	1	7	4

176

4	9	6	1	7	2	8	3	5
1	2	3	8	6	5	7	9	4
8	5	7	3	9	4	1	6	2
6	4	2	7	1	9	3	5	8
9	3	1	4	5	8	6	2	7
5	7	8	2	3	6	9	4	1
3	1	4	6	2	7	5	8	9
2	6	5	9	8	1	4	7	3
7	8	9	5	4	3	2	1	6

177

6	4	1	7	5	3	2	8	9
3	8	5	4	2	9	1	7	6
2	7	9	8	6	1	3	5	4
4	6	7	3	1	5	8	9	2
5	9	2	6	4	8	7	3	1
1	3	8	2	9	7	4	6	5
9	1	3	5	8	2	6	4	7
8	2	6	9	7	4	5	1	3
7	5	4	1	3	6	9	2	8

178

1	3	5	2	9	8	6	4	7
2	4	7	3	5	6	1	9	8
6	9	8	7	4	1	2	5	3
3	7	4	6	1	9	5	8	2
8	2	6	4	3	5	9	7	1
9	5	1	8	7	2	3	6	4
5	6	2	1	8	4	7	3	9
7	8	9	5	2	3	4	1	6
4	1	3	9	6	7	8	2	5

179

6	4	8	3	5	9	1	7	2
5	1	9	4	2	7	8	3	6
2	7	3	8	1	6	9	4	5
9	5	6	1	7	8	3	2	4
8	3	1	2	4	5	6	9	7
7	2	4	6	9	3	5	1	8
3	8	7	9	6	4	2	5	1
4	6	2	5	3	1	7	8	9
1	9	5	7	8	2	4	6	3

180

5	9	4	6	1	8	7	2	3
8	6	3	7	4	2	5	1	9
2	1	7	3	5	9	4	6	8
3	2	1	5	6	7	9	8	4
9	8	6	4	2	3	1	5	7
4	7	5	8	9	1	6	3	2
7	3	9	1	8	6	2	4	5
6	4	8	2	7	5	3	9	1
1	5	2	9	3	4	8	7	6

181

1	8	9	5	4	7	2	6	3
2	3	6	8	1	9	5	7	4
7	5	4	2	6	3	8	1	9
4	2	5	3	9	1	7	8	6
9	6	7	4	2	8	3	5	1
3	1	8	7	5	6	9	4	2
5	9	2	1	8	4	6	3	7
8	7	1	6	3	2	4	9	5
6	4	3	9	7	5	1	2	8

182

9	6	8	4	1	3	7	2	5
3	7	1	8	5	2	6	9	4
5	2	4	6	7	9	3	1	8
2	8	3	1	4	5	9	7	6
1	4	5	9	6	7	8	3	2
7	9	6	3	2	8	4	5	1
6	3	7	5	8	1	2	4	9
4	1	9	2	3	6	5	8	7
8	5	2	7	9	4	1	6	3

183

7	4	5	6	3	9	1	8	2
6	8	1	5	2	4	3	7	9
9	3	2	1	7	8	4	5	6
1	9	8	2	5	6	7	3	4
3	7	4	9	8	1	6	2	5
5	2	6	3	4	7	9	1	8
4	6	3	8	1	2	5	9	7
2	5	7	4	9	3	8	6	1
8	1	9	7	6	5	2	4	3

184

3	6	5	8	4	7	2	9	1
2	7	4	9	6	1	5	3	8
9	1	8	2	5	3	6	4	7
4	5	2	7	9	8	3	1	6
1	3	9	4	2	6	7	8	5
7	8	6	3	1	5	4	2	9
6	4	7	1	3	9	8	5	2
8	2	1	5	7	4	9	6	3
5	9	3	6	8	2	1	7	4

185

3	7	2	9	4	8	6	5	1
1	6	8	3	7	5	9	4	2
9	5	4	6	2	1	7	8	3
5	3	6	1	8	9	2	7	4
4	2	1	7	5	3	8	6	9
8	9	7	2	6	4	1	3	5
2	1	5	8	3	7	4	9	6
6	8	3	4	9	2	5	1	7
7	4	9	5	1	6	3	2	8

186

4	7	8	1	2	5	9	6	3
9	3	2	4	7	6	5	1	8
6	5	1	8	3	9	4	2	7
5	9	6	3	8	7	1	4	2
8	4	7	6	1	2	3	9	5
1	2	3	5	9	4	8	7	6
2	1	5	7	4	8	6	3	9
3	6	9	2	5	1	7	8	4
7	8	4	9	6	3	2	5	1

187

5	7	3	6	8	4	2	9	1
1	6	9	2	5	7	8	4	3
8	2	4	9	1	3	6	5	7
9	4	2	3	7	5	1	8	6
7	8	1	4	2	6	5	3	9
6	3	5	1	9	8	4	7	2
2	9	7	5	4	1	3	6	8
3	5	8	7	6	2	9	1	4
4	1	6	8	3	9	7	2	5

188

7	6	3	4	9	8	2	5	1
4	8	1	7	2	5	6	9	3
9	5	2	6	1	3	7	8	4
5	2	4	1	8	7	3	6	9
6	1	9	3	5	4	8	7	2
8	3	7	9	6	2	1	4	5
2	9	6	8	4	1	5	3	7
1	7	8	5	3	9	4	2	6
3	4	5	2	7	6	9	1	8

189

8	4	7	1	9	5	2	6	3
5	2	3	7	8	6	9	4	1
6	1	9	3	2	4	8	7	5
9	7	2	8	6	1	3	5	4
1	5	6	4	3	9	7	8	2
3	8	4	2	5	7	6	1	9
7	3	5	6	1	2	4	9	8
2	6	1	9	4	8	5	3	7
4	9	8	5	7	3	1	2	6

190

4	2	1	6	9	7	5	8	3
7	3	8	5	1	2	4	6	9
9	6	5	3	4	8	7	2	1
2	7	9	4	3	5	6	1	8
6	5	4	1	8	9	3	7	2
1	8	3	7	2	6	9	4	5
8	9	7	2	5	4	1	3	6
3	4	2	9	6	1	8	5	7
5	1	6	8	7	3	2	9	4

191

5	1	2	8	7	9	3	4	6
4	7	6	5	1	3	2	8	9
3	8	9	4	2	6	7	1	5
1	6	7	2	8	5	4	9	3
9	4	5	3	6	7	1	2	8
2	3	8	1	9	4	5	6	7
6	5	1	7	4	8	9	3	2
8	2	3	9	5	1	6	7	4
7	9	4	6	3	2	8	5	1

192

7	6	4	3	1	8	9	2	5
1	2	3	5	7	9	8	6	4
9	8	5	6	4	2	7	1	3
5	9	2	4	3	6	1	8	7
4	7	6	2	8	1	5	3	9
3	1	8	9	5	7	6	4	2
6	3	7	1	9	4	2	5	8
2	4	9	8	6	5	3	7	1
8	5	1	7	2	3	4	9	6

193

5	8	3	4	6	1	9	7	2
1	9	4	7	5	2	3	8	6
6	2	7	3	9	8	5	4	1
9	1	5	6	4	7	2	3	8
3	4	8	9	2	5	1	6	7
2	7	6	1	8	3	4	9	5
7	5	1	8	3	4	6	2	9
8	3	9	2	1	6	7	5	4
4	6	2	5	7	9	8	1	3

194

5	8	3	7	4	6	1	2	9
7	4	6	2	1	9	3	8	5
1	9	2	8	5	3	7	6	4
3	1	8	9	6	7	5	4	2
9	6	7	5	2	4	8	1	3
4	2	5	1	3	8	6	9	7
8	7	4	3	9	1	2	5	6
2	3	9	6	8	5	4	7	1
6	5	1	4	7	2	9	3	8

195

9	2	8	5	1	6	4	3	7
4	3	5	7	9	2	6	1	8
7	6	1	8	4	3	9	5	2
3	8	2	9	5	4	7	6	1
5	1	4	3	6	7	2	8	9
6	7	9	1	2	8	3	4	5
1	5	6	2	3	9	8	7	4
8	9	3	4	7	5	1	2	6
2	4	7	6	8	1	5	9	3

196

7	4	2	3	8	9	1	5	6
3	6	5	1	4	7	2	8	9
1	9	8	2	6	5	3	7	4
9	1	7	4	3	6	5	2	8
2	5	4	8	7	1	9	6	3
8	3	6	5	9	2	4	1	7
6	7	1	9	2	4	8	3	5
4	2	3	6	5	8	7	9	1
5	8	9	7	1	3	6	4	2

197

8	4	1	6	2	3	5	9	7
2	9	6	5	4	7	1	8	3
5	3	7	8	1	9	2	4	6
7	5	4	2	9	6	8	3	1
3	1	8	4	7	5	9	6	2
6	2	9	3	8	1	7	5	4
1	6	2	9	3	8	4	7	5
4	8	3	7	5	2	6	1	9
9	7	5	1	6	4	3	2	8

198

6	2	9	4	3	7	5	1	8
4	1	3	2	5	8	9	6	7
5	7	8	9	1	6	3	4	2
3	5	4	1	7	9	8	2	6
8	9	1	3	6	2	7	5	4
2	6	7	8	4	5	1	9	3
1	3	6	5	8	4	2	7	9
7	8	2	6	9	1	4	3	5
9	4	5	7	2	3	6	8	1

199

6	4	3	7	2	5	8	1	9
1	5	9	3	4	8	2	6	7
2	7	8	6	9	1	4	5	3
3	6	2	1	7	4	5	9	8
5	9	4	2	8	6	7	3	1
8	1	7	9	5	3	6	2	4
9	2	5	8	1	7	3	4	6
7	3	1	4	6	2	9	8	5
4	8	6	5	3	9	1	7	2

200

2	9	5	4	6	3	8	1	7
3	6	1	2	8	7	5	9	4
7	4	8	5	9	1	2	6	3
1	3	4	9	7	5	6	8	2
9	7	2	6	3	8	4	5	1
5	8	6	1	4	2	3	7	9
6	5	3	7	1	4	9	2	8
4	1	9	8	2	6	7	3	5
8	2	7	3	5	9	1	4	6

201

5	2	4	3	6	8	9	7	1
9	7	8	4	5	1	2	3	6
1	6	3	9	7	2	8	4	5
6	5	9	2	1	7	3	8	4
4	3	1	5	8	9	7	6	2
7	8	2	6	3	4	5	1	9
3	1	5	8	9	6	4	2	7
8	4	6	7	2	5	1	9	3
2	9	7	1	4	3	6	5	8

202

4	3	6	2	1	9	5	8	7
7	1	2	6	5	8	4	9	3
8	9	5	7	3	4	2	6	1
3	8	4	1	6	2	9	7	5
1	2	7	9	8	5	6	3	4
6	5	9	4	7	3	8	1	2
2	4	3	8	9	1	7	5	6
9	7	1	5	2	6	3	4	8
5	6	8	3	4	7	1	2	9

203

3	8	1	9	4	7	2	6	5
7	4	2	3	6	5	1	9	8
6	9	5	1	8	2	3	4	7
1	7	8	2	5	4	6	3	9
4	5	9	8	3	6	7	2	1
2	6	3	7	1	9	8	5	4
8	1	4	5	2	3	9	7	6
5	3	7	6	9	1	4	8	2
9	2	6	4	7	8	5	1	3

204

1	6	3	2	4	8	5	9	7
2	7	4	6	9	5	1	3	8
9	5	8	1	7	3	2	4	6
5	9	7	4	2	1	6	8	3
3	1	6	9	8	7	4	2	5
4	8	2	5	3	6	7	1	9
8	2	9	7	5	4	3	6	1
7	3	1	8	6	2	9	5	4
6	4	5	3	1	9	8	7	2

205

9	3	2	1	6	8	7	5	4
8	5	1	9	7	4	3	6	2
4	7	6	5	3	2	8	9	1
5	4	7	2	8	9	1	3	6
3	2	9	7	1	6	5	4	8
6	1	8	4	5	3	2	7	9
7	9	5	6	2	1	4	8	3
1	8	4	3	9	7	6	2	5
2	6	3	8	4	5	9	1	7

206

4	3	9	6	5	2	1	8	7
2	5	1	7	9	8	4	6	3
8	6	7	1	3	4	2	5	9
5	2	3	9	1	7	8	4	6
9	1	8	2	4	6	7	3	5
6	7	4	5	8	3	9	1	2
7	8	2	3	6	1	5	9	4
1	9	6	4	7	5	3	2	8
3	4	5	8	2	9	6	7	1

207

9	3	1	7	2	6	4	5	8
6	5	4	9	3	8	7	2	1
7	8	2	4	5	1	3	9	6
8	9	5	2	6	3	1	4	7
1	7	3	8	9	4	2	6	5
2	4	6	5	1	7	8	3	9
4	2	8	6	7	9	5	1	3
5	1	9	3	8	2	6	7	4
3	6	7	1	4	5	9	8	2

208

1	3	9	7	5	2	4	8	6
2	6	8	4	1	9	5	7	3
4	7	5	3	8	6	1	2	9
7	9	2	8	6	4	3	5	1
5	4	6	1	7	3	2	9	8
8	1	3	9	2	5	7	6	4
6	2	4	5	9	1	8	3	7
9	8	1	2	3	7	6	4	5
3	5	7	6	4	8	9	1	2

209

2	8	7	5	6	3	4	9	1
3	5	9	1	7	4	6	8	2
6	4	1	2	9	8	5	3	7
4	6	5	9	8	7	1	2	3
9	2	3	6	1	5	8	7	4
1	7	8	4	3	2	9	5	6
5	3	6	8	2	1	7	4	9
8	9	2	7	4	6	3	1	5
7	1	4	3	5	9	2	6	8

210

8	9	6	3	2	7	1	5	4
2	3	7	5	4	1	9	6	8
5	1	4	8	9	6	2	3	7
7	4	1	6	8	3	5	9	2
9	5	3	1	7	2	8	4	6
6	8	2	9	5	4	7	1	3
1	7	5	4	3	8	6	2	9
4	2	9	7	6	5	3	8	1
3	6	8	2	1	9	4	7	5

211

7	8	6	1	5	4	3	2	9
9	4	2	6	8	3	1	5	7
1	3	5	7	9	2	4	8	6
5	1	7	9	2	8	6	4	3
6	2	4	5	3	7	8	9	1
8	9	3	4	6	1	2	7	5
4	5	9	2	1	6	7	3	8
3	7	1	8	4	9	5	6	2
2	6	8	3	7	5	9	1	4

212

2	8	7	4	9	3	6	5	1
6	9	4	5	7	1	2	3	8
5	3	1	8	6	2	4	9	7
3	7	8	1	4	5	9	6	2
1	6	2	7	3	9	8	4	5
9	4	5	6	2	8	7	1	3
8	2	6	3	5	4	1	7	9
7	5	9	2	1	6	3	8	4
4	1	3	9	8	7	5	2	6

213

8	6	9	7	1	2	3	5	4
7	3	2	5	8	4	6	1	9
1	4	5	3	6	9	7	2	8
3	7	1	2	5	8	9	4	6
9	8	6	4	7	1	5	3	2
5	2	4	6	9	3	1	8	7
6	5	8	1	2	7	4	9	3
2	1	3	9	4	6	8	7	5
4	9	7	8	3	5	2	6	1

214

7	9	2	5	1	3	6	8	4
6	1	5	2	4	8	9	7	3
3	4	8	9	7	6	1	5	2
5	6	9	4	2	1	8	3	7
1	3	7	8	9	5	2	4	6
8	2	4	6	3	7	5	9	1
9	8	3	7	6	2	4	1	5
4	7	6	1	5	9	3	2	8
2	5	1	3	8	4	7	6	9

215

5	9	6	8	4	7	2	1	3
1	3	8	9	2	6	5	4	7
2	4	7	1	5	3	9	8	6
6	7	4	3	8	5	1	2	9
3	8	1	2	9	4	6	7	5
9	5	2	7	6	1	8	3	4
7	2	9	5	3	8	4	6	1
4	1	5	6	7	2	3	9	8
8	6	3	4	1	9	7	5	2

216

3	7	5	1	9	6	2	4	8
4	6	8	7	3	2	9	1	5
9	2	1	8	4	5	6	3	7
7	4	6	3	1	9	5	8	2
5	9	2	4	6	8	1	7	3
1	8	3	5	2	7	4	6	9
8	1	4	2	5	3	7	9	6
2	3	9	6	7	1	8	5	4
6	5	7	9	8	4	3	2	1

217

7	6	2	8	3	9	1	5	4
5	1	4	6	7	2	8	9	3
8	9	3	4	1	5	7	2	6
3	4	7	2	8	6	5	1	9
2	8	1	9	5	3	4	6	7
6	5	9	7	4	1	3	8	2
4	2	8	5	9	7	6	3	1
9	3	5	1	6	4	2	7	8
1	7	6	3	2	8	9	4	5

218

5	9	6	3	8	2	7	1	4
7	8	4	5	9	1	3	6	2
3	1	2	6	7	4	5	8	9
2	6	3	7	1	8	4	9	5
9	5	7	4	2	6	1	3	8
8	4	1	9	5	3	6	2	7
6	3	8	2	4	5	9	7	1
1	7	5	8	6	9	2	4	3
4	2	9	1	3	7	8	5	6

219

1	9	5	8	3	6	7	4	2
8	2	3	5	7	4	1	9	6
7	6	4	2	9	1	8	5	3
5	3	8	1	6	2	4	7	9
9	7	6	4	5	3	2	1	8
4	1	2	7	8	9	6	3	5
2	4	9	3	1	8	5	6	7
3	8	7	6	4	5	9	2	1
6	5	1	9	2	7	3	8	4

220

2	3	6	9	4	5	7	8	1
9	8	7	2	6	1	5	3	4
1	5	4	7	8	3	2	6	9
4	7	3	5	9	6	8	1	2
8	2	9	3	1	7	4	5	6
6	1	5	8	2	4	3	9	7
5	6	1	4	7	8	9	2	3
3	4	2	1	5	9	6	7	8
7	9	8	6	3	2	1	4	5

221

4	6	5	3	2	7	8	9	1
2	8	3	4	1	9	5	6	7
7	9	1	5	8	6	4	2	3
1	4	2	7	5	3	9	8	6
9	5	8	1	6	2	3	7	4
3	7	6	9	4	8	1	5	2
5	3	7	2	9	1	6	4	8
8	2	9	6	3	4	7	1	5
6	1	4	8	7	5	2	3	9

222

3	2	9	7	6	4	8	5	1
5	4	8	1	2	9	7	3	6
7	1	6	8	5	3	4	9	2
6	3	5	2	1	8	9	7	4
2	8	1	9	4	7	3	6	5
4	9	7	5	3	6	2	1	8
9	5	3	6	8	2	1	4	7
8	6	4	3	7	1	5	2	9
1	7	2	4	9	5	6	8	3

223

5	2	7	6	8	1	3	4	9
3	9	1	2	4	7	8	5	6
6	4	8	5	9	3	7	2	1
1	6	9	3	7	2	4	8	5
2	8	4	9	6	5	1	7	3
7	5	3	8	1	4	9	6	2
8	1	6	7	5	9	2	3	4
4	3	5	1	2	8	6	9	7
9	7	2	4	3	6	5	1	8

224

9	2	1	7	4	6	8	5	3
8	4	7	3	9	5	1	2	6
3	5	6	2	1	8	7	9	4
7	9	3	1	2	4	5	6	8
4	1	5	8	6	3	9	7	2
6	8	2	5	7	9	4	3	1
2	7	9	6	8	1	3	4	5
1	3	4	9	5	2	6	8	7
5	6	8	4	3	7	2	1	9

225

1	6	4	7	3	8	2	9	5
8	9	3	2	5	1	6	7	4
5	2	7	6	4	9	8	3	1
6	8	2	4	9	7	1	5	3
3	4	1	5	2	6	7	8	9
7	5	9	8	1	3	4	2	6
9	1	8	3	7	4	5	6	2
4	7	5	9	6	2	3	1	8
2	3	6	1	8	5	9	4	7

226

8	3	1	7	2	5	9	4	6
4	6	5	9	8	3	1	2	7
2	9	7	4	6	1	8	3	5
6	2	4	5	1	9	7	8	3
3	1	8	2	7	6	5	9	4
7	5	9	3	4	8	2	6	1
5	4	3	1	9	2	6	7	8
9	7	6	8	5	4	3	1	2
1	8	2	6	3	7	4	5	9

227

5	7	4	6	3	1	9	8	2
3	8	9	7	4	2	1	6	5
1	6	2	9	5	8	3	7	4
9	4	3	5	1	6	8	2	7
6	5	8	3	2	7	4	1	9
7	2	1	8	9	4	5	3	6
4	1	5	2	6	3	7	9	8
2	9	7	1	8	5	6	4	3
8	3	6	4	7	9	2	5	1

228

4	6	9	8	5	2	7	1	3
8	1	7	6	4	3	9	2	5
5	3	2	1	7	9	4	6	8
6	2	1	9	3	8	5	4	7
7	4	3	5	6	1	2	8	9
9	8	5	4	2	7	6	3	1
1	7	6	2	8	5	3	9	4
2	5	8	3	9	4	1	7	6
3	9	4	7	1	6	8	5	2

229

8	3	6	4	1	7	9	2	5
1	9	2	3	6	5	8	7	4
4	5	7	2	9	8	3	6	1
9	7	4	1	8	3	2	5	6
6	1	5	9	7	2	4	3	8
2	8	3	6	5	4	1	9	7
5	4	8	7	3	9	6	1	2
7	6	9	8	2	1	5	4	3
3	2	1	5	4	6	7	8	9

230

2	9	5	7	4	1	3	8	6
7	4	1	8	6	3	5	2	9
8	6	3	5	9	2	7	1	4
5	1	7	9	3	8	4	6	2
9	8	6	2	7	4	1	5	3
3	2	4	6	1	5	9	7	8
6	5	9	4	8	7	2	3	1
4	3	2	1	5	6	8	9	7
1	7	8	3	2	9	6	4	5

231

3	7	4	5	6	8	9	2	1
6	1	2	9	7	4	3	8	5
8	5	9	1	3	2	4	6	7
2	3	5	7	9	6	1	4	8
9	6	7	4	8	1	5	3	2
4	8	1	2	5	3	6	7	9
1	2	3	8	4	9	7	5	6
7	9	6	3	2	5	8	1	4
5	4	8	6	1	7	2	9	3

232

9	1	6	2	8	3	5	7	4
4	2	3	9	5	7	6	8	1
7	5	8	1	4	6	9	3	2
8	3	4	6	1	2	7	9	5
5	7	9	4	3	8	2	1	6
2	6	1	5	7	9	8	4	3
1	8	2	3	9	5	4	6	7
3	9	5	7	6	4	1	2	8
6	4	7	8	2	1	3	5	9

233

1	2	3	4	9	7	8	5	6
4	7	6	3	5	8	1	9	2
5	8	9	2	1	6	4	3	7
6	3	4	7	2	9	5	8	1
7	9	1	6	8	5	2	4	3
8	5	2	1	4	3	7	6	9
3	1	8	5	6	2	9	7	4
9	4	7	8	3	1	6	2	5
2	6	5	9	7	4	3	1	8

234

1	9	6	5	7	3	2	4	8
5	4	3	1	8	2	9	6	7
2	8	7	6	4	9	1	5	3
9	2	8	3	6	1	4	7	5
7	1	5	8	9	4	6	3	2
6	3	4	7	2	5	8	9	1
8	7	1	9	3	6	5	2	4
4	5	9	2	1	7	3	8	6
3	6	2	4	5	8	7	1	9

235

7	6	2	3	5	9	8	1	4
9	5	4	7	1	8	6	3	2
1	3	8	4	2	6	9	5	7
3	7	1	9	8	2	5	4	6
2	9	6	5	3	4	1	7	8
8	4	5	6	7	1	3	2	9
5	8	3	2	6	7	4	9	1
4	1	7	8	9	5	2	6	3
6	2	9	1	4	3	7	8	5

236

7	1	4	2	9	5	6	8	3
2	5	8	1	3	6	9	4	7
9	3	6	4	8	7	2	5	1
6	8	5	7	4	1	3	2	9
3	7	2	9	6	8	4	1	5
1	4	9	3	5	2	7	6	8
5	2	3	6	1	9	8	7	4
8	9	7	5	2	4	1	3	6
4	6	1	8	7	3	5	9	2

237

6	8	2	1	9	4	5	3	7
1	5	9	3	2	7	4	8	6
7	4	3	8	6	5	1	2	9
5	9	7	4	8	6	2	1	3
4	3	8	7	1	2	6	9	5
2	6	1	9	5	3	7	4	8
9	7	6	2	4	8	3	5	1
8	2	5	6	3	1	9	7	4
3	1	4	5	7	9	8	6	2

238

1	7	2	4	8	9	3	5	6
3	9	5	1	2	6	4	8	7
6	4	8	3	7	5	2	1	9
9	6	1	5	3	4	7	2	8
2	8	3	9	6	7	1	4	5
7	5	4	2	1	8	6	9	3
4	2	7	8	5	3	9	6	1
8	1	6	7	9	2	5	3	4
5	3	9	6	4	1	8	7	2

239

2	5	6	3	8	7	1	9	4
8	7	9	4	5	1	2	3	6
1	4	3	6	9	2	7	8	5
3	2	1	9	7	5	4	6	8
7	8	5	2	6	4	3	1	9
6	9	4	8	1	3	5	2	7
5	6	2	1	4	9	8	7	3
4	3	8	7	2	6	9	5	1
9	1	7	5	3	8	6	4	2

240

4	7	9	5	3	2	6	1	8
3	8	6	7	4	1	2	9	5
1	5	2	6	9	8	4	3	7
6	3	5	8	2	9	7	4	1
9	2	8	1	7	4	3	5	6
7	1	4	3	6	5	8	2	9
5	9	3	2	8	7	1	6	4
2	4	7	9	1	6	5	8	3
8	6	1	4	5	3	9	7	2

241

8	3	6	1	5	2	4	7	9
2	5	1	9	4	7	8	3	6
9	7	4	6	8	3	1	5	2
4	2	8	3	1	6	5	9	7
6	1	7	5	9	8	3	2	4
5	9	3	7	2	4	6	8	1
1	6	5	2	3	9	7	4	8
3	8	2	4	7	1	9	6	5
7	4	9	8	6	5	2	1	3

242

3	6	2	8	5	4	1	9	7
7	8	1	2	6	9	5	4	3
4	9	5	3	1	7	8	2	6
6	3	9	1	2	8	7	5	4
2	4	8	7	3	5	9	6	1
1	5	7	4	9	6	2	3	8
8	7	3	5	4	2	6	1	9
5	1	6	9	7	3	4	8	2
9	2	4	6	8	1	3	7	5

243

4	1	2	9	8	6	3	5	7
8	9	6	3	7	5	4	1	2
7	5	3	1	4	2	8	6	9
9	8	7	4	3	1	5	2	6
3	6	5	7	2	8	9	4	1
2	4	1	5	6	9	7	8	3
6	3	9	2	5	4	1	7	8
1	2	4	8	9	7	6	3	5
5	7	8	6	1	3	2	9	4

244

1	5	8	9	2	7	4	3	6
7	4	2	6	8	3	9	1	5
6	9	3	4	1	5	2	7	8
3	7	5	8	4	2	6	9	1
9	2	4	5	6	1	3	8	7
8	1	6	7	3	9	5	2	4
4	8	7	3	9	6	1	5	2
5	3	1	2	7	4	8	6	9
2	6	9	1	5	8	7	4	3

245

5	7	3	4	8	2	9	1	6
6	4	9	5	7	1	3	8	2
2	1	8	3	9	6	5	4	7
9	6	2	7	3	8	1	5	4
8	5	1	9	2	4	6	7	3
7	3	4	1	6	5	2	9	8
1	8	7	2	5	3	4	6	9
3	9	5	6	4	7	8	2	1
4	2	6	8	1	9	7	3	5

246

7	3	5	4	6	9	2	1	8
2	6	1	7	5	8	9	3	4
9	4	8	1	3	2	5	7	6
8	7	4	3	9	1	6	2	5
1	9	6	5	2	7	8	4	3
5	2	3	6	8	4	1	9	7
4	8	7	9	1	6	3	5	2
3	1	2	8	4	5	7	6	9
6	5	9	2	7	3	4	8	1

247

4	8	6	7	1	5	2	3	9
9	1	7	8	2	3	4	6	5
3	2	5	6	4	9	7	8	1
2	6	1	4	3	7	9	5	8
8	7	4	9	5	1	6	2	3
5	3	9	2	6	8	1	7	4
1	4	3	5	7	6	8	9	2
6	9	2	3	8	4	5	1	7
7	5	8	1	9	2	3	4	6

248

1	7	9	8	3	2	6	5	4
8	3	4	9	5	6	1	7	2
5	6	2	4	1	7	9	8	3
2	8	7	3	4	1	5	9	6
6	4	1	2	9	5	8	3	7
3	9	5	6	7	8	4	2	1
4	1	8	5	2	3	7	6	9
9	2	6	7	8	4	3	1	5
7	5	3	1	6	9	2	4	8

249

9	8	6	2	3	4	7	5	1
4	3	2	1	7	5	8	6	9
1	5	7	9	6	8	2	4	3
6	2	9	4	5	1	3	7	8
3	7	4	8	2	6	9	1	5
5	1	8	3	9	7	6	2	4
2	9	1	7	4	3	5	8	6
7	4	5	6	8	9	1	3	2
8	6	3	5	1	2	4	9	7

250

3	2	7	4	5	6	1	8	9
6	9	5	2	8	1	7	4	3
1	4	8	3	9	7	5	6	2
8	7	6	9	4	3	2	1	5
4	1	3	5	6	2	9	7	8
2	5	9	7	1	8	6	3	4
9	6	2	1	3	4	8	5	7
7	3	1	8	2	5	4	9	6
5	8	4	6	7	9	3	2	1

Word Roundup™ Solutions

251. DECEMBER, OCTOBER, AUGUST, APRIL, JUNE, JULY, MAY—SNAPPER, SALMON, SMELT, SHARK—BRUSH, COMB—CUP, MUG—RESORT

252. SNEAKER, SLIPPER, SANDAL, BOOT, SOCK, SHOE—DOLLAR, POUND, EURO, PESO, YEN—PISTOL, MUSKET, RIFLE—SOLID, GAS—SCHOOL

253. RACECAR, ROTOR, RADAR, CIVIC, LEVEL, NOON, DEED—MAROON, BLUE, PINK, TAN, RED—CATCHER, PITCHER—OAHU, MAUI—ATHENS

254. CURRENCY, MOOLAH, DINERO, BREAD, DOUGH, FUNDS, CASH, LOOT—TROUT, SMELT, TUNA, SOLE—ZOO, ZAP, ZIP, ZIG—CANOE, RAFT—COW, PIG

255. LYNX, LION, MOLE, PUMA, MULE, GOAT, SEAL, BEAR, DEER—SLEET, RAIN, SNOW, HAIL—DINNER, LUNCH—CIRCLE, OVAL—LEBANON

256. AMERICAN, CHEDDAR, GOUDA, COLBY, SWISS, BLEU—PRIME, CRIME, DIME, LIME, TIME—CAPTAIN, MAJOR—SNAIL, CLAM—ATLAS

257. LUMBERMILL, LETHAL, LABEL, LOCAL, LOYAL, LEGAL, LULL—PUMPERNICKEL, WHEAT, WHITE, RYE—OTTER, SEAL—SWAN, DUCK—TON

258. CLARINET, TRUMPET, PICCOLO, GUITAR, PIANO, OBOE, DRUM, HARP—KUWAIT, LIBYA, IRAN—GEORGE, JOHN, PAUL—ADIOS, HOLA—STUART

259. TAIPEI, DUBLIN, VIENNA, MANILA, LISBON, SEOUL, LIMA, OSLO, ROME—DRESSER, TABLE, DESK, SOFA, BED—HOUSE, TUNA, COBB—DROWSY—HAIR

260. DRINKING, BOTTLED, SPRING, TONIC, RAIN, HOT, ICE—MOUNTAIN, CANYON, VALLEY, HILL—SATURN, VENUS, MARS—WOLF, DOG, FOX—INCH

261. UNAWARE, UNCLE, UNDER, UNIFY, UNIT, URN, UMP, UGH, UP—PERIOD, COMMA, COLON—MONKEY, LEMUR, APE—GREG, JAN—DIME

262. DAUGHTER, NEPHEW, COUSIN, NIECE, AUNT, SON, MOM, DAD—ALPHA, BETA, GAMMA, DELTA—LEMON, LIME—BEAGLE—ESTATE

263. TWELVE, THIRTY, EIGHTY, ZERO, FOUR, TWO, SIX, TEN—CONNERY, BROSNAN, MOORE, CRAIG—SKUNK, PANDA, ZEBRA—ROBERTS—CRITIC

264. CYPRESS, SPRUCE, CEDAR, PALM, PINE, OAK, ELM—EMERALD, DIAMOND, OPAL, RUBY—AFRICA, EUROPE, ASIA—PARIS—VERB

265. THIRTEEN, FIFTEEN, ELEVEN, THREE, SEVEN, FIVE, NINE, ONE—TANGO, WALTZ, SALSA—ROOK, KING, PAWN—SHOE, SOCK—ABACUS

266. TERRIER, COLLIE, POODLE, BEAGLE, HOUND, BOXER, CHOW—MERCURY, EARTH, VENUS, MARS—BARLEY, MALT, HOPS—ROGER—WEST

267. LITHUANIA, LIBERIA, LIBYA, LAOS—BELUGA, KILLER, BLUE—JEEP, CAR, VAN—UNO, DOS, TRES—CHECKERS, CHESS

268. STADIUM, PLAYER, HELMET, JERSEY, COACH, FIELD, TEAM, GAME—TWELVE, TWENTY, FIFTY, TEN—HURON, ERIE—YEAR, DAY—SEOUL

269. COUNTRY, GOSPEL, BLUES, JAZZ, ROCK, RAP, POP—CHICAGO, HOUSTON, MIAMI—SPOUSE, MOUSE, LOUSE—ACORN—STATE

270. SKULL, BULL, DULL, FULL, GULL, HULL, PULL—TAURUS, PISCES, ARIES, VIRGO, LIBRA, LEO—TAILS, HEADS—RAIN, SNOW—ALIAS

271. DOLLAR, FRANC, POUND, PESO, EURO, YEN—ALPHA, BETA, GAMMA, DELTA—JACK, KING, ACE—SNAIL, CLAM—DOWN, UP

272. GRINDER, FILTER, BREAK, TABLE, CAKE, BEAN, CUP, MUG, POT—SALAMI, TURKEY, HAM—PINKY, THUMB—TROUT, TUNA—PERU

273. VIOLIN, GUITAR, BANJO, CELLO, HARP—THURSDAY, TUESDAY, MONDAY, SUNDAY—JACKAL, WOLF, DOG, FOX—YARD, FOOT, INCH—CUBA

274. GONDOLA, DINGHY, YACHT, CANOE, KAYAK, FERRY, RAFT—STRAIGHT, FLUSH, PAIR—SPLIT, PEEL—PENGUIN—EARTH

275. CUBA, LAOS, PERU, IRAN—ELEVEN, TWELVE, FORTY, TEN—CHOCOLATE, WHOLE, SKIM—TRIANGLE, CIRCLE, OVAL—LEMON, LIME

276. CLOUDY, HUMID, RAINY, SUNNY, CLEAR, FAIR, COLD, HOT—JUNK, JACK, JURY, JAY, JOB, JAB—EAST, WEST—ARM, LEG—GAMES

277. SHREW, GREW, BREW, VIEW, CLUE, BLEW, NEW, FEW, YEW—ACTIVE, ANGRY, AGILE—SWISS, COLBY—DIAMONDS, CLUBS—NASHVILLE

278. COMPANY, NUMBER, BOOTH, BILL, CALL, JACK—ORCHESTRA, ENSEMBLE, BAND—CAIRO, LIMA, ROME—CRIME, SCENE—SONY

279. TROOP, CROWD, TRIBE, CREW, GANG, BAND, CLUB, CLAN, TEAM—CHEESE, BUTTER, CREAM, MILK—STREAM, CREEK, BROOK—BOTTOM—AMBER

280. ANTARCTICA, AFRICA, EUROPE, ASIA—SCOTTY, SPOCK, KIRK, SULU—SOCCER, TENNIS, BOXING, RUGBY—SOUTH, EAST, WEST—CANASTA

281. CLERK, PERK, JERK, WORK, LURK, IRK—PANTHER, COUGAR, TIGER, LION, PUMA, LYNX—STICK, PUCK, TEAM, RINK—EVEN, ODD—MACHETE

282. SING, RING, DING, WING, KING, ZING—OLDSMOBILE, CHEVROLET, SATURN, BUICK—RUSSIAN, FRENCH, LATIN—EAGLES—GOLD

283. POWERPOINT, WINDOWS, OUTLOOK, EXCEL, WORD—THREE, ONE, TWO, SIX—MONKEY, LEMUR, APE—PLIERS, CHISEL, SAW—LONG, TALL

284. PUDDLE, HARBOR, INLET, OCEAN, GULF, POND, LAKE, BAY, SEA—CENTURY, MONTH, YEAR, DAY—GOBLET, STEIN, CUP, MUG—TROUT—ACE

285. STADIUM, JERSEY, PLAYER, FIELD, GAME, TEAM—PERIOD, HYPHEN, COMMA, COLON—FLICK, FILM—LOOT, CASH—EAST, WEST

286. SCHOOL, CHURCH, STORE, CABIN, HOUSE, BARN—AUGUST, APRIL, JUNE, JULY, MAY—ORANGE, LEMON, LIME—VENUS, EARTH, MARS—ALASKA

287. DRESSER, TABLE, CHAIR, DESK, SOFA, BED—KITTEN, PIGLET, CALF, COLT, CUB—FRASIER, NILES—BEVERAGE—GLASGOW

288. LETTUCE, PICKLE, TOMATO, ONION, BEEF, BUN—ATHENS, BERLIN, PARIS, ROME—AUTUMN, WINTER, SPRING—TODDLER, BABY—MASTERPIECE

289. SLIPPER, SNEAKER, SANDAL, SOCK, BOOT—SILVER, LEAD, GOLD, ZINC, TIN—CRICKET, HORNET, MOTH, ANT, BEE—BENNY—COLA

290. BASEBALL, BUSINESS, GREETING, CALLING, CREDIT, FACE—VIETNAM, CHINA, JAPAN, LAOS—POULTRY, BEEF, PORK—ACRES—SNOW

291. AMNESIA, ARMADA, AZALEA, ALPHA, AREA, AURA—PISTOL, MUSKET, RIFLE—GENERAL, MAJOR—BISHOP, KING—VENUS, MARS

292. NOTIFICATION, NEURON, NOTION, NATION, NYLON, NOUN, NOON, NEON, NUN—OCEAN, GULF, LAKE, SEA, BAY—LONDON, PARIS, ROME—HAMLET—ALLOY

293. ACCIDENT, DEALER, ALARM, PART, LOAN, SHOW, WASH—BOLIVIA, BRAZIL, CHILE, PERU—TREE, SODA, PEEL—APRICOT—HEALTH

294. MINUTE, SECOND, DECADE, MONTH, YEAR, DAY—VALLEY, CHASM, CLIFF, HILL—STRAIGHT, FLUSH, PAIR—ARMY, NAVY—CAPOTE

295. CHEADLE, CLOONEY, PACINO, DAMON, PITT, MAC—ELEVEN, TWENTY, FORTY, TEN—TRUCK, JEEP, CAR, VAN—BLIZZARD, TORNADO—CANCUN

296. SIBLING, COUSIN, FATHER, MOTHER, NEPHEW, UNCLE, NIECE, AUNT, SON—FRESHMAN, JUNIOR, SENIOR—GOOSE, DUCK, SWAN—DENSITY—BUNNY

297. GRIMACE, FROWN, SMILE, GRIN—GUITAR, VIOLIN, CELLO, HARP—PIG, APE, COW, BAT—HELLO, HOWDY—PECAN

298. MIDDLE, PROPER, BRAND, STAGE, FIRST, LAST—ORANGE, LEMON, LIME—GERBIL, MOUSE, RAT—DAREDEVIL—POST

299. KNIGHT, BISHOP, KING, ROOK, PAWN—LISBON, BERLIN, ATHENS, MADRID, ROME—REVERSE, DRIVE—BULB, BIB—FEDERAL

300. TRAIN, PLANE, FEET, BIKE, BUS, CAR—SALAMANDER, NEWT, FROG, TOAD—GOOSE, DUCK, SWAN—WALRUS, WHALE—KOALA

301. ADRIATIC, ARABIAN, CASPIAN, BERING, NORTH, CORAL, BLACK, IRISH, DEAD, RED—ROUGH, TOUGH, HUFF, PUFF—EAST, WEST—ATLAS—CRAB

302. BILL, FILL, GILL, HILL, KILL, PILL, SILL, TILL, WILL—MATTRESS, SLEEP, SHEET—SATURN, VENUS, MARS—SHEEN—NILE

303. CHINESE, JUNK, FAST, CAT, DOG—WORLD, WIDE, WEB—COMEDY, HORROR—HELMET, JERSEY—COUPE, SEDAN

304. FLOUNDER, HADDOCK, SNAPPER, TROUT, SHARK, PERCH, PIKE, SOLE, TUNA—ONTARIO, HURON, ERIE—LIGHT, JAM—PAGODA—INDIA

305. KNOCK, KNACK, KIOSK, KAYAK, KICK, KINK—MOOSE, MOUSE, MOLE, MULE—BAVARIAN, MOTOR, WORKS—ACROSS, DOWN—AUDIO

306. TEMPERATURE, WEIGHT, COST, TIME, AGE—SPAIN, ITALY, EGYPT, SYRIA, LIBYA—NICKEL, PENNY, DIME—GILLIGAN, SKIPPER—ANGUS

307. LEAGUE, ALLEY, BALL, LANE, PIN—JAPAN, CHILE, INDIA, SPAIN, HAITI—DEVASTATED, MANDATORY, ADVISORY, REALITY—DUMP, CAN—EAR

308. PELICAN, OSTRICH, TURKEY, EAGLE, STORK, ROBIN, HAWK, DUCK, EMU—FOUR, TWO, SIX, TEN—KRAMER, GEORGE, JERRY—JUNE, MAY—COMB

309. CHAPTER, AUTHOR, COVER, INDEX, NOVEL, PAGE—FIDDLER, HERMIT, KING, BLUE—RIGHT, LEFT—DUNK, HOOK—ANGLER

310. STALLION, ROOSTER, BUCK, BULL, STAG—DIAMONDS, SPADES, HEARTS, CLUBS—PINKY, THUMB—TALON—TULIP

311. MONGOLIA, RUSSIA, ZAMBIA, ANGOLA, LIBYA, KENYA, INDIA, CUBA—SEVEN, FIVE, NINE, ONE—EUROPE, ASIA—FLUTE, OBOE—SLICE

312. MATCH, SMOKE, BLAZE, ARSON, HEAT—GRAY, BLUE, PINK, RED, TAN—FIX, MIX, FOX, HEX, SIX—TRIANGLE, CIRCLE, OVAL—CACTUS

313. NEIGH, CHIRP, MEOW, HISS, BARK, ROAR, OINK, MOO—SCIENCE, HISTORY, MATH—HELMET, HAT, CAP—RUSSIA—BINGO

314. PINBALL, CASH, SLOT, TIME, ICE, FAX—WOLF, DOG, FOX—CORNERED, CATAPULT, DIPLOMAT—ENGLISH, LATIN—SNOW, RAIN

315. TANGERINE, ORANGE, LEMON, LIME—LOBSTER, LIZARD, LLAMA, LION—PULP, PUMP, PLOP, PEEP—JEEP, CAR, BUS, VAN—WEST

316. PLAYER, RINK, GAME, PUCK, TEAM—AUDIENCE, BARBARIC, COLONIAL, ECONOMIC, RINGSIDE—SAFE, OUT—BOOT, SOCK—ACRONYM

317. YOUNGSTER, TODDLER, INFANT, CHILD, ADULT, BABY, GIRL, BOY, MAN—LAKE, GULF, SEA, BAY—LITER, PINT—ITALY, PERU—PEAR

318. CAMERON, MADISON, SPADER, GARNER, BROWN, WOODS, BOND, CAAN—HASH, HUSH, HIGH—ROOT, BARK, LEAF—BOTTOM, TOP—HAGGIS

319. STRAIGHT, FLUSH, RAISE, FOLD, PAIR, HAND, ANTE, BET—KNUCKLE, ANKLE, ELBOW—MONTREAL, TORONTO—SNOWMAN—SOLO

320. KEYBOARD, SOFTWARE, PROGRAM, MONITOR, MOUSE, VIRUS, GAME—ZERO, ZINC, ZEST, ZEAL, ZEBU, ZONE—DEUCE, JACK, ACE—MANILA—PADRE

321. HIGHWAY, AVENUE, STREET, LANE, ROAD—CHAIR, SOFA, DESK, BED—DONOR, COUNT, CELL, BANK—BOUNTY—CIVIC

322. RACK, SACK, HACK, LACK, JACK, YAK—SUNDAY, MONDAY, FRIDAY—AUSTRIA, SPAIN, CHILE—SOLID, GAS—JOE

323. GARBAGE, SPRAY, SODA, BEER, TIN—FISH, DOG, CAT—SCANDINAVIAN, DICTATORSHIP—FLOOR, WALL—SILVER, GOLD

324. HARRISON, FOREMAN, CLOONEY, STRAIT, LUCAS, BUSH—BEIGE, BROWN, GREEN, IVORY, WHITE—ARIES, VIRGO, LEO—BUCKLE—VENUS

325. INNING, COUSIN, DEGREE, PLACE, FLOOR, BASE, DOWN, DATE, NAME, AID—CITY, TOWN—FRONT, BACK—NIGHT, DAY—STOP, GO

Hidato™ Solutions

326

(16)	15	12	13
9	11	14	2
8	10	3	(1)
7	6	5	4

327

(16)	15	3	4
(1)	2	14	5
8	10	6	13
9	7	11	12

328

30	29	28	25	24	22
31	27	26	20	21	23
32	34	35	(36)	19	18
33	5	3	(1)	13	17
6	4	2	12	14	16
7	8	9	10	11	15

329

24	25	26	2	(1)	7
23	27	4	3	6	8
22	29	28	5	9	11
19	21	30	32	10	12
20	18	31	33	13	35
17	16	15	14	34	(36)

330

33	34	35	9	10	12
30	32	8	(36)	11	13
31	29	7	17	16	14
28	20	18	6	15	(1)
27	19	21	23	5	2
26	25	24	22	4	3

331

8	10	6	4	2	(1)
9	7	11	5	3	22
13	12	25	24	23	21
14	15	16	26	18	20
(36)	35	32	17	27	19
34	33	31	30	29	28

332

22	24	25	26	27	30
23	21	19	28	29	31
3	20	18	17	32	33
2	4	10	11	16	34
(1)	5	9	15	12	35
6	7	8	14	13	(36)

333

(1)	21	22	23	26	27
2	3	20	25	24	28
5	4	19	18	15	29
6	8	17	16	30	14
35	7	9	10	31	13
(36)	34	33	32	11	12

334

35	34	33	32	25	26
(36)	20	21	24	31	27
19	17	23	22	30	28
16	18	3	4	5	29
14	15	(1)	2	9	6
13	12	11	10	8	7

335

(36)	34	3	2	29	28
35	4	33	(1)	27	30
5	6	14	32	31	26
12	13	7	15	25	24
11	8	16	17	23	21
9	10	18	19	20	22

336

(36)	34	33	32	25	24
35	4	5	31	23	26
7	6	3	30	22	27
8	9	2	29	28	21
12	11	10	(1)	17	20
13	14	15	16	18	19

337

21	23	24	5	4	3
22	20	25	6	(1)	2
19	26	7	9	12	11
18	27	8	15	10	13
28	17	16	33	14	35
29	30	31	32	34	(36)

338

21	20	18	17	12	10	9
22	19	16	15	13	11	8
26	23	24		14	7	6
27	25				4	5
28	33				3	(42)
32	29	34	36	39	41	2
30	31	35	38	37	40	(1)

339

37	36	34	6	5		
(40)	38	33	35	7	4	3
39	32	31		9	8	2
28	30				10	(1)
29	27	21		16	15	11
26	22	24	20	17	14	12
25	23	19	18	13		

340

	34	33	4	5	9	10
35		32	3	8	6	11
36	31		2	7	13	12
37	30	(1)		41	14	15
29	38	39	40		(42)	16
28	24	23	22	20		17
27	26	25	21	19	18	

341

	32	34	35	44	43	46	47	
30	31	33	36	38	45	42	50	48
29	18	19	37	39	40	41	51	49
28	17	20	21	55	53	52	2	(1)
27	16	22	56	57	54	3	4	(68)
26	23	15	58	60	61	62	5	67
25	24	14	59	10	8	6	63	66
	13	12	11	9	7	64	65	

342

52	51	50	49	61	62	64		
54	53	58	59	60	48	63	43	65
55	57	33	34	47	45	44	42	66
56	32	31	35	46	39	40	41	67
29	30	36	37	38	14	13	11	(68)
28	22	20	19	17	15	12	6	10
27	21	23	18	16	4	5	7	9
26	25	24	3	2	(1)	8		

343

	11	10	13	16	17	21	23	
8	9	12	14	15	18	20	22	24
7	6	4	3	2	19	27	26	25
57	56	5	53	▓	(1)	28	30	32
58	55	54	52	▓	45	29	31	33
59	60	49	51	44	46	38	36	34
61	63	50	48	47	43	37	39	35
	62	64	65	(66)	42	41	40	

344

		7	12	13	14	16		
	3	6	8	11	15	17	(60)	
2	4	5	9	10	49	20	18	59
(1)	41	42	46	48	21	50	19	58
40	37	45	43	47	22	51	52	57
38	39	36	44	23	29	54	53	56
	35	34	32	30	24	28	55	
		33	31	25	26	27		

345

48	49	51	53	55	2	64	63	62
47	50	52	54	56	3	(1)	65	61
46	45	▓	▓	4	57	58	60	(66)
43	44	▓	5	6	8	10	59	12
42	41	30	28	7	9	▓	11	13
40	35	31	29	27	▓	▓	19	14
39	36	34	32	25	26	20	18	15
38	37	33	24	23	22	21	17	16

346

8	7	59	60	61	62	64	65
9	10	6	58	55	(72)	63	66
11	4	5	56	57	54	71	67
12	3	2	21	52	53	68	70
13	14	(1)	20	22	51	45	69
15	17	19	23	50	49	44	46
16	33	18	26	24	48	47	43
32	29	34	27	25	37	42	41
31	30	28	35	36	38	39	40

347

(1)	5	7	9	10	11	12	14
4	2	6	8	20	19	13	15
3	70	69	21	62	63	18	16
(72)	71	68	24	22	61	64	17
27	29	25	67	23	65	60	58
28	26	30	40	66	56	57	59
32	31	39	38	41	42	55	54
33	35	37	48	45	44	43	53
34	36	47	46	49	50	51	52

348

51	50	54	55	56	69	68	67
49	52	53	71	70	57	58	66
47	48	43	(72)	3	59	61	65
46	44	42	4	2	60	62	64
45	41	40	5	10	(1)	18	63
36	38	39	9	6	11	17	19
35	37	8	7	15	16	12	20
34	32	30	28	14	13	23	21
33	31	29	27	26	25	24	22

349

33	2	(1)	4	6	8	11	12
34	32	3	5	7	9	10	13
35	31	30	20	19	17	15	14
37	36	29	21	18	66	16	64
38	28	27	22	68	67	65	63
39	41	26	69	23	58	59	62
42	40	70	25	24	57	60	61
43	71	(72)	47	49	50	56	54
44	45	46	48	51	52	53	55

350

56	54	53	51	50	46	45	44
55	57	52	49	47	40	42	43
58	64	66	67	48	41	39	37
59	65	63	68	4	5	38	36
60	62	2	3	69	6	34	35
61	①	14	⑦72	70	7	31	33
16	15	13	71	8	30	24	32
17	12	11	21	9	23	29	25
18	19	20	10	22	28	27	26

351

21	20	19	18	9	8	①	2
22	16	17	14	10	7	5	3
24	23	15	13	11	6	39	4
25	29	30	12	37	38	40	43
26	27	28	31	36	41	42	44
63	64	65	32	35	47	48	45
62	61	66	34	33	70	46	49
59	60	67	68	69	53	71	50
58	57	56	55	54	52	51	⑦72

352

23	22	21	14	13	⑦72	71	70
24	19	20	15	11	12	68	69
26	25	18	16	10	8	65	67
27	29	60	17	9	64	7	66
30	28	59	61	62	63	5	6
33	31	58	56	①	54	3	4
32	34	41	57	55	2	53	52
35	37	40	42	44	46	49	51
36	38	39	43	45	48	47	50

353

3	4	5	25	26	21	19	18
2	①	6	27	24	22	20	17
31	29	28	7	9	23	14	16
32	30	35	8	10	11	13	15
33	34	36	48	49	50	12	53
39	38	37	47	46	51	52	54
40	⑦72	42	45	65	64	56	55
71	41	43	44	66	57	63	62
70	69	68	67	58	59	60	61

354

42	40	39	38	13	14	15	18
43	41	37	12	11	16	17	19
44	36	35	33	9	10	20	5
45	46	34	32	8	21	6	4
50	47	48	31	22	7	3	2
51	49	54	55	30	23	24	①
52	53	56	29	27	26	25	68
61	62	63	57	28	⑦72	67	69
60	59	58	64	65	66	71	70

355

53	59	58	57	6	7	4	①
52	54	60	56	8	5	3	2
51	61	55	9	13	12	18	17
50	62	63	10	11	14	19	16
49	47	64	68	69	71	15	20
48	46	65	67	70	25	⑦72	21
44	45	66	33	34	26	24	22
43	40	38	35	32	27	28	23
42	41	39	37	36	31	30	29

356

99	⑩⑩	29	30	35	36	37	38	44	45
98	96	28	32	31	34	39	42	43	46
97	95	27	85	33	82	40	41	79	47
94	26	86	87	84	83	81	80	78	48
25	93	88	89	3	74	75	77	49	50
24	92	90	5	4	2	73	76	53	51
23	8	91	6	①	70	71	72	54	52
22	9	7	14	15	69	67	61	60	55
10	21	13	18	16	68	62	66	59	56
11	12	20	19	17	63	64	65	58	57

357

18	19	9	10	7	5	4	2	56	57
17	20	11	8	89	6	①	3	58	55
16	12	21	22	90	88	86	53	54	59
15	13	23	92	91	85	87	50	52	60
97	14	95	24	93	84	49	51	62	61
98	96	25	94	45	83	82	48	63	64
99	26	34	35	44	46	47	81	80	65
27	⑩⑩	33	43	36	70	69	67	66	79
28	30	32	42	37	71	68	74	75	78
29	31	41	40	39	38	72	73	77	76

358

95	93	92	90	88	87	54	55	57	58
96	94	98	91	89	86	85	53	56	59
①	97	99	47	48	49	52	84	60	62
2	4	46	⑩⑩	50	51	83	82	63	61
5	3	44	45	42	40	38	36	81	64
6	8	10	43	41	39	37	35	65	80
7	9	11	18	19	30	34	66	77	79
13	12	17	20	29	33	31	67	76	78
14	16	21	24	28	32	68	70	75	74
15	22	23	25	26	27	69	71	72	73

359

76	75	74	31	30	29	35	36	37	38
77	73	71	32	33	34	28	43	42	39
78	79	72	70	25	27	44	46	41	40
87	80	68	69	26	24	45	47	48	50
86	88	81	67	66	65	23	19	49	51
85	82	89	90	62	64	22	20	18	52
83	84	91	61	60	63	21	54	53	17
97	92	2	(1)	59	58	56	55	11	16
96	98	93	3	4	7	57	10	12	15
95	94	99	(100)	5	6	8	9	13	14

360

93	94	5	6	7	10	11	12	13	14
95	92	4	3	8	9	24	23	15	16
96	97	91	90	2	(1)	25	22	21	17
98	71	89	87	86	85	26	27	20	18
99	70	72	88	84	37	28	29	30	19
69	(100)	73	79	83	36	38	39	32	31
68	74	78	76	80	82	35	33	40	42
67	65	75	77	55	81	34	50	41	43
66	64	61	56	57	54	49	51	47	44
63	62	60	59	58	53	52	48	46	45

361

39	40	49	51	52	53	55	57	77	78
38	41	48	50	71	54	56	76	58	79
37	42	47	70	68	72	74	75	80	59
36	43	44	46	69	67	73	82	81	60
35	33	32	45	66	84	83	63	62	61
34	30	31	89	85	65	64	3	4	5
29	28	90	88	87	86	2	99	(100)	6
22	21	27	91	92	93	98	(1)	7	9
23	26	20	17	94	15	96	97	8	10
24	25	18	19	16	95	14	13	12	11

362

(100)	94	92	91	90	86	85	84	82	80
95	99	93	27	28	89	87	83	79	81
96	98	26	11	29	30	88	3	78	(1)
97	25	12	10	34	31	32	4	2	77
24	14	13	35	9	33	5	69	67	76
15	23	22	36	8	6	70	68	75	66
16	18	20	21	37	7	40	71	65	74
17	19	45	44	38	39	41	72	73	64
47	46	50	52	43	42	56	58	60	63
48	49	51	53	54	55	57	59	61	62

363

82	83	46	48	39	38	36	35	34	33
84	81	47	45	49	40	37	30	31	32
85	80	43	44	41	50	54	29	28	26
86	79	78	42	51	52	53	55	27	25
87	99	98	77	76	66	65	56	24	23
(100)	88	97	75	69	67	64	62	57	22
89	96	71	70	74	68	63	58	61	21
95	90	72	73	6	7	59	60	20	19
91	94	(1)	4	5	8	12	13	15	18
92	93	2	3	9	10	11	14	17	16

364

85	86	87	88	67	66	65	63	61	60
(96)	84	90	89	68	76	64	62	59	56
95	91	83	81	69	77	75	58	57	55
94	92	80	82	78	70	72	74	54	53
12	93	14	79	■	■	71	73	51	52
11	13	15	16	■	■	32	50	49	48
10	(1)	17	19	21	31	33	34	35	47
9	2	18	20	22	28	30	45	46	36
8	6	3	23	27	29	43	44	37	38
7	5	4	24	25	26	42	41	40	39

365

		77	89	90	91	(92)	47	45	
	86	78	88	76	51	49	48	46	44
85	87	79	52	75	50	57	43	42	41
84	82	80	53	54	74	56	58	40	39
83	4	81	6	73	55	59	34	36	38
(1)	3	5	13	7	72	60	35	33	37
2	15	14	12	11	8	71	61	62	32
16	17	19	20	10	9	70	30	31	63
		18	22	21	27	69	29	66	65	64
		23	24	25	26	28	68	67	

366

	3	2	14	15	17	18	19	20	
5	4	13	(1)	16	31	29	21	22	23
6	7	12	11	32	30	28	26	25	24
84	8	9	10	33	34	27	69	67	66
85	83	95	(96)	35	36	71	70	68	65
86	94	82	38	37	73	72	61	62	64
87	93	81	39	74	75	77	58	60	63
92	88	40	80	79	78	76	59	57	56
91	89	41	44	45	47	49	51	53	55
90	42	43	46	48	50	52	54		

367

37	35	33	32	29	27	25	24	22	21
38	36	34	30	31	28	26	23	20	19
39	40	■	■	■	■	■	■	16	18
42	41	■	79	80	81	(82)	■	15	17
43	44	■	78	71	69	68	■	13	14
47	45	■	77	72	70	67	■	12	11
48	46	■	76	75	73	66	■	9	10
49	51	■	■	74	65	■	■	8	6
50	52	57	58	59	62	64	(1)	7	5
53	54	55	56	60	61	63	2	3	4

368

(76)	75	74	73	69	71	30	31	35	34
47	46	45	68	72	70	29	36	32	33
		48	44	67	■		37	28	26
		49	66	43	■		38	27	25
50	65	■	■	42	39	■		24	23
51	64	■	■	40	41	■		21	22
		52	63	62	■		17	18	20
		53	60	61	■		16	15	19
58	59	54	4	5	6	8	9	14	13
57	56	55	3	2	(1)	7	10	11	12

369

71	72	75	76			36	35	34	31
70	73	74	77			37	33	32	30
69	68	80	78			38	25	27	29
82	81	67	79			24	39	26	28
47	83	66	65	43	41	40	23	2	3
48	46	(84)	44	64	42	22	(1)	5	4
49	51	45	63			21	20	6	7
50	52	56	62			19	17	9	8
53	55	57	61			18	16	13	10
54	58	59	60			15	14	12	11

370

29	30	31	36	35	38	39	40	47	48
28	26	32	34	37	44	41	46	50	49
27	25	24	33	43	42	45	51	54	53
19	21	23	■	■	■	■	55	52	60
18	20	22	■	■	■	■	56	61	59
17	15	14	■	■	■	■	62	57	58
16	13	10	■	■	■	■	63	70	69
12	11	9	7	79	80	65	64	68	71
3	4	8	6	78	82	81	66	67	72
2	(1)	5	(84)	83	77	76	75	74	73

371

55	53	51	50			6	8	9	10
54	56	52	49			7	5	12	11
57	58	61	48	47	45	15	4	13	2
59	60	62	63	46	44	16	14	3	(1)
		64	41	42	43	18	17		
		65	40	83	(84)	19	36		
79	66	81	82	39	20	37	35	33	32
78	80	67	68	69	38	21	34	29	31
76	77	71	70			23	22	28	30
75	74	73	72			24	25	26	27

372

	51	64	65	66	70	69			
53	52	63	50	49	67	68	71	72	73
54	56	58	62	47	48	(78)	44	76	74
55	59	57	61	26	46	45	77	43	75
	60	24	25	27	28	42			
	21	23	■	■	29	41			
3	20	19	22	■	■	30	32	40	39
4	2	18	17	■	■	31	33	35	38
5	6	(1)	16	9	10	11	34	36	37
	7	8	15	14	13	12			

373

57	58	52	51	78	79	81	88	87	86
56	53	59	50	74	77	80	82	89	85
55	54	60	73	49	75	76	(90)	83	84
70	71	72	61	48					
69	67	63	62	47	45	44	43	42	41
68	66	65	64	46	25	26	28	40	39
			24	27	29	31			38
11	12	13	15	16	17	23	30	32	37
10	8	6	14	3	18	19	22	33	36
9	7	5	4	(1)	2	20	21	34	35

374

	55	54	61	52	51	50	48	47	
56	58	60	53	62	19	49	44	45	46
57	59	64	63	20	18	30	43	40	41
68	66	65	21	28	29	17	31	42	39
69	67	22	24	25	27	32	16	36	38
70	72	23	74	26	33	34	35	15	37
71	85	73	75	90	91	(92)	14	13	12
84	86	87	76	89	3	5	6	11	10
	83	81	88	77	2	4	7	9	
		82	80	79	78	(1)	8		

375

15	13	12	27			(92)	82	85	84
16	14	11	26	28	29	81	91	83	86
17	19	10	25	79	80	30	90	89	87
18	20	24	9	78	7	6	31	32	88
	23	21	77	8	3	5	33	34	
	22	76	63	2	(1)	4	36	35	
66	67	64	75	62	61	52	37	48	49
68	65	74	59	60	53	38	51	50	47
69	73	58	57	55	54	39	41	43	46
70	71	72	56			40	42	44	45

376

(121)	106	105	104	103	102	101	93	99	98	97
107	120	109	87	88	89	92	100	94	10	96
119	108	112	110	86	90	91	12	11	95	9
118	113	83	111	85	15	14	13	6	7	8
117	114	82	84	66	16	17	18	5	4	(1)
116	115	81	79	65	67	68	69	19	3	2
55	56	80	64	78	77	76	70	20	22	24
54	53	57	58	63	62	75	71	21	23	25
51	52	59	60	61	38	74	73	72	28	26
50	46	45	43	41	39	37	35	32	29	27
49	48	47	44	42	40	36	34	33	31	30

377

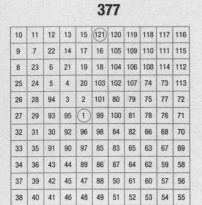

10	11	12	13	15	(121)	120	119	118	117	116
9	7	22	14	17	16	105	109	110	111	115
8	23	6	21	19	18	104	106	108	114	112
25	24	5	4	20	103	102	107	74	73	113
26	28	94	3	2	101	80	79	75	77	72
27	29	93	95	(1)	99	100	81	78	76	71
32	31	30	92	96	98	84	82	66	68	70
33	35	91	90	97	85	83	65	63	67	69
34	36	43	44	89	86	87	64	62	59	58
37	39	42	45	47	88	50	61	60	57	56
38	40	41	46	48	49	51	52	53	54	55

378

10	9	(1)	2	3	53	54	55	57	58	59
11	12	8	7	4	52	51	50	56	61	60
13	19	20	6	5	44	45	48	49	62	63
14	16	18	21	22	43	46	47	67	66	64
15	17	31	23	33	42	41	40	68	69	65
29	30	24	32	35	34	39	110	70	71	72
28	27	95	25	97	36	38	109	111	113	73
93	94	26	96	98	37	108	107	112	74	114
92	87	100	99	82	81	105	106	75	76	115
91	88	86	101	83	104	80	(121)	77	119	116
90	89	85	84	102	103	79	78	120	117	118

379

32	31	30	28	26	25	13	23	22	20	18
33	35	37	29	27	12	24	14	21	17	19
34	36	38	39	11	10	8	15	16	4	(121)
55	56	57	60	40	9	7	6	5	120	3
52	54	59	58	61	41	115	116	117	119	2
51	53	44	43	42	62	114	112	111	118	(1)
49	50	45	71	69	63	113	110	109	108	106
48	46	72	70	68	66	64	91	92	105	107
47	75	74	73	67	65	90	102	104	93	94
76	78	80	83	85	89	88	103	101	98	95
77	79	81	82	84	86	87	100	99	97	96

380

37	48	49	50	52	54	55	57	67	59	60
36	38	47	46	51	53	56	68	58	66	61
33	35	39	43	45	71	70	69	65	64	62
34	32	40	42	44	72	73	74	97	98	63
31	30	26	41	■	■	96	75	99	77	
29	27	24	25	■	■	95	100	76	78	
28	23	9	10	■	■	101	94	79	80	
21	22	8	11	(112)	110	102	93	91	81	82
20	18	12	7	111	103	109	108	92	90	83
19	17	13	6	4	(1)	104	107	85	84	89
16	15	14	5	2	3	105	106	86	87	88

381

	3	4	52	53	54	55	57	58	60	
2	(1)	■	5	51	7	8	56	■	59	61
45	■	■	50	6	9	79	81	■	■	62
44	46	49	48	10	78	82	80	66	64	63
43	42	47	11	84	83	77	76	65	67	69
41	39	15	14	12	85	86	75	74	68	70
40	16	38	13	33	32	30	87	88	73	71
17	37	36	35	34	29	31	90	89	72	(105)
18	■	■	26	25	28	93	91	■	■	104
19	20	■	24	27	94	98	92	■	102	103
	21	22	23	95	96	97	99	100	101	

382

	55	56	58	66	74	75	76	77	78	
54	52	57	59	65	67	73	84	83	82	79
53	49	51	60	64	72	68	85	88	81	80
47	48	50	61	63	69	71	86	87	89	90
46	43	42	62	14	70	8	7	95	96	91
45	44	41	39	15	13	9	6	94	92	97
(117)	37	38	40	16	12	11	10	5	93	98
36	116	115	112	113	17	18	20	3	4	99
34	35	28	114	111	22	21	19	105	2	100
33	29	30	27	23	110	109	106	(1)	104	101
	32	31	26	25	24	108	107	103	102	

383

2	3	118	117	115	114	107	104	103	101	100	99
4	(1)	119	116	113	112	108	106	105	102	97	98
5	6	16	120	121	111	109	90	92	94	95	96
7	14	15	17	21	122	110	91	89	93	135	136
13	8	18	20	22	123	124	125	128	88	137	134
12	9	19	23	27	28	126	127	87	129	138	133
11	10	24	26	31	29	85	86	130	131	132	139
47	48	25	32	30	84	82	79	75	74	73	140
46	49	39	33	34	83	81	80	78	76	72	141
45	40	50	38	36	35	61	62	64	77	71	142
44	41	51	37	55	56	60	63	65	67	70	143
43	42	52	53	54	57	58	59	66	68	69	(144)

384

30	32	33	34	47	49	50	51	69	70	71	101
29	31	35	44	46	48	52	67	68	72	100	102
28	36	41	43	45	53	65	66	74	73	99	103
27	37	40	42	54	63	64	75	85	86	98	104
26	38	39	55	61	62	76	82	84	87	97	105
25	24	58	56	60	77	79	81	83	88	96	106
22	23	57	59	2	128	78	80	89	94	95	107
18	21	20	3	(1)	127	129	90	92	93	109	108
17	19	4	9	126	130	124	91	122	121	110	113
16	11	10	5	8	125	131	123	120	111	112	114
12	15	6	7	142	132	139	134	135	119	115	117
13	14	(144)	143	141	140	133	138	137	136	118	116

385

113	112	110	109	108	126	127	128	(144)	143	131	132
115	114	111	124	125	107	106	(1)	129	130	142	133
116	117	123	100	101	105	3	2	140	141	138	134
118	120	99	122	102	104	4	38	37	139	135	137
119	92	121	98	103	8	7	5	39	36	35	136
90	91	93	97	96	10	9	6	25	40	33	34
88	89	94	95	12	11	23	24	26	32	41	43
87	85	83	13	14	15	22	21	27	31	42	44
86	84	82	72	70	16	18	20	28	30	47	45
80	81	73	71	69	62	17	19	29	48	49	46
79	77	74	64	63	68	61	58	56	55	53	50
78	76	75	65	66	67	59	60	57	54	52	51

386

64	65	66	67	68	69	27	26	24	17	16	15
63	62	61	60	70	74	28	25	23	18	19	14
55	57	58	59	73	71	75	29	22	20	13	11
54	56	48	47	72	79	77	76	30	21	12	10
53	49	50	46	80	81	78	32	31	4	8	9
52	51	45	44	43	84	82	33	34	5	3	7
91	90	88	86	85	42	83	35	134	133	6	2
92	89	87	40	41	37	36	136	135	132	(1)	130
94	93	104	39	38	(144)	143	137	138	122	131	129
95	97	103	105	109	110	142	140	139	121	123	128
96	98	102	106	108	111	141	115	117	120	127	124
99	100	101	107	112	113	114	116	118	119	125	126

387

6	7	8	10	11	12	16	17	18	19	20	99
5	4	2	9	13	14	15	24	23	21	100	98
51	3	(1)	41	40	38	25	26	27	22	101	97
52	50	49	42	39	37	35	28	29	104	102	96
54	53	48	46	43	36	34	32	30	105	103	95
(144)	55	47	45	44	66	33	31	106	107	94	92
143	56	58	59	60	65	67	69	109	108	93	91
142	57	139	61	64	71	70	68	110	112	89	90
141	140	138	63	62	73	72	75	111	113	88	87
129	130	137	136	135	134	74	76	115	114	84	86
128	125	131	123	133	120	118	116	77	80	83	85
126	127	124	132	122	121	119	117	78	79	81	82

388

15	13	11	9	7	5	30	29	28	33	34	35
16	14	12	10	8	6	4	31	32	27	37	36
17	18	19	20	21	22	23	3	25	26	38	40
63	61	59	57	55	53	52	24	2	(1)	41	39
64	62	60	58	56	54	51	49	48	47	(144)	42
65	67	69	70	110	111	118	50	46	44	43	143
66	68	72	71	109	112	117	119	45	140	141	142
76	75	74	73	107	108	113	116	120	121	139	138
87	77	78	79	106	104	114	115	130	122	123	137
86	88	80	90	105	103	101	100	129	131	124	136
85	81	89	92	91	102	97	128	99	125	132	135
84	83	82	93	94	95	96	98	127	126	134	133

389

65	64	69	70	72	73	3	5	7	9	11	12
66	68	63	71	49	74	2	4	6	8	10	13
67	62	61	48	50	(1)	75	78	140	141	15	14
44	60	46	47	51	76	77	79	139	16	142	(144)
43	45	59	56	55	52	81	80	136	138	17	143
42	41	58	57	54	53	82	83	137	135	18	19
38	40	35	34	86	85	84	28	25	26	134	20
39	37	36	87	33	30	29	119	27	24	21	133
90	89	88	32	31	106	118	117	120	22	23	132
91	102	103	104	105	107	108	116	115	121	122	131
101	92	93	94	96	110	109	114	126	124	123	130
100	99	98	97	95	111	112	113	125	127	128	129

390

70	69	68	64	63	62	60	59	116	115	121	120
71	72	67	65	105	108	61	58	114	117	119	122
74	73	66	104	107	106	109	113	57	118	123	124
75	78	77	102	103	110	111	112	56	(128)	127	125
79	76	100	101					55	48	47	126
80	81	99	98					54	53	49	46
82	83	96	97					52	50	45	44
85	84	95	27					51	35	41	43
86	88	94	26	28	29	30	33	34	40	36	42
87	89	93	25	24	23	31	32	9	5	39	37
90	92	18	17	22	15	12	10	8	6	4	38
91	19	20	21	16	14	13	11	7	3	2	(1)

391

11	12	7	6	(1)	125	126	127	129	130	131	(132)
10	8	13	5	2	123	124	128	116	115	114	112
9	14	15	4	3	122	121	120	119	117	111	113
21	20	16			76	78			118	109	110
19	22	17		75	65	77	79		86	108	107
23	18	73	74	66	64	80	81	85	87	89	106
24	72	70	68	67	60	63	82	84	88	90	105
25	71	69		59	62	61	83		91	93	104
26	27	28		58	55				92	94	103
36	37	38	29	57	56	47	54	53	95	97	102
35	31	30	39	41	45	46	48	52	96	98	101
34	33	32	40	42	43	44	49	50	51	99	100

392

	65	67	68	69	71	73	75	76			
	64	60	66	22	21	70	72	74	77	78	
63	61	59	23	20	16	15	13	9	8	79	80
62	58	54	24	19	17	14	12	10	7	83	81
57	55	53	25	18			11	4	6	84	82
56	52	48	26					3	5	85	87
51	49	47	27					2	101	86	88
50	46	42	28					(1)	102	100	89
45	43	41	29					104	103	90	99
44	40	36	30					105	91	98	97
39	37	35	31					106	92	96	95
38	34	33	32					107	(108)	93	94

393

85	86	88	90	(108)	92	93	94	98	2	3	4
82	84	87	89	91	107	95	99	97	(1)	5	7
81	83		105	106	100	96				6	8
80	78		104	101					11	9	
79	71	77		102	103			18	12	10	
69	70	72	76				17	13	19	20	
68	67	73	75			16	14	21	23		
65	66	74		42	41		15	22	24		
62	64		43	40			26	25			
61	63		52	44	39	37		27	28		
60	57	56	51	53	49	45	38	36	33	32	29
59	58	55	54	50	48	47	46	34	35	31	30

394

67	66	65	64	61	60	59	58	44	43	42	
97	68	70	62	63	53	55	57	45	41		39
96	98	69	71	52	54	56	47	46		40	38
94	95	99	72	51	77	49	48		28	35	37
93	100	73	75	76	50	78		29	34	27	36
92	90	101	74	80	79		30	31	33	26	24
91	102	89	82	81		130	(132)	(1)	32	23	25
103	87	88	83		129	124	131	2	3	5	22
104	86	84		128	125	117	123	122	4	6	21
105	85		127	126	116	118	120	121	7	8	20
106		109	110	111	115	119	12	11	10	9	19
	107	108	112	113	114	13	14	15	16	17	18

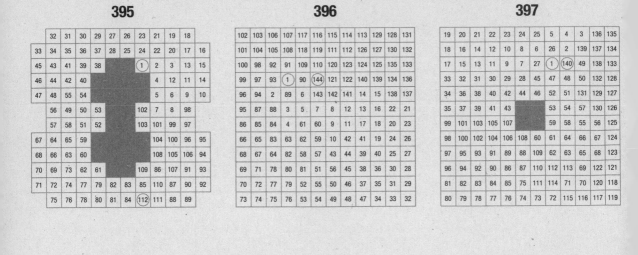

395

396

397

398

399

400